Jørgen Dige Pedersen
GLOBALIZATION, DEVELOPMENT AND THE STATE
The Performance of India and Brazil Since 1990

Markus Perkmann and Ngai-Ling Sum
GLOBALIZATION, REGIONALIZATION AND CROSS-BORDER REGIONS

K. Ravi Raman and Ronnie D. Lipschutz (editors)
CORPORATE SOCIAL RESPONSIBILITY
Comparative Critiques

Ben Richardson
SUGAR: REFINED POWER IN A GLOBAL REGIME

Marc Schelhase
GLOBALIZATION, REGIONALIZATION AND BUSINESS
Conflict, Convergence and Influence

Herman M. Schwartz and Leonard Seabrooke (editors)
THE POLITICS OF HOUSING BOOMS AND BUSTS

Leonard Seabrooke
US POWER IN INTERNATIONAL FINANCE
The Victory of Dividends

Timothy J. Sinclair and Kenneth P. Thomas (editors)
STRUCTURE AND AGENCY IN INTERNATIONAL CAPITAL MOBILITY

J.P. Singh (editor)
INTERNATIONAL CULTURAL POLICIES AND POWER

Fredrik Söderbaum and Timothy M. Shaw (editors)
THEORIES OF NEW REGIONALISM

Susanne Soederberg, Georg Menz and Philip G. Cerny (editors)
INTERNALIZING GLOBALIZATION
The Rise of Neoliberalism and the Decline of National Varieties of Capitalism

Helen Thompson
CHINA AND THE MORTGAGING OF AMERICA
Economic Interdependence and Domestic Politics

Ritu Vij (editor)
GLOBALIZATION AND WELFARE
A Critical Reader

Matthew Watson
THE POLITICAL ECONOMY OF INTERNATIONAL CAPITAL MOBILITY

Owen Worth and Phoebe Moore
GLOBALIZATION AND THE 'NEW' SEMI-PERIPHERIES

International Political Economy Series
Series Standing Order ISBN 978-0-333-71708-0 hardcover
Series Standing Order ISBN 978-0-333-71110-1 paperback

You can receive future titles in this series as they are published by placing a standing order. Please contact your bookseller or, in case of difficulty, write to us at the address below with your name and address, the title of the series and one of the ISBNs quoted above.

Customer Services Department, Macmillan Distribution Ltd, Houndmills, Basingstoke, Hampshire RG21 6XS, England

Globalization and Labour in China and India

Impacts and Responses

Edited by

Paul Bowles
Professor of Economics and International Studies, University of Northern British Columbia, Canada

and

John Harriss
Director, School for International Studies, Simon Fraser University, Canada

First published 2010 by
PALGRAVE MACMILLAN

Palgrave Macmillan in the UK is an imprint of Macmillan Publishers Limited,
registered in England, company number 785998, of Houndmills, Basingstoke,
Hampshire RG21 6XS.

Palgrave Macmillan in the US is a division of St Martin's Press LLC,
175 Fifth Avenue, New York, NY 10010.

Palgrave Macmillan is the global academic imprint of the above companies
and has companies and representatives throughout the world.

Palgrave® and Macmillan® are registered trademarks in the United States,
the United Kingdom, Europe and other countries.

ISBN 978–0–230–23088–0   hardback

This book is printed on paper suitable for recycling and made from fully
managed and sustained forest sources. Logging, pulping and manufacturing
processes are expected to conform to the environmental regulations of the
country of origin.

A catalogue record for this book is available from the British Library.

Library of Congress Cataloging-in-Publication Data

Globalization and labour in China and India: impacts and responses /
   edited by Paul Bowles, John Harriss.
       p. cm.
   ISBN 978–0–230–23088–0
   1. Labor policy—China. 2. Labor policy—India. 3. Globalization—
   China. 4. Globalization—India. I. Bowles, Paul. II. Harriss, John.
   HD5830.A6G56 2010
   331.12'0420951—dc22   2010023771

Printed and bound in Great Britain by
CPI Antony Rowe, Chippenham and Eastbourne

Contents

List of Tables

List of Figures

Acknowledgements

This collection originates from a workshop held at the University of Northern British Columbia, Canada in September 2008. Funding from the Social Sciences and Humanities Research Council of Canada is gratefully acknowledged.

Nine papers from that workshop were originally published in the *Global Labour Journal*, volume 1, no. 1, 2010 (see http://digitalcommons. mcmaster.ca/globallabour). These papers are: Harriss; Bowles; Dong, Bowles and Chang; Pun Ngai, Chan and Chan; Blecher; Ramachandran and Rawal; Harriss-White; Hensman; and Flynn and O'Brien. These papers were subsequently revised and abridged to appear here.

To these papers, four others, by Sanyal and Bhattacharya, RoyChowdhury, Wang et al., and Bienefeld were added to complete this collection.

A longer version of Sanyal and Bhattacharya's chapter was published in *Economic and Political Weekly, Review of Labour*, vol. 44, no. 22, 30 May 2009. RoyChowdhury's chapter is a slightly abridged version of an article that appeared first in *Economic and Political Weekly, Review of Labour*, vol. 43, no. 22, 2008.

Wang, Appelbaum, Degiuli, and Lichtenstein's chapter is a slightly revised version of their paper which was published in *Third World Quarterly*, vol. 30, no. 3, April 2009, pp. 485–501 (see http://www.informaworld.com). We acknowledge permission to republish from Taylor and Francis.

Notes on Contributors

Richard P. Appelbaum is Professor of Sociology and Global and International Studies at the University of California at Santa Barbara, where he also serves as Director of the Institute for Social, Behavioral, and Economic Research. His most recent book is *Critical Globalization Studies* (co-edited with William I. Robinson, 2005). He is currently engaged in a multi-disciplinary study of supply chain networks in the Asian-Pacific Rim.

Rajesh Bhattacharya is with the Center for Popluar Ecnomics at the University of Massachusetts, Amherst. He recently completed a doctoral thesis on 'Capitalism in Post-Colonial India: Primitive Accumulation Under Dirigiste and Laissez Faire Regimes'.

Manfred A. Bienefeld is a Professor in the School of Public Policy and Administration at Carleton University. His current research interests include development policy, wages/employment, commodity/capital markets, human capital, technology/industrialization, development and the environment, and development in a historical perspective; his area interests include Africa, Canada, the Pacific and East Asia and his issue interests include the debt crisis, protectionism, industrial policy, planning, privatization, and the 'newly industrializing countries'. He is the editor (with Jane Jenson and Rianne Mahon) of *Production, Space, Identity* (1993).

Marc Blecher is Professor of Politics and East Asian Studies at Oberlin College, USA. He is the author of four books and several dozen articles on Chinese politics, society and political economy, focusing on local politics and political economy in rural and urban China. The third edition of *China Against the Tides* is out in 2010. His current research focuses on working-class formation and the role of urban governments in north China in shaping economic development and its social consequences.

Paul Bowles is Professor of Economics at the University of Northern British Columbia. His research focuses on globalization, regionalism and the political economy of Chinese development. Previous research has included studies of China's financial system, rural industries and labour systems. He recently published *National Currencies and Globalization:*

Endangered Specie? (2008). He is currently engaged in a project analysing China's foreign exchange rate regime and currency choices.

Chris King-Chi Chan is Assistant Professor at City University of Hong Kong.

Jenny Chan is a doctoral candidate at the University of London, Royal Holloway.

Hongqin Chang is a PhD candidate at the School of Management, Xi'an Jiaotong University. Her research focuses on rural development and institutional change and on gender/women's issues in China.

Francesca Degiuli is a Faculty Fellow in the Department of Global and International Studies at the University of California, Santa Barbara. She has published articles in journals such as the *European Journal of Women Studies, Work, Employment, and Society* and has a chapter in *Labour, Globalisation, and the New Economy* edited by Gyorgy Széll.

Xiao-yuan Dong is Professor of Economics at the University of Winnipeg, an adjunct professor of the China Centre of Economic Research (CCER), Peking University, China, and co-director of the Chinese Women Economic Research and Training Programme at CCER. Her research focuses on China's economic development and labour and gender issues. She has published in a variety of journals, including *Journal of Political Economy, Journal of Development Economics, Journal of Comparative Economics, Cambridge Journal of Economics* and *New Left Review*. She is an associate editor of *Feminist Economics* and has served on the editorial boards of *Journal of Socio-Economics* and *Journal of Comparative Economics*.

Greg Flynn is a lawyer and an Assistant Professor of Political Science at McMaster University. He graduated with a PhD from McMaster in 2009 with a specialization in comparative public policy. His research focuses on the role of the courts, law and legal process in policy-making and citizen engagement in democratic institutions and practices, including political parties and elections.

John Harriss is Professor, and Director of the School for International Studies at Simon Fraser University, having previously been the Director of the Development Studies Institute at the London School of Economics. His recent research has been concerned with civil society and politics in India's metropolitan cities, and he has research ongoing on social policy and agrarian change in Tamil Nadu. His most recent book is *Power Matters: Essays on Institutions, Politics and Society in India* (2006).

Barbara Harriss-White is Professor of Development Studies at Oxford University and Director of Oxford's new Contemporary South Asian Studies Programme and the Master's in Contemporary India. She teaches and researches the Indian political economy. Her recent books include *Trade Liberalization and India's Informal Economy* (2007), *Defining Poverty in the Developing World* (co-edited with Frances Stewart and Ruhi Saith) (Palgrave, 2008), *Rural Commercial Capital: Agricultural Markets in West Bengal* (2008 – Edgar Graham Prize), and *The Comparative Political Economy of Development: Africa and South Asia* (edited with Judith Heyer) (2010).

Rohini Hensman is an independent scholar and writer based in Bombay who has been active in the trade union, women's liberation and anti-war movements in India and Sri Lanka. She has written extensively on all these issues, and in recent years has also been researching and writing on globalization. Her publications include two novels, *To Do Something Beautiful*, inspired by working women and union activists in Bombay, and *Playing Lions and Tigers*, inspired by anti-war activists and human rights defenders in Sri Lanka.

Nelson Lichtenstein is Professor of History at the University of California, Santa Barbara, where he directs the Center for the Study of Work, Labor and Democracy. His newest book is *The Retail Revolution: How Wal-Mart Remade American Business, Transformed Global Trade, and Put Politics in Every Store* (2009).

Pun Ngai is Associate Professor at Hong Kong Polytechnic University and Deputy Director of the Joint Peking University – Hong Kong Polytechnic University China Social Work Research Centre.

Robert O'Brien is the LIUNA-Mancinelli Professor of Global Labour Issues and Chair of the Department of Political Science at McMaster University. He teaches courses in international relations and global political economy. His books include: *Solidarity First: Canadian Workers and Social Cohesion* (2008); with M. Williams, *Global Political Economy: Evolution and Dynamics*, 2nd edition (Palgrave, 2007); with Paul James, *Globalizing Labour* (2007); and with Jan Aart Sholte, A. M. Goertz and Marc Williams, *Contesting Global Governance: Multilateral Economic Institutions and Global Social Movements* (2000). He is also co-editor of *Global Social Policy*.

V. K. Ramachandran is with the Social Sciences Division, Indian Statistical Institute, Kolkata, India.

Vikas Rawal is with the Centre for Economic Studies and Planning, Jawaharlal Nehru University, New Delhi, India.

Supriya RoyChowdhury is Professor, Centre for Political Institutions, Governance and Development at the Institute for Social and Economic Change in Bangalore, India. Her areas of research interest are globalization and labour, urban poverty, social movements and comparative development.

Kalyan Sanyal is Professor of Economics at the University of Calcutta, India. His research interests are international economics and development economics.

Haiyan Wang is a Lecturer and Assistant Director of the China and Asia-Pacific Studies Program at Cornell University. Her research interests focus on capital–labour relations, global trade and regional economic integration in East Asia.

Part I
Introduction

1
Globalization's Problematic for Labour: Three Paradigms

Paul Bowles

1. Introduction

Workers in all parts of the world have seen their working conditions and rewards affected by the forces of globalization. These changes have been complex, often ambiguous and have had differential impacts leading to new inter- and intra-class frictions and fissures. A coherent response from labour has, not surprisingly, been difficult to formulate either locally, nationally or internationally. Yet the task remains pressing. As the global recession's impacts are felt by workers across the globe, solidaristic responses to globalization's dynamics are more important than ever.

The re-emergence of China and India as global economic powers has added further dimensions. Analysing the impacts of globalization on the vast labour forces of these two countries is itself a large undertaking; other chapters in this volume are focused on this question. They remind us of the differentiated nature of the working class, the difficulties, possibilities and limits of organized responses in these two countries and the complexities of the interactions between globalization, state and labour.

Many of the impacts which they discuss have specific roots in the Indian and the Chinese economic, social and political systems. Included here are the continued informalization of work in India and the expansion of the informal sector despite exposure to the 'modernizing' forces of globalization as analysed by Harriss-White in Chapter 7 and Sanyal and Bhattacharya in Chapter 8 of this volume. The agricultural crisis in rural India and its historic links to 'landlordism', analysed by Ramachandran and Rawal in Chapter 6, present a picture of India far removed from that usually portrayed by the western media and Indian politicians alike. For the latter, the emphasis is more likely to be on the promise of India's burgeoning IT sector but the new 'flexi workers' in these firms are facing their own forms of insecurity. In China, the particular role of migrant workers in China's export-oriented sector, constrained by residency categories and shaped by gender relations, demonstrates how the 'Chinese model' has affected many of its workers, as Chan, Pun Ngai and Chan show in Chapter 3, in an environment where labour has been effectively controlled by the state as Blecher explains in Chapter 4.

Notwithstanding these specificities, the experience of labour in these two countries of the South also bears some comparison with the generic changes which have affected workers worldwide as a result of contemporary global capitalism's dynamics. In the advanced industrial countries of the North, there have also been trends towards the informalization of work, often termed casualization, with the growth of largely non-unionized service sector jobs organized in 'flexible' labour regimes. The emergence of so-called 'Third World' sweatshop working conditions, gendered and racialized, in the core countries has been shocking but perhaps not surprising. To these similarities, we can also add factors specific to labour in the advanced industrialized countries. The holes in social safety nets have become larger and more have slipped through as many states have sought to reduce expenditures and add further disciplines to the labour force. Trade union and employment rights have been scaled back in many countries and real wages have stagnated with income growth coming largely through more hours being worked and higher labour force participation rates. Labour market flexibility, enshrined in OECD policy reports, and welfare state retrenchment have been the dominant policies across the industrialized world for the past two decades. This aspect of neoliberalism remains largely unchallenged despite its spectacular failures in other areas such as the under-regulation of financial institutions and markets.

Labour in both the advanced industrial core and in the developing world has therefore been challenged by many factors in the period marked by contemporary globalization. For the working classes of India and China, their integration into global capitalism has been complex and as other chapters in this volume document, their responses have been primarily local; Blecher in Chapter 4 and Hensman in Chapter 10 provide analyses of labour responses in China and India respectively. Labour in the advanced industrial countries has also engaged in local and national responses; but, in addition, organized labour particularly from North America and the European Union has been vocal in pursuing redress at the international level. It is labour in these countries, often in conjunction with sections of capital, which has lobbied its states for international labour standards. As Singh and Zammit (2004: 85–6) have written, 'for the last 20 years the

United States and a group of advanced countries, US trade unions, and the International Confederation of Free Trade Unions (ICFTU) have led a concerted campaign at the General Agreement on Tariffs and Trade (GATT) and subsequently at the World Trade Organization (WTO) for instituting higher labour standards in developing countries. Developing countries have, however, resolutely opposed any discussion of labour standards at the WTO, regarding these as thinly veiled protectionist devices.'

And yet while these debates have occurred at the international level, others have argued that labour's response should be primarily national in focus. This is pointedly the case for Gindin (2004: 6) who argues that 'the greatest international contribution the American left can make involves coming to grips with their own state'. The appropriate level(s) for progressive responses to globalization remain enduring problems.

But questions of strategy and response depend on the problematic being addressed. And here, we are in need of greater conceptual clarity so that the widely cited but too often ill-specified 'forces of globalization' are subject to greater scrutiny. If we are to find solidaristic labour responses to globalization in countries as diverse as China and India and the advanced industrial countries, then globalization's problematic for labour needs careful analysis. The possibilities for local and national labour struggles and their potential contributions to internationalist solutions, depend on the precise specification of the problematic to be addressed. That is, how the various levels of response and resistance are linked depends on how 'globalization' is analysed.

The purpose of this chapter is to provide a contribution to this analysis. Many interpretations of the concept of globalization have been formulated with very different implications for labour. While some authors choose to ignore this fundamental point and proceed as if the meaning of globalization was self-evident and non-contentious, an essential first step must be an interrogation of the term globalization itself, an examination of some of the main ways in which it has been conceptualized, as a prelude to a detailed analysis of its workings. Here, I identify three leading paradigms of globalization and set out what each implies about globalization's 'problematic' for labour. I also explore the policy responses that each paradigm suggests.

2. Mapping the dynamics of globalization: three paradigms and their implications for labour

There is no agreement on the meaning of 'globalization'. Instead of proposing a generic interpretation, I distinguish here between three different paradigms and present their interpretations of the dynamics of globalization highlighting what they identify as globalization's problematic for labour. As I will show, specifying the problematic that must be addressed depends crucially on how the dynamics of globalization are conceptualized.

The three paradigms I identify are, firstly, the *neoclassical liberal paradigm*. Based on trade theory developed by economists over the past two hundred years, this paradigm views a liberal global trading order as the main manifestation of globalization and as beneficial to the majority; the policy issue becomes how to prevent the minority obstructing globalization's march and how to minimize the adverse effects on them. The second paradigm I term *anti-neoliberal globalism*. This paradigm starts from the proposition that globalization is better viewed as an ideology, an 'ism', that of globalism. Moreover, the dominant form of this ideology over the past two decades has been that of neoliberal globalism. The problematic that this presents for labour stems from the (deliberate) shift of power to capital and away from labour and the state. The response varies from arguments in favour of a social democratic form of globalism ('counter-hegemonic globalization' for Evans, 2008), to support for de-globalization. The third paradigm, that of *multi-centred statism*, argues that globalization is a process that has a number of sources and is driven by a number of states, including non-western ones. Here the problematic concerns the space available to these states and how their internal socio-economic dynamics might work to ensure that labour receives a fair share of the gains. Each of these three paradigms is analysed in more detail below.

2.1 Neoclassical liberalism

Neoclassical economics typically privileges trade liberalization and trade flows as evidence of global integration. In general, financial liberalization is also seen as beneficial but, even before the current crisis, this tenet was more controversial than trade liberalization even among neoclassical economists with some recognizing the destabilizing and welfare-reducing costs of financial liberalization.[1] As a whole, neoclassical economics has been more comfortable dealing with the case for trade liberalization. Starting from Ricardian trade theory, the argument runs that globalization increases global welfare by reaping the benefits of greater specialization. As Deepak Lal puts it 'if the newly reconstructed [liberal international economic order] can be maintained, it offers the prospect (as did the first to the Victorians) of a sustained period of universal prosperity' (1999: 212). However, while global welfare may increase, it is not necessarily the case that all participants in the globalizing and liberalizing economy will benefit. 'Universal prosperity' notwithstanding, as Lal recognizes, 'for developed countries the major threat perceived from globalization is to the living standards of their poorest and least-skilled workers from trade with the Third World' (1999: 216).

Given the perceived threat to labour in the North from increased trade with the countries of the South, it is not surprising to find that much of the economics literature has been concerned with finding and measuring the extent of globalization's impact on the wages of workers in industrialized countries (see, for example, Feenstra, 1998; Jones, 2000; Leamer, 1998).

Widening income inequality in the core countries has been attributed at least in part to the decline in the incomes of unskilled workers whose jobs have disappeared, been offshored, or whose wages have declined as a result of competition from the unskilled labour from developing countries embodied in their exports to the industrialized countries. Labour, especially low-skilled labour, in industrialized countries competes directly with labour from developing countries.

Globalization, on this reading, is likely to lead to protectionist sentiment among workers in industrial countries, pitted as they are against lower cost labour imports from developing countries. Neoclassical economists prefer longer-term retraining programmes which shift workers in industrial countries out of those industries in which developing countries have a comparative advantage.

The natural unfolding of the market, therefore, results in some workers in industrialized countries being pitted against their developing country counterparts. Neoclassical economics has the interesting but troublesome prediction that globalization as trade liberalization is a positive sum game but it nevertheless necessarily involves losses for workers in some countries. Most of the academic and policy attention has been focused on how to ease the transition costs for these workers.

Empirical studies initially focused on particular industries with high import content, especially footwear and textiles (although in theory the depressing wage effect should be felt by all in the tradable goods sector). But the rise of China and India has subjected much broader segments of the industrialized countries' working class to the threat of competition from labour abroad. Now everyone from computer programmers and software engineers to workers in the highly capital-intensive auto sector are threatened with job losses and lower wages. The response has been for industrialized countries' governments to place even greater stress on the importance of education for the knowledge-based economy; with those who fail to accept the challenge facing a low-wage future. The 'globalization problematic', as far as labour is concerned, concerns relatively highly paid, typically unionized, relatively low-skilled workers in core countries. Workers in developing countries are generally presumed to be the beneficiaries of globalization.

Whether the driving force behind globalization is the technology which allows communication and coordination to take place globally and/or the rational wisdom of trade negotiators in liberalizing trade (and investment) rules, the result is a redistribution of income from the trade-exposed part of labour's aristocracy in the core to labour in developing country export sectors. 'Transition' and 'retraining' strategies are the policy response. The possibilities for common responses by labour are limited to impossible as labour is conceived in national terms (as are capital, and the underlying explanandum, relative capital/labour ratios).

One way out of this conflict recently highlighted by Rodrik (2008) occurs if competition from imports spurs productivity growth in the import competing sector in core countries, a possibility ignored in static trade theory. If this is the case, then wages need not fall if workers in the core retain some of the ensuing productivity gains (although whether this happy outcome arises through agency or the market is unclear) and the problem shrinks to being one of adjustment for displaced workers. Indeed, other workers in developed countries may gain from China's export of cheap consumer goods; in many cases, workers in the core are not threatened by China's low wages but benefit from them.

2.2 Anti-neoliberal globalism

This paradigm starts from the proposition that globalization represents a global shift in power towards capital and away from labour. Globalization has effectively empowered multinational corporations in their relations with nation states and labour so that they are able to play off states and workers against each other in their global search for profits. Associated with the neoliberal revolution of the 1980s, globalization is viewed as a response to the profits crisis and capital–labour impasse of the 1970s (Harvey, 2005). The deliberate policies enacted to unleash market liberalization, or market fundamentalism, through the auspices of the international financial institutions freed capital from its national fetters and created the conditions for global capital accumulation directed by the emerging 'transnational capitalist class' (Sklair, 2001). Labour, in all countries, has been weakened as a result, its bargaining power reduced by mobile transnational capital and compliant national elites.

While weakening labour everywhere, the globalization problematic is likely to be felt most intensely where labour rights are weakest. In China, for example, Anita Chan (2001) describes China's workers as being metaphorically, and often literally, 'under assault' from the forces and agents of globalization; while in India enterprise surveys show 'an aggressive shift in employment from permanent to temporary, casual and contract employment [with] a systematic transfer of jobs from the bargainable or unionized category' (Sharma, 2006: 2083). Globalization sceptics would point out, though, that the informalization of labour in India precedes globalization and that the Supreme Court has sometimes ruled against labour rights. In core countries, where previous expansions of the market led to extensive and successful Polanyian reactions with the establishment and expansion of national welfare states, there are still important challenges – but the rawness of global capitalism's new power is most often found in the periphery where such a countermovement against the attempt to establish the 'self-regulating market' is still only weakly developed.

Transnational capital does have pressure points, however, on which action is possible. One such pressure point is through consumers and non-governmental organizations (NGOs). With the state (intentionally) weakened by neoliberalism, the governance of the corporation becomes a matter of direct public interest. Thus, NGOs such as the Clean Clothes campaign publicly challenge corporations to ensure that working conditions in their global supply chains meet some minimum standards. Corporate codes of conduct, voluntarily developed by private agents, become a key regulator to raise working conditions at the most exploitative links of the supply chain by setting minimum standards. Private sector agencies become the monitors and enforcers of these standards through site visits, and working conditions in the global economy may gradually become governed perhaps by a combination of private actors and governments (see Seidman, 2007). Flynn and O'Brien, in Chapter 11, propose an innovative approach beyond voluntary codes of conduct by arguing that western labour movements could bring their own states' multinationals to account through legal means.

International labour standards may play a role, not as a defensive action by globally privileged sections of the working class as suggested under neoclassical liberalism, but as a collective defence by workers against the enhanced powers of capital. International labour standards, in this framing, can be part of a response aimed at reclaiming for labour some of the rights and bargaining power that it has lost under the neoliberal onslaught. This type of approach, often championed by the ILO through its 'decent work' agenda, could contribute to raising global labour standards; such a strategy might be widely supported since labour solidarity is more readily achievable if globalization is interpreted in its neoliberal form. There is the possibility that the expansion of transnational corporations gives workers across different countries shared objectives, and the consequent development of 'global unions' and of global bargaining (Lerner, 2007). The objection to this is that the focus of labour standards on formal sector work (and unions) runs the risk of pushing work back into the informal sector, a move which would be socially regressive and counter-productive (Kabeer, 2004).

Campaigns over labour standards and moves to establish global unions and global bargaining broadly describe attempts at constructing a 'fair globalization', to use the preferred term of the World Commission on the Social Dimensions of Globalization, through strengthening the power of global labour in its dealings with global capital and opening up a space for global social democracy. This response accepts globalization as a technologically driven reality, but seeks to change its neoliberal governance to a more benign, labour-friendly, form. As the World Commission, which included such anti-neoliberal globalism luminaries as Joseph Stiglitz, writes, 'we judge that the problems we have identified are not due to globalization as such but to deficiencies in its governance. Global markets have grown rapidly without the parallel development of economic and social institutions necessary for their smooth and equitable functioning. At the same time, there is concern about the unfairness of key global rules on trade and finance and their asymmetric effects on rich and poor countries' (2004: xi). Here, the 'unfairness' lies in the trade rules used by advanced countries.

There are other responses on offer too. For example, Walden Bello (2002) has promoted the idea of 'de-globalization', a strategy which places much greater weight on the nation state as a site of democracy, control and regulation of social outcomes. The approach is again based on the assumption that neoliberal globalism is a political project and, as such, politically reversible. The push for liberalization under the WTO can be halted and the neoliberal agendas of the World Bank and IMF reversed. In their place will be the return of an international, not global, economy in which nation states serve as the basic units of analysis. It is within these political spaces that each society can forge its own path and solve its own distributional conflicts; states are linked together through trade and investment but no longer harmonized along neoliberal lines. In this response, therefore, it is both neoliberalism and globalism that need to be opposed. But in so far as the argument seems to suggest 'bringing back the nationalist developmental state' it may be reckoned problematic. Is it likely that 'national bourgeoisies' and their political representatives will reform neoliberal globalization? (Evans, 2008).

Still, many accounts of 'neoliberal globalization' place the action at the global level, with global capital confronting global civil society and/or global labour, and Bello does a great service by re-emphasizing the importance of the nation state. Analyses focusing on the global level run the risk of missing the important global–nation state–local complexities that determine how globalization processes play out in practice. In the Chinese case, the local state has been a key player in shaping the interactions with global capital, often as 'compradors' with foreign capital to the detriment of workers, as Chan, Pun Ngai and Chan document in Chapter 3. In India, too, different states have pursued different strategies, and though most are now seeking to persuade capitalists, both local and international, that they provide an attractive 'investment climate', they differ widely in terms of the social protection that they offer. All of this points to the need for including more detailed examinations of the state, at its various levels, in determining globalization's impacts. The global financial crisis has led to a major rethinking of the role of the state in regulating national and global political economies as neoliberalism's dominance fades. It is not so much the state that is withering away as neoliberalism's appeal.

2.3 Multi-centred statism

The necessity of examining the state is central to analyses of globalization which suggest that the neoliberal phase has run its course and that a new dynamic is emerging. Of course, states have always been central to accounts of globalization which equate it with imperialism. Here, the US and, to a lesser extent, European countries are seen as adopting globalization as a project, backed by state power, to open up foreign markets for 'their' firms (see Petras and Veltmeyer, 2001, for example). But these accounts are all premised on the assumption that globalization – aka imperialism – is a western-centric process. The places of China and India are under-explored in these accounts; they are typically viewed as being incorporated *tout court* into global capitalism's expansion. Implicitly it is typically western capital and western interests that drive global integration with western state policy geared to promoting this.

But this account misses the possibility that globalization might be a multi-centred process. It is in this possibility that the importance of China and India are particularly evident, not simply as repositories of western capital and outsourcing but as potentially important emerging centres of global power, both economic and political. This requires a rethinking of the dynamics of globalization. Instead of equating globalization with Americanization, and with US imperial power, the concept needs to be refined to allow multiple centres and dimensions. Befu (2007) has made the case with respect to Japan. He argues that the concept of 'Japanization' parallels such concepts as 'Westernization' and 'Americanization', which have sometimes been equated with globalization. 'Japanization' has as much utility for the understanding of globalization' and 'there is no intrinsic reason why "universal theory" or concepts applicable globally must be born out of the Western experience' (2007: 151).

Certainly the evidence of the rise of multinationals from the South (Goldstein, 2007) suggests that western capital is not unchallenged in the global market. Multinationals from China and India have been prominent among them and many Chinese firms, typically state-owned, have 'gone global' as part of their growth strategy and have been actively supported by the government in this process. In this regard, China is unique in that, as Williamson and Zeng (2007) note, China's own global firms have emerged at a much earlier stage of capitalist development than they did elsewhere. Both China and India are now significant sources of foreign direct investment in some sectors with, for example, the Indian group Tata having acquired Corus, the last surviving at least partially British steelmaker, and more recently such iconic former British companies as Jaguar and Land Rover, and China's Lenovo acquiring IBM Thinkpad. Politically, too, China has 'gone global' where 'the early years of the twenty-first century have witnessed a growing awareness on the part of the CCP's theorists and leaders that globalization offers China an opportunity to project its influence and power beyond the boundaries of the Chinese nation-state, and that China could operate throughout the world in a far more proactive and energetic manner than had hitherto been the case' (Knight, 2008: 171).

But this strategy of 'going global' is premised on a particular interpretation of globalization. Of course, the term 'globalization' has been debated in China as elsewhere (see Knight, 2008) with a spectrum of views evident; the dominant view, however, is that globalization should be seen as an objective, technologically driven process and, as such, capable of being used by a variety of social systems. That is, it (allegedly) transcends debates over capitalism and socialism and can be fashioned to be consistent with either. As Yu (2007: 59) has noted, 'in the discussion of globalization ... Chinese intellectuals, for the most part, no longer regard it as a synonym for capitalism, although they know clearly that the developed capitalistic countries control the progress of globalization.' This opens the possibility that 'unlike some Western political leaders who downplay state sovereignty in the global age, Chinese leaders make sovereignty the basis on which all political and economic activities take place, including economic globalization' (Yu, 2007: 57). As a result, China's leaders have sought integration into the global economy but on the basis of retaining state sovereignty, a path which has included the training of high-level state cadres to 'become the pivotal force of the Chinese government in dealing with the process of globalization' (Yu, 2007: 55).

The central point of this 'globalization with Chinese characteristics' is that it is consistent with national sovereignty and the pursuit of a national developmentalist agenda. Such an agenda requires that globalization be governed in such a way as to allow development space. If the term the 'Beijing Consensus' (Ramos, 2004) means anything it means this (see also Dirlik, 2007). In this respect, this paradigm bears similarities with the 'de-globalization' route outlined above. But there are some differences. The multi-centred statist approach places much greater emphasis on the state – and multiple states – as the drivers and continued occupants of the driving seat of globalization. The frictions in the global political economy are between globalizing states (and their firms) rather than between global capital and global civil society with states relegated to the back seat. Rather, the emerging powers of China and India are growing in their influence on global governance. As the Doha round collapsed in the summer of 2008, it was significant that it was not the result of the usual US versus European disagreements but because developing countries led by India refused to sign off a deal that would adversely affect their agricultural sectors. And as the global financial crisis has unfolded it is the G20, not the G8, which has become the key forum for the discussion of solutions.

There are many debating points here. One of them is whether the Chinese state can really be viewed as a unitary state capable of following a developmentalist strategy (Howell, 2006), a question which is certainly also applicable to India. But let us assume for the moment that both countries are capable of making use of the development space which they seek. What are implications of this for labour?

In a neoclassical world, rising productivity would fuel both growth and rising real wages in both countries. However, history is more complex than this. While East Asian developmental states have seen tremendous increases in real wages this has been in no small degree the result of the often bloody struggles that workers there have waged against brutal regimes for labour and union rights, as Japan circa 1960 and South Korea circa 1980 testify.

On this reading of globalization, the problematic for labour is how to ensure that it receives its share of the benefits from, and has voice in, the economic success of the globalizing developmental state. This requires assessment of internal political structures and dynamics. What are the prospects, for example, for Chinese labour? Is the state monopoly ACFTU capable of playing a more independent role as China advances economically? Or will rents continue to be captured by the new elite of entrepreneurs and cadres with income inequality increasing further? How do the Chinese leaders and cadres, guiding globalization as they see it in the 'national interest', view workers? To many, the answer may seem all too depressingly obvious. But it is of interest to note that as many western governments continue to dismantle labour protections in the face of globalization, China after years of systematically dismantling the 'iron rice bowl' now appears to be moving in a somewhat different direction with a succession of upgrades to the labour law in recent years. While this is of interest, research is needed to determine if this is also of significance; Wang, Appelbaum, Degiuli, and Lichtenstein provide us with exactly that research in Chapter 5.

It is certainly hard to see, to put it mildly, China – or India – as the agents of globally emancipatory politics. Advocates of counter-hegemonic globalization have good reason for arguing that while 'diminishing disparities among nation states is a valuable agenda ... unless the behaviour of nation states themselves is constrained domestically and globally, by a more powerful "movement of movements" they will remain primarily agents of elite interests' (Evans, 2008: 285). Even so, elite interests in both China and India do suggest that some kind of 'counter-movement from above' is underway. Dong, Bowles and Chang, in Chapter 2, explore the extent to which this is occurring, and has been successful, in the Chinese countryside. Harriss, in the concluding Chapter 13, reviews all of the chapters in this volume and provides a Polanyian interpretation of the dynamics at play.

I return to the question of whether 'globally constraining' policies, perhaps such as international labour standards, provide a possible mechanism for bringing about the types of societal change that would strengthen labour organizations and movements in developmental states. That is, should there be a quid pro quo for the development space that China and India demand in terms of measures that would permit or even encourage the transition to a developmental state in which labour is able to bargain for its share of the productivity gains? The possibility of a specifically 'democratic developmental state' was raised by Gordon White (1998). He argued that such a state would need to have broad control over three functions: regulatory, infrastructure and, importantly for our theme here, redistributive. But for such a state simultaneously to achieve both developmental and democratic objectives would require a specific constellation of institutional design of the state, political society and civil society. It is no surprise that he concluded that 'given the particular characteristics of the democratic developmental state ... it would be reasonable to be sceptical about their feasibility. Democratic developmental states may turn out to be the exception rather than the rule' (1998: 42). Are there external pressures or spaces that might make such exceptions more likely to occur and succeed?

China and India present different challenges in this respect. China as an authoritarian state poses one set of challenges as outlined above. India, as a democratic polity which has shifted to neoliberalism but which nevertheless wishes to claim greater development space, offers a different set. The almost standard account that portrays the organized Indian working class as having been co-opted and rendered politically inconsequential may be overdrawn (Teitelbaum, 2006). RoyChowdhury, in Chapter 9, analyses the changing nature of class in India and its continued relevance for understanding industrial disputes. In the era of neoliberal economic reforms, unions have had some success in resisting measures proposed to enhance the powers of employers (as by the Second National Labour Commission in 2002). However, it is the case that poverty is recognized as a major issue but that redistribution is not. As Mooij and Dev (2004: 117) noted in an analysis of social policy, 'the human development framework [to which India moved in the later 1990s], sympathetic as it may be, helped to divert attention from the more structural characteristics of poverty' including the availability of employment and the possibilities of 'decent work'. 'Poverty' is a powerful factor politically. Labour is not.

Refashioning the governance of the global economy to allow more development space raises questions, therefore, of how that space can best be used to advance the cause of labour. This relies on analyses of 'internal' political dynamics as well as the possible mechanisms that might be available to influence them from 'outside'. Bienefeld, in Chapter 12, analyses how the 'internal' and 'outside' pressures are shaping Chinese capitalism and the paths it could take. If greater development space is either ceded by the core or grabbed by emerging powers then the implications for labour in the core also require consideration. If economic and political power continues to shift to China and India, analyses of how labour in the core can be accommodated within this beyond the neoclassical emphasis on 'retraining' are required.

One important consideration here is the international policy environment. This reflects the ways in which global shifts are managed. The current environment, with large imbalances as developmental states run large surpluses and the US acts as the consumer of last resort, is fraught with instability as the current global situation, triggered by the credit crisis, demonstrates. New forms of global economic governance which allow developmentalist strategies but which also stress the importance of domestic demand and coordinated international policy responses might be prerequisites for ensuring that the insecurities for labour arising from global power shifts are minimized. That is, in seeking to manage the shifts that are presently underway in the global economy, greater autonomy for the state might also paradoxically require closer international macroeconomic policy coordination for the new configurations to be beneficial to labour.

Even those who are sceptical of the size of the impacts of the global shifts, nevertheless see a new international governance structure as desirable. Singh and Zammit (2004: 99–100), for example, argue that 'the alternative path is essentially one of an international Keynesian regime of managed world trade and controlled international capital movements with measures to increase worldwide demand for labour. The national and international institutions required to provide the basis for such a regime are, not surprisingly, rather different from those underpinning the current globalization project. The alternative model, it is suggested, would not only bring closer North–South cooperation, but also lead to full employment of the world's resources and to a faster rate of economic growth, thereby reducing poverty and helping promote labour standards in both the North and the South.' The space to discuss such alternatives has been opened by the current crisis.

Understanding the dynamics of globalization is therefore a critical task for examining the impacts on labour and formulating effective strategies in response. The three paradigms discussed here propose different theoretical frameworks and analytical tools for addressing the question. These are summarized in Table 1.1.

3. Conclusions

Globalization's 'problematic' – its understanding and implications – for labour depends upon the conceptual framework used to understand the term 'globalization'. Much confusion has surrounded this term and its multiple uses have been an obstacle to the analysis of its effects on, and desirable responses by, labour throughout the world. In this chapter, I have demonstrated this by analysing three different paradigms for interpreting globalization. All three posit their own particular problems, identify specific sites where the effects of globalization are expected to be most keenly felt and suggest which strategies at the local, national and international levels are likely to be most appropriate for labour. In so doing, the paradigms assist us in understanding how globalization's impacts in China and India can be best interpreted, what dynamics are at play and what responses can forge solidaristic responses.

In adopting any of the three paradigms, it is necessary to ask, as an empirical matter, the extent to which 'globalization', however interpreted, is a key explanatory factor. That is, all three paradigms are subject to the globalization sceptic's critique that the forces of globalization have been exaggerated. The case studies of China and India in the chapters in this volume provide rich terrain in this regard. They present us with careful analysis of the ways in which local and national politics act as critical filters through which globalization must pass and which limit and refract the ways in which globalization is experienced.

If we follow the reasoning of the multi-centred statist argument – or that of de-globalization – as outlined above, then this suggests that the way forward is to develop analysis of the politics of labour within the developmentalist states of China and India, and to examine the possible ways in which transnational connections are – or could be – involved in these politics. Would such connections be seen as useful by labour organizations in India? Are there even such possibilities for China? Where should the strategic focus of resistance be: at the local, national or global levels? To what extent have international labour standards proven of practical value in expanding democratic space for labour, or what role might they play? Relatedly, what has been the contribution, or what could the contribution be, of consumer-NGO campaigns? What are the connections between workers in different industries in the advanced countries with their counterparts in the re-emergent Asian

Table 1.1 Globalization paradigms, the problematic for labour, and responses

Paradigm	Assumptions/ characteristics	Globalization's problematic for labour	Policy issues and responses
Neoclassical liberalism	Globalization characterized as trade and investment liberalization	Job losses and wage reductions in advanced countries especially in the import competing sectors	Local: Individual human capital upgrading
	Globalization as welfare-enhancing in the aggregate	Increasing wage inequality in the advanced countries	National: Job retraining for workers in the core
	Comparative advantage, based on factor endowments, explains processes	The natural unfolding of the market pits the interests of workers in North against those in the South	International: Protection against imports advocated by labour in the core
			International labour standards as a means to prevent low labour standards acting as an 'unfair endowment' for developing countries
Anti-neoliberal globalism	Globalization as a political project to increase the power of capital over states and labour	Increasing power of capital (corporations) everywhere	Local: Collective forms of resistance
	A response to the profits crisis of the 1970s	Increased insecurity and deteriorating working conditions for workers everywhere as capital is able to play off jurisdictions and workers against each other	National: Adaptive and competition states too weak but there is still the possibility of varied outcomes based on extent of state elite's embrace of neoliberalism
		Most adversely affected workers are those in the weakest bargaining positions, e.g. migrant women in export processing zones	International: Corporate codes of conduct/CSR
			Global unionism

Multi-centred (developmental) statism	No single model or source of globalization	Internal dynamics of developmental states determine labour organizations' ability to claim productivity gains	International minimum wage campaigns
	Rise of southern multinationals		Global social democracy as a way to regulate global capital or, more radically, a counter-hegemonic globalization
	Evolving global governance structures with developing states seeking to wrestle back policy space	Impact on workers in the advanced countries of expanding developmental states in a deflationary/recessionary world economy	International labour standards as a way of reclaiming labour's lost power at the global level
			De-globalization as a mechanism to re-establish the political autonomy of the state
			Local: Collective forms of resistance and voice
			National: Using national sovereignty to benefit labour; the possibilities for voice in, or more strongly a democratic, developmental state
			International: Importance of global macroeconomic policy environment
			Possibilities for promoting labour rights in developmental states (a role for international labour standards?)
			Defining policy space; what is 'fair'?

economies? Are there points of leverage that would create opportunities for global unionism and global bargaining? Or are there positive as well as normative arguments in favour of counter-hegemonic globalization as a promising way forward? Zolberg (1995) has characterized the post-1945 international regime as 'labour friendly'; how can a 'labour friendly' international regime be constructed now as a response to the current global crisis? In clarifying the conceptual terrain of 'globalization' it is hoped this chapter and this volume can contribute to the answers to these questions.

Note

1. For a neoclassical liberal critique of financial liberalization see, for example, Bhagwati (1998).

References

Befu, H. (2007) '"Japanization", "Asianization of the West" and "Creolization": a Perspective from Japan', in Paul Bowles, Henry Veltmeyer et al. (eds), *National Perspectives on Globalization*, Basingstoke: Palgrave Macmillan, pp. 139–53.
Bello, W. (2002) *Deglobalization: Ideas for a New World Economy*, London: Zed Books.
Bhagwati, J. (1998) 'The Capital Myth: the Difference Between Trade in Widgets and Dollars', *Foreign Affairs*, May/June, 77, 3: 7–13.
Chan, A. (2001) *China's Workers Under Assault: the Exploitation of Labor in a Globalizing Economy*, Armonk, NY: M. E. Sharpe.
Dirlik, A. (2007) 'Global South: Predicament and Promise', *The Global South*, Winter, 1, 1: 12–23.
Evans, P. (2008) 'Is an Alternative Globalization Possible?' *Politics and Society*, 36: 271–305.
Feenstra, R. (1998) 'Integration of Trade and Disintegration of Production in the Global Economy', *Journal of Economic Perspectives*, 12, 4: 31–50.
Gindin, S. (2004) 'Globalization and Labour: Defining the "Problem"', paper presented at Brandeis University, 24 April.
Goldstein, A. (2007) *Multinational Corporations from Emerging Economies: Composition, Conceptualization and Direction in the Global Economy*, Basingstoke: Palgrave Macmillan.
Harvey, D. (2005) *A Brief History of Neoliberalism*, Oxford: Oxford University Press.
Howell, J. (2006) 'Reflections on the Chinese State', *Development and Change*, 37, 2: 273–97.
Jones, R. (2000) *Globalization and the Theory of Input Trade*, Cambridge, MA: MIT Press.
Kabeer, N. (2004) 'Globalization, Labour Standards, and Women's Rights: Dilemmas of Collective (In)Action in an Interdependent World', *Feminist Economics*, 10, 1: 3–35.
Knight, N. (2008) *Imagining Globalization in China*, Cheltenham: Edward Elgar.
Lal, D. (1999) 'Globalization: What Does it Mean for Developed and Developing Countries?' in Horst Siebert (ed.), *Globalization and Labour*, Institut für Weltwirtschaft an der Universität Kiel, pp. 211–21.

Leamer, E. (1998) 'In Search of Stolper-Samuelson Linkages between International Trade and Lower Wages', in S. Collins (ed.), *Imports, Exports and the American Worker*, Washington, DC: Brookings Institution, pp. 141–202.

Lerner, St, (2007) 'Global Unions: a Solution to Labour's Worldwide Decline', *Labour Forum*, 16, 1: 23–37.

Mooij, J. and Dev, M. (2004) 'Social Sector Priorities: an Analysis of Budgets and Expenditures in India in the 1990s', *Development Policy Review*, 22, 1: 97–120.

Petras, J. and Veltmeyer, H. (2001) *Globalization Unmasked: Imperialism in the Twenty-first Century*, London: Zed Books.

Ramos, J. (2004) 'The Beijing Consensus', The Foreign Policy Centre, May.

Rodrik, D. (2008) 'Stolper-Samuelson for the Real World', 16 June blog available at http://rodrik.typepad.com/dani_rodriks_weblog/2008/06/stolper-samuelson-for-the-real-world.html

Seidman, G. (2007) *Beyond the Boycott*, New York: Russell Sage Foundation.

Sharma, A. (2006) 'Flexibility, Employment and Labour Market Reforms in India', *Economic and Political Weekly*, 41: 2078–85.

Singh, A. and Zammit, A. (2004) 'Labour Standards and the "Race to the Bottom": Rethinking Globalization and Workers' Rights from Developmental and Solidaristic Perspectives', *Oxford Review of Economic Policy*, 20, 1: 85–104.

Sklair, L. (2001) *The Transnational Capitalist Class*, Oxford: Blackwell.

Teitelbaum, E. (2006) 'Was the Indian Labour Movement Ever Co-opted? Evaluating Standard Accounts', *Critical Asian Studies*, 38, 4: 389–417.

White, G. (1998) 'Constructing a Democratic Developmental State', in M. Robinson and G. White (eds), *The Democratic Developmental State: Politics and Institutional Design*, Oxford: Oxford University Press, pp. 17–51.

Williamson, P. and Ming Zeng (2007) 'The Global Impact of China's Emerging Multinationals', in C. McNally (ed.), *China's Emergent Political Economy: Capitalism in the Dragon's Lair*, London: Routledge, pp. 83–101.

World Commission on the Social Dimension of Globalization (2004) *A Fair Globalization: Creating Opportunities for All*, available at http://www.ilo.org/fairglobalization/report/lang--en/index.htm

Yu, K. (2007) 'From Sino-West to Globalization: a Perspective from China', in P. Bowles, H. Veltmeyer et al. (eds), *National Perspectives on Globalization*, Basingstoke: Palgrave Macmillan, pp. 44–60.

Zolberg, A. (1995) 'Response: Working-Class Dissolution', *International and Working-Class History*, March, 47: 28–38.

Part II
China: Impacts and Responses

2
Managing Liberalization and Globalization in Rural China: Trends in Rural Labour Allocation, Income and Inequality

Xiao-yuan Dong, Paul Bowles and Hongqin Chang

1. Introduction

China's rural economy has undergone radical change since the onset of economic reforms in 1978. In the thirty years since then, rural China has experienced successive waves of liberalization. The dismantling of the commune system in 1978 was the opening, and dramatic, salvo in a continued and protracted extension of the market into the organization and coordination of the rural economy. The household responsibility system, which replaced the commune system, was followed by the expansion of off-farm rural industrial employment in township and village enterprises (TVEs) in the mid-1980s. These enterprises were rapidly privatized themselves in the mid to late 1990s. At the same time, rural–urban migration became a major feature of the Chinese economy as tens of millions of peasants moved around the country in search of work. Then, in 2001, China joined the World Trade Organization (WTO) in a move which further opened the agricultural and rural economies to the forces and logic of global capitalism.

These changes enriched many peasant households but sparked resistance from others, especially those dispossessed of their land as local governments reallocated land to more profitable industrial uses with little regard to those farming it (see Guo, 2001). And yet, despite the extension of the market into every facet of rural life, it has not been a process which has been wholly spontaneous or unregulated. In fact, quite the opposite. The central government has made conscious efforts to manage the process of rural market liberalization over the past thirty years. The Chinese state, far more than in most developing countries, has sought to manage the path of liberalization and globalization so as to both take advantage of the market and to constrain its more negative dynamics (see Naughton, 2007; Qian, 2003).

In this chapter, we argue that a Polanyian framework can be used fruitfully to explain the dynamics of government policy in rural China. We set out this framework in the next section and discuss rural change in China through this prism in detail in section 3. We examine the ways in which liberalization and globalization have been introduced into China's rural economy and survey the ways in which the central state has sought to manage these processes by policy interventions, particularly since the early 2000s.

We then analyse the outcomes of this dual process of liberalization and globalization on the one hand and government-sponsored amelioration efforts on the other in section 4. We focus on changing patterns of labour allocation in response to market expansion, rural incomes and intra-rural income inequality. The data show that the state has been successful in managing liberalization and globalization in such a way as to reduce poverty, raise average real incomes, and reduce inter-regional rural income inequalities. The evidence on inter-group income inequality, however, points to widening intra-rural income gaps. We conclude that the biggest test of the leadership's ability to manage globalization comes with the fallout from the current global recession.

2. Karl Polanyi in China

The path of liberalization and globalization in China has been heavily managed by the central state. The unleashing of market forces has been rapid and dramatic but has also been heavily influenced by the government policy of 'economic reform' which has set the parameters for market expansion. This has been the case not only for promoting the rapid development and intensification of market processes but also in attempts to control the outcomes of those processes.

This 'managing the market' approach is suggestive of possible Polanyian processes at work. For this to be a plausible interpretation, a careful recasting of Polanyi in the Chinese context is required. The changes occurring over the past thirty years in rural China certainly qualify as being a 'great transformation' in their own right. The liberalization and globalization of the rural sector with the ever increasing roles of local, national and international markets have already been noted. But this expansion of the market has been used to facilitate the structural transformation of the Chinese countryside. That is, the rural economy has been transformed from a largely non-market self-sufficient sector to one increasingly reliant on wage labour much of which is employed in the industrial sector. The developmental transition from an agricultural to an industrial economy has transformed the rural sector with the creation of a rural-based waged labour force which is employed in both rural and urban centres. The absorption of labour into local enterprises at the township and village levels as well as the mass migrations to the coastal cities for export-oriented employment have fundamentally changed the income sources and labour allocation patterns of households in rural China (Taylor et al., 2003).

This multi-dimensional transformation of rural China has been facilitated by the expansion of the market. And yet, while there has undoubtedly been a progressive increase in the scope and scale of the market, and this has been a consistent thrust of government policy over the past three decades, this has also been a process which has spawned some kind of 'counter-movement'. While there have been many instances of peasant protest and backlash, it would be far too much to suggest that there has been an organized civil society counter-movement. Indeed, while local spontaneous protests and grievances have typically been addressed, any semblance of organized resistance – a 'counter-movement' from below – has been swiftly destroyed.

But the constraining of markets can come from many sources and not just from civil society, from below. Munck (2006: 176) also reminds us that a 'counter-movement' can also come from above, from 'enlightened managers of capitalism' or from 'reactionary backward-looking forces'. Munck (2006: 184) approvingly quotes Evans that 'elites, no less than the rest of us, need to resolve the Polanyi problem'.

This clarification of Polanyi's message opens up new ways of interpreting changes in the Chinese countryside. It suggests a dialectic at work between the policy thrust to sequentially liberalize the rural sector and integrate it into the global economy as well as a desire to manage this process to protect society – and maintain social stability – against the worst excesses of an unregulated market. In China, with civil society effectively suppressed and confined to numerous but uncoordinated acts of local protest and resistance, the main agents in this dialectic are state elites themselves as both using the institution of the state to promote the extension of the market and to seek to regulate its workings – to 'create a degree of sustainability for the machine they had created' (Munck, 2006: 180) – and outcomes. Of course, the Chinese state operates at multiple levels but, as a first mapping of this process, we focus here primarily on the policies of the central state. Here the rhetoric of the 'harmonious society' promoted by the current leadership under Hu Jintao speaks directly to the need to ensure the social stability and sustainability of the reformed economy, making use of the market where possible but intervening to ensure equitable outcomes where necessary. It is this type of elite-driven Polanyian process that characterizes the Chinese leadership's outlook, especially under the new leadership.

This interpretive framework has been explicitly used to examine China's reform path by Wang. He argues (2008: 18) that in the reform period 'the Chinese moral economy was transformed into a market society' from 1979 to 1999 with market society emerging as the 'dominating factor' by the end of this period. The problems associated with market domination, including 'increasing social polarization between rich and poor (e.g. regional disparities, urban/rural divide, inequality within urban China, and inequality within the countryside)' required a change in policy and led to a 'protective countermovement to re-embed the economy into the society' (ibid.: 21) He argues that this 'counter-movement' can be dated back to 1999 although 'most social policies were introduced after Hu Jintao and Wen Jiabao took office in 2002' (ibid.: 22) with 'protective legislation and other interventions [as] the characteristics of this countermovement' (ibid.: 47). Wang provides examples in both urban and rural areas of policies which have been introduced to reduce inequality and to provide social security. In this way, he argues that China has moved from the initial reform period concentration on 'economic policies' to one now which concentrates on 'social policies'.

We find Wang's basic argument instructive and consider in more detail its application to the rural economy in the next section. In so doing, we argue that the temporal division suggested by Wang (i.e. reforms prior to 1999 and afterwards) has some traction but that the division he presents is too stark. In particular, the period since the turn of the millennium has been one in which it is true that social protections have increased but it is also one in which the expansion of the market has intensified with WTO accession. That is, the latter period has been one in which *both* market expansion and counter-movement have been promoted by government policy rather than one in which there has been a simple switch from one to the other. The outcomes of this dynamic are discussed in section 4.

3. Reforming China's rural economy: liberalization, globalization and social protection

Prior to 1978, nearly three-quarters of the Chinese population lived in rural areas and most of the rural residents were primarily engaged in agricultural production. Rural income was low with the majority of the rural population living below the dollar a day poverty line. Despite low levels of absolute income, the social protections offered by the commune system were extensive through the 'iron rice bowl'. The commune system also emphasized self-sufficiency over trade and so internal markets were poorly developed. This was the case for goods and for factors of production; with respect to labour, the household registration system (*hukou*) clearly separated rural from urban workers, a characteristic of a long-standing and enduring 'urban bias' in China's policy formation, and intra-rural labour mobility was also highly constrained (Cheng and Selden, 1994). The role of the market in rural China was, therefore, strictly limited and subservient to the political logic of Maoist planning. However, this socialist legacy did mean that the subsequent expansion of the market took place against a backdrop of assets such as land and education being relatively equally distributed by developing country standards (Lardy, 1983).

The economic reforms that began in 1978 were initially focused on agriculture with the liberalization of prices and a greater role for the market in allocating and rewarding labour, and consequent eroding and abolition of the previous commune-provided social protections, the main policy thrusts. The main policy objective in promoting the expansion of the market as the primary labour allocation mechanism has been to facilitate the transfer of surplus out of the agricultural sector and into higher productivity industrial wage labour, thereby moving the rural economy towards fuller employment and higher earnings.

The first step was the implementation of the household responsibility system which significantly improved the work incentives of farmers and generated unprecedented growth in agricultural production and farm incomes between 1978 and 1984 (Lin, 1987). Households were given limited use rights to land in return for fulfilling grain quotas. Output above this quota could be sold on free markets and led farmers to diversify into higher value crops. After the initial post-1978 boost in production, agricultural growth slowed but has still maintained a respectable average rate of output growth of 5.8 per cent per year in years since 1984. Since the early 1980s, however, off-farm work has emerged as a main source of income growth for many rural households (Kung, 2002; Lohmar, 1999). From 1985 to the early 1990s, TVEs grew rapidly, providing jobs for nearly 120 million rural workers (Bowles and Dong, 1994; Weitzman and Xu, 1994). This marked the first large structural transformation of the rural economy as farmers were transferred from agricultural to industrial work within their home towns and average incomes rose as a result.

Since the early 1990s, rural–urban migration has become the most common way for rural labourers to get a job off the farm (de Brauw et al., 2002). It is estimated that in 1994 and 1995, about 80 million migrant workers went to the cities, a number which roughly doubled over the following decade. Consistent with the experience of industrial countries, this second large structural transformation which moved labourers from agricultural to non-agricultural activities and rapidly increased rural–urban migration, fuelled sharp rises in labour productivity and income in China's rural sector. As a result, the proportion of the rural population living below the dollar a day poverty line fell sharply, from 65 per cent in 1981 to 12.5 per cent in 2001 (Ravallion, 2006).

While the transformation of China's rural economy is indisputable, there remain many challenges which government policy has sought to address. Farm size is small and agricultural productivity remains low. There have therefore been attempts, from the late 1990s onwards, at agricultural 'modernization' which have sought to increase production scale mainly though the government promotion of so-called 'dragon head' agribusinesses which supply urban markets through large-scale rurally located agribusiness operations (in poultry, livestock and food processing). Government policy seeks not only to expand the market but to shape the forms that it takes. Zhang and Donaldson (2008) document how these enterprises have led to the development of agrarian capitalism with the rise of wage labour but conditioned by continuing strong norms of collective land rights which have led to a distinctive, and more egalitarian, form of agrarian capitalism than found in other developing countries.

The development of rural industry, however, has been unbalanced and concentrated in coastal regions while the less developed western regions experienced great difficulty generating off-farm employment with the result that inter-regional inequalities were exacerbated (Cai et al., 2002). Moreover, while restrictions on labour movement were relaxed, the *hukou* system still deprived rural migrant workers of equal access to employment, health care and education. All of these problems were evident in the 1990s and the economic slowdown following the Asian financial crisis in 1997 created additional hurdles for rural economic structural change. In the face of rising urban unemployment, rural migrants found it hard to find jobs in the cities and a large number of migrants returned to the countryside (Zhao, 2002). In the countryside, many TVEs went bankrupt, forcing workers to return to agricultural production. Thus, the growth of rural income decelerated, the gap between rural and urban incomes increased, and progress in poverty reduction came to a standstill in the mid-1990s (Ravallion and Chen, 2004; Sicular et al., 2007).

Against this backdrop, China's accession to the WTO in 2001 marked a further stage in the transformation of the rural economy. This time the transformation was spurred not just by domestic market expansion but by greater exposure to international market forces as well. This intensification of market pressures might be expected to further enhance the role of the market in allocating labour and hastening the transfer of surplus labour into non-agricultural activities (Sicular and Zhao, 2004).

WTO accession also committed China to opening up its domestic agricultural markets to foreign competition and reducing subsidies to agriculture, raising the fear that it might further hinder income growth for rural households and exacerbate inter-regional and rural–urban income disparity (Blum, 2002; Fewsmith, 2001). This outcome would be expected from analyses of globalization which argue that the employment and income gains from trade liberalization in developing countries are captured disproportionately by the already better-off groups, with negative implications for inequality and for the poor (Cornia, 1999).[1]

China's WTO membership was predicted to reduce the prices of crops that use land intensively, such as wheat, corn and soybeans, but increase the prices of crops and manufactured goods that use labour intensively.[2] The changes in relative prices of crops and goods would lead to labour reallocation between sectors. However, with labour market barriers and poor infrastructure and a shortage of human capital in China's less developed interior regions, it would be difficult for farmers to switch from grain production to other high value-added crops or to non-farm activities. The difficulty in switching between activities would, *ceteris paribus*, contribute to rising income inequality among households and between regions and worsening rural poverty. Even commentators in favour of greater liberalization through WTO accession accepted that this would likely create problems for the agricultural sector (Lin, 2000).

The legacy of inter-regional inequalities and rural–urban disparities which resulted from the liberalization policies of the 1990s were threatened with being further exacerbated by exposure to global market forces in the 2000s through WTO membership. The commitment to expanding market forces and allocation mechanisms in the rural economy is common to both periods but, since the early 2000s, the further integration of the rural economy into the global market has brought forth responses from the central leadership attempting to manage this integration to counter the potential adverse effects on rural labour. That is, while the leadership has sanctioned and championed the extension of the market in the rural economy, it has also sought to manage this by securing distributional outcomes which will maintain social stability. A partial, limited and elite-driven (Polanyian) attempt to counter the unfettered market's potentially destabilizing effects is evident.

The 16th National Congress of the Communist Party (CPC) in 2002 announced that one of the main goals of the next decade was to increase the income of rural households, continue to shift massive amounts of labour out of farming as a way of doing this, and ensure a more balanced growth between city and countryside and between the east and west regions. The aim was to manage the distributional outcomes of further market liberalization and globalization to maintain social stability.

The increased importance accorded to addressing the rural economy and to managing the impact of further liberalization and globalization is reflected in 'Number 1' policy documents (*yihaowenjian*). This document is the first policy document the Chinese government issues each year and indicates the policy priority for that year. Since 1978 the central government has issued eight 'Number 1' policy documents concerning rural development, five of which were issued in the early reform period from 1982 to 1986. The remaining three, however, were all issued after WTO entry in 2004, 2005 and 2006. For these three consecutive years, rural development was placed as the central government's highest priority. All three of the recent policy documents intended to address problems concerning agriculture, farmers and rural areas (*sannong wenti – nongye, nong min* and *nongchun*).

The three Number 1 documents from the 2000s stipulate that governments at all levels adopt measures to raise rural income and reduce rural–urban income disparities. Included in the policy initiatives are: reforming the *hukou* system so that rural migrants have more formal rights in the urban areas; increasing land tenure security; providing subsidies for grain production; reducing, and abolishing in 2006, all agricultural tax and rural levies, taxes which were regressive in nature and whose abolition has been estimated will raise rural household income by approximately 15 per cent per year; increasing off-farm employment and urban–rural migration; increasing infrastructural investment targeted at the poorest regions (see Zhang et al., 2006); free nine-year compulsory education in rural areas (see Knight, 2008); and developing rural social programmes such as the 'rural health cooperative scheme' and rural pension programme. This represents an extensive set of policy measures designed to both enable rural labour to engage in the market economy on better terms and to increase levels of social protection when they are unable to do so.[3]

To sum up, the security of the previously collectivized sector is now but a distant memory for residents in rural China. In its place has come a relentless wave of liberalization and now globalization, in the form of WTO accession; the market has consequently expanded its role in allocating labour and facilitating the transfer of labour from agricultural to non-agricultural activities, a process which has been the central leadership's main policy for raising rural incomes. However, with the inequalities arising from this process, combined with rising levels of economic insecurity, the central leadership has also sought to manage the distributional consequences of the market-led reallocation of labour within the rural economy. These policies have intensified since the 2001 WTO accession, as indicated by the designation of rural development as a Number 1 policy for example. All have intended to mitigate the effects of market liberalization on the poorest and to equip them with the tools to participate in the new market-driven economy rather than be submerged beneath it. In the next section, we discuss the extent to which this objective has been realized.

4. Trends in labour allocation, income and inequality

To anlayse these trends we use data from the China Health and Nutrition Survey (CHNS).[4] The advantage of this survey data is that it has been collected for the years 1989, 1991, 1993, 1997, 2000, 2004 and 2006. Each survey is carried out over a three-day period, and covers about 3,800 households and 14,000 individuals in both urban and rural areas from nine of China's thirty provinces, namely, Heilongjiang, Liaoning, Shandong, Henan, Jiangsu, Hubei, Hunan, Guizhou and Guangxi (autonomous region). These provinces are geographically dispersed and contain both coastal and inland areas, and range from the north to the south. The survey provides rich socio-economic information on individuals, households and communities in the sample. In order to focus sharply on rural conditions and rural dynamics, we exclude villages in suburban areas and communities around the county centres. Our sample is strictly a *rural* sample and its coverage is therefore reduced to about 2,000 households in the villages from the nine provinces for the period from 1991 to 2006.[5] A typical household in our sample is poorer than its counterpart in the full survey.

The data from the survey demonstrate the extent to which the structural transformation of the rural economy has taken place over the past decade and a half and its acceleration in the 2000s. Column 1 of Table 2.1 shows that in the early 1990s less than 12 per cent of rural households had no members engaged in agricultural activities; by 2006 this has risen to just under 30 per cent.[6] Column 2 shows even more dramatically the extent to which agriculture has ceased to be the exclusive employment for rural households. In 1991 nearly three-quarters of rural households had members who worked only on-farm. By 2006 this was the case for only 13 per cent of households. This decline was particularly dramatic after 2000 when the rural economy was further transformed by exposure to the logic of global market forces in the form of WTO accession – a change which made land-intensive farming less attractive and which led to a rapid rise in China's labour-intensive manufacturing exports. As farm employment decreased, wage employment rose dramatically, fuelled by rising levels of migration. By 2006 over 40 per cent of rural households had at least one member working as a migrant worker in an urban centre and over 80 per cent of households had at least one member in waged employment (whether in rural agribusiness, rural industry or urban industry).

These patterns are also evident if we look, in Table 2.2, at the allocation of work hours by rural households.[7] We see that the percentage of time spent in agricultural work was halved between 1991 and 2006, from 72.2 per cent to 35 per cent of household hours while wage

Table 2.1   Labour force allocation over activities in rural China (%)

| | Household farm | | Non-farm self-employment | Waged labour | Migration |
	(1)	Farm only (2)	(3)	(4)	(5)
1991	88.52	73.23	9.72	18.88	–
1993	84.92	69.33	10.31	20.98	–
1997	83.25	69.23	11.95	19.77	16.5
2000	78.26	61.55	13.91	25.74	24.8
2004	76.35	21.36	15.76	75.56	34.8
2006	70.07	13.19	15.06	84.21	41.2

Source: Data taken from CHNS.
Notes: (1)–(4) present proportion of rural population aged between 16 and 64 engaged in the respective activity and (5) presents proportion of the rural households which have at least one member living and working outside the village on either a temporary or more long-term basis.

Table 2.2 Labour hour allocation over activities (annual hours/household)

	Household farm		Non-farm self-employment		Waged labour		Total hours	No. households
	hours	%	hours	%	hours	%	hours	
1991	3,018	72.2	347	8.3	817	19.5	4,181	1,758
1993	2,402	66.0	395	10.9	841	23.1	3,638	1,646
1997	2,249	64.9	457	13.2	760	21.9	3,467	1,792
2000	1,722	54.6	498	15.8	933	29.6	3,154	1,903
2004	1,405	39.1	483	13.4	1,709	47.5	3,596	1,832
2006	1,205	35.0	444	12.9	1,797	52.1	3,447	1,836

Source: Data taken from CHNS.

employment expanded from less than 20 per cent of household labour hours to over 50 per cent.

The dramatic shift of labour out of agriculture and into waged labour and, to a lesser extent, into self-employment, is rational given the much lower returns to farm labour than to employment in the other two activities.

This reallocation of labour into higher return activities has been behind the growth of rural incomes over the survey period. In real terms, average household income in the survey has increased by 90 per cent over the period 1991–2006. However, within this, real earnings from farming have decreased while earnings from wage labour have risen substantially as Table 2.3 indicates. The higher rates of return offered in waged work in conjunction with the reallocation of labour into that sector has meant that wage income has gone from contributing just a fifth of total household earnings in 1991 to contributing three-fifths in 2006. Noticeably, both earnings growth and structural change were accelerated after 2000.

This dramatic structural transformation of the rural economy has raised average real earnings as shown in Table 2.3. To investigate the income inequality trends around this rising average, we can consider measures such as the Gini coefficient. The Gini coefficients reported in Table 2.4 suggest very little change in earnings inequality over the period, a conclusion also supported by the Theil index. It is perhaps noteworthy that the dramatic structural transformation of the rural economy occurred without increasing earnings inequality but it is also

Table 2.3 Household annual earnings in rural China

	Total earnings	Farm income		Non-farm self-employment		Wage income		Earnings per worker
	yuan	yuan	%	yuan	%	yuan	%	yuan
1991	3,477	2,461	70.8	281	8.1	735	21.2	1,465
1993	3,656	2,197	60.1	508	13.9	950	26.0	1,576
1997	4,176	2,382	57.0	531	12.7	1,263	30.2	1,826
2000	4,548	1,921	42.2	902	19.8	1,725	37.9	2,009
2004	6,022	2,004	33.3	590	9.8	3,428	56.9	3,174
2006	6,601	1,806	27.4	875	13.3	3,920	59.4	3,821
Average annual rate of growth %								
1991–2000	3.0	-2.7		13.0		9.5		3.5
2000–2006	6.2	-1.0		-0.5		13.7		10.7
1991–2006	4.3	-2.1		7.6		11.2		6.4

Source: Data taken from CHNS.
Note: Earnings are measured in 1991 constant price.

Table 2.4 Earnings inequality in rural China

Year	1991	1993	1997	2000	2004	2006
Gini coefficient	0.480	0.459	0.438	0.476	0.434	0.461
95% C.I.	0.447	0.436	0.424	0.448	0.414	0.431
	0.513	0.481	0.453	0.504	0.454	0.491
Theil index	0.508	0.387	0.337	0.438	0.342	0.427
95% C.I.	0.412	0.329	0.304	0.339	0.284	0.331
	0.603	0.445	0.370	0.536	0.399	0.524

Source: Data taken from CHNS.
Note: Inequality indexes are calculated based on earnings per worker in 1991 constant price.

the case that the rapid growth of wage labour might have been expected to reduce earnings disparities.

Government policies discussed above, such as the central government infrastructure spending projects, were designed to increase rural productivity and to reduce inter-regional inequalities by being disproportionately targeted to the poorer provinces. As an indicator to gauge the success of this strategy, we report average earnings per worker by region in Table 2.5.

The results show that real earnings per worker were higher in rural areas in coastal provinces than in provinces in the other three regions. However, earnings per worker in the latter three regions all moved to convergence with the coastal provinces over the fifteen-year period. By the end of the period, earnings per worker in rural areas in the central region had reached parity with those in the coastal region, while those in the north-east had reached 90 per cent of the coastal region's value and the west over 77 per cent. Thus, rural inter-regional inequality declined significantly over the period with much of the decrease occurring after 2000.

The Gini coefficient reported above provides insights into the changing dynamics of rural income inequality and its sources. However, as a summary measure, it does not provide evidence of what is happening in the tails of the income distribution, a matter of policy significance and important for any assessment of income trends. Furthermore, the data reported so far have analyed how changing patterns of labour allocation have affected rural households' earnings profiles. To consider inequality further we also need to take into account non-labour incomes which include remittances from long-term migrants, gifts, subsidies and asset

Table 2.5   Regional earnings disparity in rural China (yuan/worker)

	Coast	North-east		Central		West	
	(1)	(2)	(2)/(1)	(3)	(3)/(1)	(4)	(4)/(1)
1991	2,269	1,591	0.701	1,262	0.556	929	0.409
1997	2,302	1,842	0.800	1,824	0.792	1,391	0.604
2000	2,665	2,237	0.839	1,591	0.597	1,717	0.644
2006	4,182	3,762	0.900	4,138	0.990	3,241	0.775

Source: Data taken from CHNS.
Note: Earnings per worker are calculated in 1991 constant price.

income. We therefore use the sample to construct income per capita for each income decile in 1991, 2000 and 2006. These results are presented in Table 2.6 and provide some startling evidence on the different fortunes of the richest and poorest households in rural China over the period.

The results show that between 1991 and 2000 the real income of the poorest two deciles decreased while that of all other deciles increased, with the rate of increase uniformly rising as income level increases. This suggests a clearly rising trend in income inequality. In the post-2000 period the pattern changes. In this period, all income deciles experienced rising real income growth. The average real income growth rate of the poorest decile was 5.7 per cent per year although this was still lower than that of all other deciles, which now experienced similar income growth rates.

The post-2000 period corresponds to the large shift in labour allocation from farm to wage labour, itself a result of the structural transformations induced by globalization. More households were able to benefit from the higher incomes provided by the expansion in wage labour and this was the case for all deciles. In addition, this period is also the one in which government policy was particularly active in pursuing redistributive policies such as the abolition of the regressive agricultural taxes and investing in education and infrastructure in less developed western regions. This combination of globalization and redistributive policies seems to have led to an increase in the average real incomes of each income decile although the poorest decile still saw the lowest income growth rate, indicating that income inequality worsened although at a slower rate than in the 1991–2000 period.

The transformation of the rural economy and the increased reliance on market labour has also led to an increase in the percentage

Table 2.6 Per capita income by decile in 1991, 2000, 2006 in rural China (constant prices)

Decile	Income per capita			Annual rate of growth (%)	Change as percentage of the 10th decile income increase	Annual rate of growth (%)	Change as percentage of the 10th decile income increase
	1991	2000	2006	1991–2000		2000–2006	
1	327	264	371	−2.4	−1.9	5.7	1.9
2	451	427	744	−0.6	−0.7	9.2	5.6
3	584	627	1146	0.8	1.3	10.0	9.1
4	708	858	1554	2.1	4.5	9.9	12.3
5	841	1101	1966	3.0	7.8	9.7	15.2
6	990	1420	2547	4.0	12.9	9.7	19.8
7	1194	1810	3193	4.6	18.5	9.5	24.4
8	1469	2254	4002	4.8	23.6	9.6	30.8
9	1935	3111	5927	5.3	35.3	10.7	49.6
10	4565	7897	13575	6.1	100.0	9.0	100.0
No. of households	716	1,036	942	—	—	—	—

Source: Data taken from CHNS.
Note: Income is the sum of labour earnings plus assets income, various subsidies, and gifts and remittances of relatives and friends. Income per capita is measured in 1991 constant prices.

of unemployed rural labourers in the survey as shown in Table 2.7. That is, the number of people who no longer have access to household farmland – the traditional rural social safety net – has increased with the marketization process. As a result, rural open unemployment has increased significantly.

5. Conclusion

China's rural economy has undergone radical change since 1978. The dismantling of the commune system and the shift to household farming responding to both plan and market forces signalled the start

Table 2.7   Unemployment rates in rural China

Year	Unemployment rate (%)
1991	0.55
1993	0.94
1997	1.77
2000	2.19
2004	3.92
2006	4.08

Source: Data taken from CHNS.
Note: The unemployment rate is the number of unemployed as a percentage of the total number of labour force participants.

of this change. Since then, liberalization and an increasing role for the market have, as in the urban sector, been the consistent reform programme. Globalization must be seen within this context. That is, the globalization of the rural economy has been a part of the general liberalization programme with accession to the WTO and its attendant price and regulatory effects, a further conscious development of this programme rather than a purely 'external' force. That is, 'globalization' is in many ways just another step on the Chinese leadership's chosen path of 'opening up to the outside world' and market-oriented reform. Nevertheless, it did have a direct impact on the rural economy by depressing the relative price of land-intensive crops such as grain and encouraging the shift into other crops and earnings activities; at the same time, the rise in exports following WTO succession increased the demand for migrant labour which the rural areas provided.

But just as the pace of 'opening up' has been managed by the Chinese policy elite so has its effects. The market-oriented reforms, with globalization marking its latest phase, have been planned by the leadership through a multitude of policy initiatives. And yet, at the same time as this progressive unleashing of the market has been facilitated and encouraged, the central leadership has also sought to constrain its most deleterious social effects. This has been most evident since the early 2000s when the rural economy again ranked highly in elite policy priorities and when the current leadership's goal of building a 'harmonious society' is premised on the need to ensure that the rural population enjoys the benefits of the rapid growth sustained over three decades. Thus, policies to invest heavily in the poorer regions, to abolish agricultural taxes and fees, to increase tenure security and to continue with grain subsidies all point to ways in which the central government has sought to manage the markets' inequalizing tendencies on rural inhabitants. In this limited and constrained way, we can see a Polanyian dynamic at work at the elite level in China; especially so after 2001 when the rural sector was exposed to greater international competition and integration as a result of WTO entry and when it became a recipient of increased central government redistributional attention.

To assess the success of this management of liberalization and globalization we have used data from the rural areas of nine provinces from the period 1991 to 2006. This structural transformation shifted labour out of relatively low productivity agriculture and into higher productivity industrial wage employment. As a result, average real earnings grew significantly over the period. Summary measures of income inequality, such as the Gini coefficient, indicate that the distribution of rural earnings around this rising trend was roughly constant over time. However, more disaggregated data including all income sources show that at the bottom end, real incomes decreased over the 1991–2000 period and that the incomes of the richest income groups grew the fastest. Post-2000 the pattern changed with all income groups experiencing real income growth with the growth rates being comparable for all income deciles except the poorest which continued to lag behind. The post-2000 period witnessed a more rapid shift into wage employment, greater liberalization through WTO-governed integration into the global market, and a more concerted effort on the part of the central leadership to address the rural economy and raise rural living standards.

Given the complexity of processes at work, it is not possible to separate out the effects on rural income distribution of global market integration and more aggressive government intervention but we can say that the net effect has been positive in terms of real earnings growth and poverty reduction but negative in terms of the rise in open unemployment, and in terms of increasing income inequality (although this was noticeably more pronounced in the 1991–2000 period than in the 2000–6 period).

However, the greatest test for managed liberalization is now to come in the wake of the global financial crisis and accompanying global recession. The transformation of the rural economy to a greater reliance on wage labour served to raise rural real incomes while the industrial sector was expanding rapidly. However, this situation has changed dramatically in the wake of global recession. Similar to the experience of rural workers during the Asian financial crisis but now intensified, many rural enterprises have gone bankrupt and rural migrant workers are being sent back to the countryside as a result of the export growth slow-down. Official estimates indicate that 26 million rural migrants have been sent back from the coastal cities already in the first two months 2009. At any rate, the wage labour boom is now at least temporarily ended and rural households are now faced with the challenge of how to survive in its absence. With an increasing rural landless population and increasing numbers of unemployed rural labourers, the prospects for social strife are considerably increased. The central government has sought to manage liberalization and globalization to date and to constrain their negative impacts on economic insecurity and inequality although this has still stopped well short of a programme of rural social welfare provision. Large-scale infrastructure spending has been announced to generate employment in the wake of the global recession but whether this will be sufficient remains to be seen; economic growth has already slowed sharply. The post-reform period has seen China's leadership manage liberalization and globalization in the rural sector and, thousands of local disputes notwithstanding, has seen its strategy of elite management prove effective. The latest and still unfolding crisis of globalization, however, much more severe and long-lasting than the regional crisis of 1997, threatens to create the conditions for the rural 'counter-movement from below' which the leadership has sought so assiduously to prevent from emerging in the past.

Notes

1. For a contrary view see, for example, Dollar and Kraay (2004).
2. See Dong et al. (2006) for the challenges facing China's rural sector under the WTO.
3. See Wang (2008) for more extensive discussion of some of the rural social protections which are discussed only briefly here.
4. The CHNS is jointly sponsored by the Carolina Population Center at the University of North Carolina at Chapel Hill, the Institute of Nutrition and Food Hygiene of China and the Chinese Academy of Preventive Medicine. Detailed information about the CHNS is available at the website www.cpc. unc.edu/china/home.html.
5. Urban–rural inequalities, very important though they are, are therefore beyond the scope of this chapter.
6. The 30 per cent of households who report no income from farming consist of those who do not have use-rights to land, those who lease land to others and those who use land for non-agricultural purposes. We are unable to ascertain the proportions in each category from the data set. We do, however, report figures on open unemployment in Table 2.7 which would largely be drawn from those that have no access to land.

7. The data reported in Table 2.2 and subsequent earnings tables exclude household members who were long-term migrants and hence not reporting their activities and earnings in the survey. The activities and earnings of short-term migrants who were still considered by respondents to be part of the household are included.

References

Blum, S. (2002) 'Rural China and the WTO', *Journal of Contemporary China*, 11, 32: 459–72.

Bowles, P. and Dong, X.-Y. (1994) 'Current Successes and Future Challenges in China's Economic Reforms: an Alternative View', *New Left Review*, 208: 49–76.

Cai, F., Wang, D. and Du, Y. (2002) 'Regional Disparity and Economic Growth in China: the Impact of Labor Market Distortions', *China Economic Review*, 13 (2–3): 197–212.

Cheng, T. and Selden, M. (1994) 'The Origins and Social Consequences of China's Hukou System', *China Quarterly*, 139: 644–68.

Cornia, G. (1999) 'Liberalization, Globalization and Income Distribution', Working Paper, UNU/WIDER.

de Brauw, A., Huang, J., Rozelle, S., Zhang, L. and Zhang, Y. (2002) 'China's Rural Labor Market', *China Business Review* (March–April): 2–8.

Dollar, D. and Kraay, A. (2004) 'Trade, Growth, and Poverty', *Economic Journal*, 114 (February): 22–49.

Dong, X.-Y., Song, S. and Zhang, X. (eds) (2006) *China's Agricultural Development: Challenges and Potentials*, Burlington: Ashgate Publishing Ltd.

Fewsmith, J. (2001) 'The Social and Political Implications of China's Accession to the WTO', *China Quarterly*, 167: 573–91.

Guo, X. (2001) 'Land Expropriation and Rural Conflicts in China', *China Quarterly*, 166: 422–39.

Knight, J. (2008) 'Reform, Growth and Inequality in China', *Asian Economic Policy Review*, 3, 1: 140–58.

Kung, J. K. (2002) 'Off-Farm Labor Markets and the Emergence of Land Rental Markets in Rural China', *Journal of Comparative Economics*, 30, 2: 395–414.

Lardy, N. (1983) *Agriculture in China's Economic Development*, Cambridge: Cambridge University Press.

Lin, J. (1987) 'The Household Responsibility System Reform in China: a Peasant's Institutional Choice', *American Journal of Agricultural Economics*, 69, 2: 410–15.

Lin, J. (2000) 'WTO Accession and China's Agriculture', *China Economic Review*, 11, 2: 405–8.

Lohmar, B. (1999) 'Household Labor, Migration and China's Rural Development', unpublished PhD Dissertation, Department of Agricultural and Resource Economics, Davis: University of California.

Munck, R. (2006) 'Globalization and Contestation: a Polanyian Problematic', *Globalizations*, 3, 2: 175–86.

Naughton, B. (2007) *The Chinese Economy: Transitions and Growth*, Cambridge, MA: MIT Press.

Qian, Y. (2003) 'How Reform Worked in China', in D. Rodrik (ed.), *In Search of Prosperity: Analytic Narratives on Economic Growth*, Princeton, NJ: Princeton University Press, pp. 297–333.

Ravallion, M. (2006) 'Looking Beyond Averages in Trade and Poverty Debate', *World Development*, 34, 8: 1374–92.

Ravallion, M. and Chen, S. (2004) 'China's (Uneven) Progress against Poverty', World Bank Policy Research Working Paper 3408.

Sicular, T. and Zhao, Y. (2004) 'Earnings and Labor Mobility in Rural China: Implications for China's WTO Entry', in D. Bhattasali, S. Li and W. Martin (eds), *China and the WTO: Accession, Policy Reform, and Poverty Reduction Strategies*, Washington, DC: World Bank.

Sicular, T., Xue, X., Gustafsson, B. and Li, S. (2007) 'The Urban–Rural Income Gap and Inequality in China', *Review of Income and Wealth*, 5, 1: 93–126.

Taylor, J., Rozelle, S. and de Brauw, A. (2003) 'Migration and Incomes in Source Communities: a New Economics of Migration Perspective from China', *Economic Development and Cultural Exchange*, 52: 75–101.

Wang, S. (2008) 'The Great Transformation: the Double Movement in China', *boundary 2*, 35, 2: 15–47.

Weitzman, M. and Xu. C. (1994) 'Chinese Township Village Enterprises as Vaguely Defined Cooperatives', *Journal of Comparative Economics*, 18, 2: 121–45.

Zhang, L., Luo, R., Liu, C. and Rozelle, S. (2006) 'Investing in Rural China: Tracking China's Commitment to Modernization', *Chinese Economy*, 39: 1–40.

Zhang, Q. and Donaldson, J. (2008) 'The Rise of Agrarian Capitalism with Chinese Characteristics: Agricultural Modernization, Agribusiness and Collective Land Rights', *China Journal*, 60: 25–47.

Zhao, Y. (2002) 'Causes and Consequences of Return Migration: Recent Evidence from China', *Journal of Comparative Economics*, 30, 2: 376–94.

3

The Role of the State, Labour Policy and Migrant Workers' Struggles in Globalized China

Chris King-Chi Chan, Pun Ngai and Jenny Chan

1. Introduction

The financial crisis of 2008 brought the world economy into a new stage. While the western capitalist countries suffered seriously, China seems to stand out as one of the few countries that could resist the economic tsunami. There is a general belief that this ability arises from China's strong state which has reshaped the role of China in the new international division of labour and which also has the ability to resume its economic development internally. Our study of labour policy and workers' struggles challenges this belief.

China has deeply transformed itself into 'a factory of the world'. We argue that this transformation is state-initiated and has been achieved with the collusion of the interests of transnational capital in its search for offshore production relocation. This state-driven process of globalization has created a new millions-strong working class in China. A paradox is that this state-driven process of economic globalization has been accompanied by a state withdrawal process in the areas of social reproduction and social protection. The socialist legacy of contracting agricultural lands to individual rural households is one of the enabling factors for China in creating a pro-business environment: employers do not need to pay their peasant-workers a living wage or the full cost of social reproduction of labour, which are supposed to be subsidized by the workers' rural communities. Local host governments likewise have shunned the responsibility for improving the livelihoods of internal migrant workers and their families under their jurisdiction. This state withdrawal process shapes a specific pattern of proletarianization of Chinese labour and a specific capital–labour relationship which contributes to a growing number of migrant workers' struggles in China.

Persistent struggles by Chinese workers themselves have created huge pressure on the post-Mao state to redefine its position towards labour conflicts. From 2003 onwards, the new Hu Jintao and Wen Jiabao leadership has emphasized harmony and stability in society, even over the pursuit of economic growth and efficiency. The labour rule of law – regulating labour contracts, wages, work hours, social insurance, compensations, and official trade union membership – has been vastly expanded. The goal is to demobilize worker discontent through the institutionalized legal and bureaucratic systems.

Labour protests, however, will likely increase in frequency as the market reforms deepen and generate new forms of social as well as class inequalities in China. State power and capital have become more closely associated than ever, giving rise to class polarization and income inequality. By the early 2000s, China had become a more unequal country than many other Asian countries including Indonesia, India and Bangladesh (World Bank, quoted in Khan and Riskin, 2005). In 2006, China surpassed the level of inequality in the United States (Andreas, 2008). Demanding economic justice and social rights, Chinese workers have pushed for changes from the bottom up. Their ability to improve working and living conditions will be significant for both local class struggles and global labour politics.

In the next section we document the ways in which the state has been instrumental in transforming China into a world factory. In section 3, we show how the dynamics of this process have created a new migrant working class. Included here is an analysis of how the state's withdrawal from the provision of social protection has been central to this. Despite efforts by the new leadership since 2002 to address issues of social protection, for the great majority of migrant workers these efforts remain at the level of rhetoric not substance. In section 4, we discuss how labour protests have been escalating and analyse one particular strike in Shenzhen in 2007 to illustrate how class consciousness is developing among the new migrant working class. The rising labour struggles have led the central authorities to change labour laws and to channel labour disputes through bureaucratic legal structures. This is discussed in section 5 where we argue that these legal measures fall far short of providing the necessary protection for workers. We conclude, in section 6, that workers' struggles are likely to intensify as a result of the current global economic crisis.

2. State-driven transformation: China as a 'world factory' in globalization

> Capitalist encroachment on the family labour sector and the relentless displacement of small enterprises by larger ones is fundamentally market-driven, but it is also state policy. China's political leaders do not want backward produce markets, they want modern supermarkets, and state officials are expected to identify and support 'winners' in the economic competition. (Andreas, 2008: 140)

Western commentators, from the political left to the right, typically admire China's economic achievement symbolized by the iconic skylines of Beijing and Shanghai as well as by the stunning economic figures frequently reported by the media. Following WTO entry in 2001, China surpassed the United States as the largest recipient of world foreign direct investment (FDI) in 2002 (China's Ministry of Commerce, 16 January 2003). In 2002, China became the top world producer of 80 products, including garments, colour TVs, washing machines, DVD players, cameras, refrigerators, air-conditioners, motorcycles, microwave ovens, PC monitors, tractors and bicycles (*The Economist*, 28 July 2005). In 2005 China became the world's third largest trading country, surpassed only by the US and Germany. In 2006, China climbed to fourth place in the world in terms of the size of the economy. Alongside the dramatic economic growth, the manufacturing structure also moved into high-end goods. Electronics products made up 56 per cent of total exports in 2006 (*China News Net*, 12 November). Advanced technology exports are second only to the US, and China overtook Japan to become the world's second largest investor in research and development in 2007.

Much of this success has relied on foreign firms. In 2005, overseas funded enterprises in China accounted for 57.3 per cent of China's overall exports and they took a huge share – 87.9 per cent – of high-tech exports (China's Ministry of Commerce, 12 June 2006). Even with China's absorption of FDI down 26.2 per cent over that of 2007, newly approved foreign funded companies in the country totalled 22,736 between January and October 2008 (China's Ministry of Commerce, 17 November 2008).

The rise of China as a major economic power, however, is not a natural consequence of the free market in the age of globalization as neoliberal economists assume. Thirty years of socialism left a powerful state authority to drive the process of 'reform and open' policies forwards.

Zooming inside China's global factory, labour costs are as low as one-sixth those of Mexico and one-fortieth those of the United States (Lee, 2004). Chinese municipal governments in the Pearl River Delta regions in southern China increased the statutory minimum wages by as little as 68 yuan (approximately US$10) over a twelve-year period between the 1990s and early 2000s (China's Ministry of Labour and Social Security, 2004). The state has strategically produced an inexpensive Chinese workforce absorbed from the countryside since the 1980s and at the same time absolved itself of the responsibility of providing this new workforce with minimal protections and rights. This process is discussed in more detail in the next section.

3. The making of new generations of a Chinese migrant working class

The rapid development of export processing and technology experimental zones across China was based on a massive harnessing of young peasant-workers, in particular of women, who are often the cheapest and most compliant labour (Gaetano and Jacka, 2004; Pun, 2005). Officials have partially relaxed the decades-old household registration system and actively coordinated the transfer of rural 'surplus labour' to the booming cities. By the mid-1990s, rural surveys estimated that the number of internal migrant labourers ranged from 50–70 million nationwide (Roberts et al., 2004: 49). Some sources attest that the size of the migrant working population is now over 130 million (China's State Council, 2006: 4).

The formation of this new working class of internal rural migrant labourers – the *dagong* class – is taking shape. Young peasant-workers are *dagongmei/zai* (female and male migrant workers) who embrace new gendered identities. *Dagong* means 'working for the boss' or 'selling labour', connoting commodification and a capitalist exchange of labour for wages. Labour is sold to capitalists and, this time, under the auspices of the state. In contrast to the term *gongren* or urban worker, which carried the highest status in the socialist rhetoric of Mao's day, the new term *dagong* signifies a lesser status as a hired hand in the market (Pun, 1999, 2005).

Peasant-workers are not new in China. They were well represented in big cities such as Tianjin and Shanghai in pre-1949 China (Hershatter, 1986; Perry, 1993) and they were employed as temporary labourers in state-owned and collective enterprises in the socialist period (Walder, 1984). However, the new generations of peasant-workers are radically different from previous ones. We observe new life expectations and dispositions and more collective labour action among those who have grown up in the reform period and entered the labour market in the late 1990s to early 2000s (Pun and Lu, forthcoming). The characteristics of the new generations include greater individualism, attraction to urban consumer culture (Davis, 2000; Pun, 2003), driven more by the personal pursuit of development and freedom (Jacka, 2005), higher rates of job turnover and less loyalty to their work, but simultaneously they are more likely to be involved in spontaneous collective action at the workplace (Chan and Pun, 2009; Lee, 2007).

3.1 The process of unfinished proletarianization of Chinese migrant labour

The process of proletarianization in post-Mao China – turning rural bodies into industrial waged labour – is specific to the way in which the state has promoted massive rural-to-urban labour migration over the past three decades. The first level of analysis is structural: owing to the deep rural–urban divide, largely shaped by national development strategies, rural authorities have submitted to the central government's direction by exploring inter-provincial labour cooperation and coordination programme initiatives, facilitating rapid urban economic growth. From the 1990s onwards Hunan and Guangxi provinces, for example, have systematically exported their peasant labour to Guangdong in the south. In exchange, these interior provinces benefit from the remittances sent back by rural migrant workers. This migration policy also assures a continuous replenishment of internal migrant labourers to the production power-bases in the coastal cities. Strong state initiatives support the labour needs of emerging industries and facilitate labour supply flow to the manufacturing sites (Solinger, 1999). The government's labour management offices serve as the agency coordinating this market: first by screening and recruiting young female applicants and then transferring the applicants directly to the factories in the booming regions. These labour offices sometimes go into details such as arranging long-distance coaches to transport rural women to work, in return for management fees from the hiring company.

The second level of analysis is from an individual and familial viewpoint. Young rural men and women alike must contend with low prices for agricultural products in the post-WTO accession era, limited educational opportunities, and limited village employment opportunities – indeed, these last two challenges are particularly intolerable for younger generations who have grown up in the reform period. Rural youth have no choice but to go to work at 16 or 17 years old. Some rural women also aspire to escape arranged marriages, familial conflicts and patriarchal oppression. Still others want to widen their horizons and to experience modern life and cosmopolitan consumption styles in the cities. Thus, personal decisions in out-migration – shaped by the state-led pro-city development strategy – support the goal of the state in channelling labour from rural areas to coastal industrial areas.

The official categorization of peasant-workers – wage labourers of rural household registration – means that their social status and class identities are ambiguous. The post-socialist Chinese state has permitted them to go out to work but has not granted them the right to urban permanent residence. Maintenance of the distinction between permanent and temporary residents through the household registration system enables the state, at all levels, to escape from their obligations to provide housing, job security and welfare to rural migrant workers. As a result, they live mostly either in factory-provided collective dormitories or in substandard migrant villages within the city.

3.2 The retreat of the state from the costs of social reproduction of migrant workers

We have argued that the household registration system, combined with the interests of domestic and foreign capital, have created exploitative mechanisms of labour appropriation in post-socialist China. This is the 'state-out' process of societal globalization: China's economy needs the labour of the rural population but does not need the city-based survival of that population once market demand for rural-to-urban migrants' labour power shifts in either location or industry. This newly forming working class is not permitted to form permanent roots and gain legal identity in the city. The ambiguous identity of rural migrant labour simultaneously deepens and obscures the exploitation of this huge population. Hence, this subtle and multi-faceted marginalization of rural labourers has created a contested, if not a deformed, citizenship that has greatly disadvantaged Chinese migrant workers who attempt to transform themselves into urban workers.

Being extraordinarily dislocated in the cities, migrant labour is distinguished by its transient nature. A worker, especially a female worker, will usually spend a number of years working as a wage labourer in an industrial city before getting married. Upon reaching marriageable age, most of the women have to return to their rural homes because of their difficulty in finding partners in the city. Rural communities have long exercised – and have long been expected to exercise – the extended planning of life activities such as marriage, procreation and family. The reproduction of labour of the next generation is hence left to the rural villages which bear the cost of industrial development in urban areas, even though the ability of the rural communities to meet reproduction costs is often highly constrained. Furthermore, physical or mental rehabilitation in cases of serious industrial injuries and occupational diseases are also presumed to be taken care of in the rural areas.

Under the new leadership of Hu Jintao and Wen Jiabao, since 2002 there have been pressing demands for the Chinese state to introduce more extensive social policies. However, most of the social policies subsequently introduced – such as employment policies, health policies and education policies – were designed either for the urban or the rural populations and hence excluded the migrant population. One notable policy regarding migrant workers is the compulsory social insurance scheme comprising five items: pension, injury compensation, medical care, maternity leave and unemployment pension. This insurance system, and the benefits arising from it, is only available to workers with written labour contracts. However, the percentage of migrant workers who have written labour contracts remains low. According to survey findings provided by the State Council in 2006, 46.3 per cent of all migrant workers were still not protected with a labour contract, and 51.4 per cent of them were not paid on time (quoted in J. Chan, 2009). In the construction sector, the percentage of workers who had signed a labour contract was much lower than in the manufacturing and service sectors; in our current studies in Beijing, over 90 per cent of the construction workers were not provided with a labour contract. Many of them have suffered from industrial accidents and injuries but were left with no compensation (Pun and Lu, 2009). In the area of social protection and social policies, the majority of migrant workers remain unprotected; the new policies exist much more in form than in substance for migrant workers. Furthermore, the 'humanistic' social policies launched by the central government have been largely ignored by the local governments whose priority is still pro-capital development. The floating nature of the migrant population also created excuses for the local state to escape its responsibility, and the local state, in turn, blamed the migrant labourers for lacking the incentive to participate in the social insurance scheme. These current social reforms pay only lip service to the needs of migrant workers due to the nature of the existing state which serves the interests of capital, not society.

This results in the unfinished proletarianization of Chinese labour, driven by the state but at the same time crippled by it. It is not surprising that this has produced a rising tide of labour protest as we discuss in the next section.

4. Labour disputes and protests in China since the 1990s

Resisting multi-fronted injustice and exploitation, Chinese workers have increasingly fought for their rights. Official statistics from various departments attest to the pervasiveness and intensification of labour unrest since the early 1990s throughout the country. There are two major types of labour conflicts: labour strikes and labour disputes via legal systems. In this section, we will discuss trends in both forms of conflict drawing on official statistics and our own case study work on strikes.

According to China's Ministry of Public Security, the number of mass incidents and demonstrations, such as collective suicide attempts, traffic blockage and other public forms of civil disobedience taken by desperate workers, increased tenfold from 8,700 in 1993 (quoted in Pei, 2003) to 87,000 in 2005 (*New York Times*, 20 January 2006). Unofficially, at least one strike involving more than 1,000 workers occurs every day in the manufacturing hub of the Pearl River Delta region in Guangdong, to say nothing of the many smaller spontaneous strikes (AFP, 15 January 2008).

We provide an analysis of one such strike here to provide an example of the emerging forms of migrant working-class resistance. Our study is based on our longitudinal fieldwork in the industrial town of Shenzhen between 2003 and 2007. During the period, we conducted intensive research into migrant workers' working life and social life in the town by participant observation, interviews and documentary research in dormitories, migrant communities and workers' centres. The strike we discuss here occurred in a German electronics company in one of the industrial towns in Shenzhen in 2007. This strike encouraged a series of strikes in other factories leading to wage increases across the town.

4.1 German factory strike in 2007[1]

Factory X is a German-funded enterprise which produces batteries, power cords and other components for mobile phones. Since setting up in 1993, it has expanded into two large plants at two industrial towns in Shenzhen. It employs about 8,000 workers, of whom 80 per cent are women aged between 18 and 30. The wage level in Factory X was comparatively high in the town. The minimum hourly wage rate was basically observed and social insurance was provided for all of the workers. The factory operates two shifts. The day shift is from 7:00 a.m.

to 6:30 p.m. with a one-hour lunch break, while the night shift is from 7:00 p.m. to 6:45 a.m. with a 45-minute midnight break. Ordinary workers usually work six days per week and their monthly salary is from 1,000 to 1,400 yuan (approximately US$150–200).

In this factory, production workers are called *yuan gong*, employees, while others, including managers, supervisors, engineers, technicians and office clerks, are collectively called *zhi yuan*, staff. Most of the workers, *yuan gong*, live in the factory-provided dormitories where eight or twelve workers share a room. Thirty yuan are deducted from wages as rent. The factory pays an accommodation subsidy from 200 to 300 yuan per month to *zhi yuan* to rent private rooms outside of the factory.

In July 2005, when the minimum wage rate in Shenzhen was raised to 580 yuan, the factory adjusted the salary accordingly. The minimum wage was further increased to 700 yuan in 2006. Workers in Factory X also got a pay rise accordingly. After two years' consecutive pay rises, however, the factory steadily began to increase the work quotas of the production line and units. If workers could not finish the quota unilaterally set by the management for the eleven daily working hours, they were 'requested' to perform extra work the next day without payment. The practice created conflict between experienced, and hence more efficient, workers and the inexperienced, as well as between the front line supervisors, who announced the new quota and forced their subordinates and the production workers to work faster. Therefore, feeling 'too exhausted' rather than 'low pay' was the most common cause of discontent in the factory. Many workers quit the factory after a few months or a year, but most of them were not permitted to do so and there was always a long queue of those who had applied to leave. For those without proper 'permission', the factory would confiscate their salary and they were prohibited from returning to the factory for employment for six months.

A special 'rationalization reform' was also made to lower the wage costs of the *zhi yuan* by restricting their overtime working hours in March 2007. From July, the maximum overtime hours of *zhi yuan* was set at 72 per month. They would not get extra pay for any hours worked beyond that level. The impact for front line supervisors was that they had to take care of more lines when other supervisors were on leave. For technicians, a smaller number was on duty in each shop.

The immediate cause of the strike was due to the wage policy of the city government. As mentioned, the city had significantly raised the minimum wage rate in July 2005 and 2006, and workers generally expected a similar pay rise in July 2007, but the government finally decided not to raise the legal minimum rate but maintained it at

700 yuan. A strike was immediately sparked on the second day after the workers got their July payslip in August.

4.2 Collective action for a reasonable wage

Workers got their payslips on Thursday, 16 August. Workers' salaries had not been raised. Furthermore, technicians and supervisors found their incomes were severely reduced due to the overtime restrictions. For example, one of the technicians, whose salary was always well over 2,000 yuan, only received 1,400 yuan. On the Friday evening, when the managers (who only work during the day) had left the factory, a public letter was posted on the notice-board of all of the workshops.

The letter was issued in the name of all of the Factory X workers and entitled 'voices from *zhi yuan* and *yuan gong*'. It began by pointing out that the management had attempted to lower their salary from the end of 2006, and now their income had been reduced by 50 per cent from the same period last year, while work quotas and living costs had doubled. 'We have reasonable demands', the letter stated:[2]

1. To adjust our current wage standard. We all know the market wage standard now, and thus demand it should be adjusted in the following ways: *yuan gong*, 1,500 yuan or more; second level *zhi yuan*, 2,000 yuan or more; third level *zhi yuan*, 2,500 yuan or more; fourth level *zhi yuan*, 3,000 yuan or more; the above does not include any subsidy.
2. To raise the accommodation and food subsidy for living outside.
3. To improve welfare conditions, provide reasonable allowances for high temperature, toxic, outdoor and occupational disease-prone posts and regular occupational disease and body checks.
4. To provide night shift subsidy and snack allowance for those working on the night shift.
5. The company should buy unemployment, maternity, medical care and all of the other insurances requested by the labour law.
6. To solve the hygiene problem of drinking water.
7. To improve the reasonableness of overtime work.
8. The trade union should function appropriately and its core members should invite the grassroots *yuan gong* to participate in it.

The letter ended by stating that the workers requested that the company answer these demands in written form and that they would not accept an oral reply from anybody, including the company CEO. News began to circulate among the workers that the technicians would start a strike soon.

After more and more workers, mostly young women, joined in, the technicians then led the crowd onto a crossroads in the industrial town. It was not a busy road and not many cars came, several policemen just stood by the workers peacefully. 'One policeman even told us that it was useless to stay there and we should go to the major national road', a worker said. Half an hour later, the mass walked out to the national highway and occupied one half of the main road. Hundreds of security forces came, including patrol police, military police, transport police and local government security guards, followed by labour bureau officers, the town Party general-secretary and the factory managers. The local Party head, labour bureau representative and top manager spoke to the strikers with loudspeakers and asked them to go back to the factory for negotiation. Officers said that it was illegal to stand there and that anything could be discussed in the factory while the manager asked the workers to elect their representatives. Some of the workers responded that 'we are all representatives' or 'we have no representatives'.

One of the significant features of this strike was that it also happened almost simultaneously at the subsidiary factory in a different town. This strike soon spread to other factories around the industrial town. It had a significant knock-on effect on other factories in the same community and in the same business group. In our observation, the strike wave from 2003 to 2007 at least partially accounted for the dramatic rise of the legal minimum wage rate and the local state's improved labour law inspections. Moreover, it was a breakthrough that organizers in Factory X were able to coordinate workers in two factories to stage a strike together in order to enhance their bargaining power. The strike resulted in a wage increase of 10 per cent to the technicians and supervisors and 5 per cent to the production workers.

This strike demonstrates an important process in the formation of the new Chinese working class. The alliance between the supervisory staff and the production workers in Factory X and the knock-on effect from Factory X to another factory in the industrial district show an increasing maturity of the working class in China which has learned how to take collective action step by step. In recent years, workers in foreign-owned enterprises in coastal China have resorted to strikes more frequently to express their grievances and discontents. We argue that recent labour protests are mostly interest-based, purposively induced to improve working conditions and oppositional against capital. Without strong leadership or formal organization, most of the labour conflicts are triggered off squarely at the point of production, with the reproduction space as the bedrock for labour mobilization.

Turning to labour disputes referred to legal bodies, these too have been soaring since the early 1990s. To restore social stability, the Chinese government has attempted to resolve labour disputes through institutional means. In August 1993, the State Council promulgated its Regulations on the Handling of Enterprise Labour Disputes. Employees of all kinds of enterprises were legally entitled to raise complaints concerning wages, benefits, occupational health and safety, and termination of contracts to labour dispute arbitration committees at the county, city and provincial levels. The number of arbitrated labour disputes was 19,098 in 1994 and it reached an all-time high of 317,162 in 2006, involving 679,312 workers nationwide. Also significant has been the rapid rise of arbitrated collective labour disputes, involving three or more workers. In 1994, 1,482 cases were recorded. By 2006, the number had increased to 13,977. The climate of deteriorating labour relations shows no sign of abating as a result of the global economic crisis and the threat of unemployment; in fact, quite the opposite. In the first six months of 2008, Ministry of Human Resources and Social Security statistics revealed that arbitrated labour disputes soared by 145 per cent in Chongqing and 92.5 per cent in Shanghai (*Southern Weekly*, 31 July 2008). In the same period, courts in Guangdong province received nearly 40,000 new labour dispute cases – a 157.7 per cent increase from 2007, in which the Pearl River Delta area accounted for 96.5 per cent of all cases (*China Daily*, 22 July 2008). Between January and September 2008, labour arbitration departments in Beijing handled 32,954 labour disputes, up 104 per cent from the same period in 2007 (*Beijing Review*, 20 January 2009).

Furthermore, there is ample evidence that Chinese migrant workers are becoming more pro-active in defending their rights. We observe the radicalization of labour in which strikes, street actions and public demonstrations are increasingly used (Leung and Pun, 2009). Indeed, despite institutional barriers to labour self-organization, migrant workers have expressed their discontent and demanded changes by staging factory-level strikes, bargaining on wages and other terms, launching collective complaints, and/or resorting to media exposure for the redress of their problems.

5. Channelling labour conflicts into state institutions

The increasing number of labour protests and labour conflicts has pressured the central government into setting up a new legal regulation framework. A national Labour Law came into effect on 1 January 1995. The law laid down a foundation for workers' legal rights as well as collective contracts and collective consultations between official trade unions and management (Clarke et al., 2004; Taylor et al., 2003).

The huge discrepancy between legal entitlements and the actual delivery of protection, however, was so telling that the legitimacy of the Chinese state has been undermined. Labour contracts in written form, if provided at all, have been predominantly short-term. Workers' rights are blatantly disregarded. Officials have responded by speeding up labour disputes into an expanded system of arbitration committees and courts. The goals are to individualize and demobilize worker discontent through the bureaucratic and legal procedures, to continue driving forward economic reforms and holding on to the one-party regime.

In 2007, the state promulgated three new national labour laws: the Labour Contract Law, the Labour Dispute Mediation and Arbitration Law and the Employment Promotion Law.

The first of these laws, the Labour Contract Law, which came into effect on 1 January 2008, is considered the most significant piece of Chinese labour law reform in more than a decade (Ngok, 2008). Faced with strong corporate opposition at home and abroad, or a 'sweatshop lobby', to the proposed legislation on labour contracts, the Chinese government eventually pushed through the law. Important provisions include: mandatory labour contracts for new employees for all employment relations; strengthening worker representatives' and workplace-based trade unions' roles in representing their workers' interests; worker entitlement to severance pay upon the expiration or termination of contracts under certain conditions; the regulation of contingent labour; and the imposition of disciplinary measures on officials who neglect their responsibilities or abuse their authority. By mid-March 2008, the Vice-President of the All China Federation of Trade Unions (ACFTU) reported to the media that up to 80–90 per cent of employees nationwide had already signed their written employment contracts (*China News*, 15 March 2008), notwithstanding findings to the contrary analysed by a number of Hong Kong and Chinese NGOs based in southern China (Chan, 2009). The second law on the mediation and arbitration of employment disputes was enacted on 1 May 2008, International Labour Day. It facilitates access to the arbitration system by waiving arbitration fees, amounting to several hundred yuan. It further streamlines the process of arbitration and extends the time limit for aggrieved and injured workers to bring their claims to arbitration. The third law on equal employment opportunities mandates local governments to take measures to eliminate discrimination and to promote equality in all forms of employment.

Last, but not least, the state-run union aims to set up more branches in the workplace (at the grassroots level), thereby mediating labour disputes from the start. By March 2008, the ACFTU had a 193-million strong membership – the largest in the world – and more than 1.5 million enterprise-based unions nationwide, across the state and non-state sectors (*China News*, 15 March 2008). Union officials are mandated to promote the rule of law and foster a harmonious relationship between employers and employees.

5.1 State absence in defending workers' rights in struggles

Despite the formulation of a better legal framework, in the critical realm of workplace collective bargaining and labour strikes, the Chinese state is almost entirely absent. Workers' fundamental right to strike – the clause removed from China's 1982 constitution – remains absent under the twice-amended Trade Union Law in 1992 and 2001. Although the state has actively engaged in workplace relations through labour legislation, workers' basic economic rights, especially those of strike, association and collective bargaining as benchmarked by international standards, are all still absent in the reforms (Chan 2008a, 2008b). The intention to weaken workers' associational power is explicit.

In reality, official unions are politically constrained in confronting employers, leaving workers to fight on their own. In collective bargaining and negotiation, union cadres are the only legal labour organization to represent the interests of workers. As Cai (2006: 66) puts it: the ACFTU would never 'assume the role of organizers for the workers' collective action against the management, not to mention against the government'. Without the rights to organize, Chinese workers do not have institutionalized associational power to bargain with employers. The existing collective contract system in China, which is supposed to be based on collective negotiation, is therefore unable to reflect workers' collective right in any meaningful sense (Chen, 2007).

Worse still, the unpredictability of the decisions made by arbitrators or judges, if not their overt unfairness, has caused very tense labour relations. Under fiscal and administrative decentralization policies, local states are driven to retain revenues and accumulate resources rather than to implement labour laws and regulations. Intense competition among localities to lure foreign investment has resulted in the 'flexible' enforcement of labour laws. Lower courts continue to depend on funding from local governments, and local judges lack autonomy and independence to uphold the law, especially in cases where outcomes are contrary to powerful interests. Despite the fact that the lower courts are increasingly reaching out to other courts of equal rank for guidance in making difficult legal decisions – an impressive development of 'horizontal networking' between the courts in fostering legal innovations – extensive external interference from higher courts and party officials persists (Liebman, 2007). Under these circumstances, workers' rights often end at the courtroom door.

At times of financial slowdown, Chinese workers' structural position becomes even more precarious: about 8,500 enterprises in Guangdong province alone shut their doors in October 2008 (Associated Press, 19 October 2008). China's manufacturing sector contracted for the fifth consecutive month in December 2008, leaving tens of thousands of workers from the export-oriented manufacturing industries jobless. At the critical moment, the Dongguan municipal government, fearing a break-out of popular protest, paid more than 24 million yuan to compensate for the unpaid wages of the 7,000 protesting workers of two toy factories owned by Smart Union Group (Holdings) Limited, a Hong Kong publicly listed company, when the owner secretly fled and production was suspended in mid-October 2008 (Associated Press, 19 October 2008; *China Daily*, 23 October 2008). However, much-needed social security programmes, such as unemployment insurance for migrant workers, have never been put in place. Indeed, the state is still largely outside of the urban reproduction of migrant workers by denying them basic social and political rights.

Subject to continuing class and social deprivations, disgruntled workers are standing up to fight for their interests. China's judicial departments predict that the number of labour disputes is likely to keep rising across provinces, autonomous regions and municipalities, amid the downturn in the global economy.

6. Conclusion

In this chapter we have argued that the great transformation of China's socialist economy was largely driven by the role of the state. The launch of Deng Xiaoping's reform and open policies in 1978 was historic and unprecedented. It has changed not only the path of Chinese socialism but also the road of global capitalism. The Chinese state has brought the country into the WTO, further demonstrating this state-driven process of economic globalization.

The state-initiated process is, paradoxically, accompanied by a state retreat process from the key areas of social reproduction and social protection. Alongside the rise of a new working class in the industrial and urban areas, the state (at various levels) is almost absent in providing collective consumption such as housing, education, medical care and other basic necessities for migrant workers in particular to live in the towns and cities. This has laid the groundwork for proletarianization of Chinese peasant-workers which has resulted in a sharp increase in the number of migrant worker struggles in China.

In summary, this paradoxical role of the state has resulted in the formation of a new working class in China which is left unprotected, despite the pro-active role of the state in promulgating new labour laws and regulations. The absence of the ACFTU in cases of collective labour disputes and workers' strikes further weakens the associational power of the workers who, due to their peasant-worker identity, already suffer acutely from their lack of market bargaining power. Worker radicalism has intensified, as workers have learned how to organize collective action on their own. In concrete, lived space – in the workers' dormitories and social communities – Chinese workers are developing higher levels of class awareness and identification that make them more capable of forming mutual support networks based on shared interests. Their resilience is likely to intensify further in the face of the current global economic recession.

Notes

1. This section draws upon the material presented in Chan and Pun (2009).
2. Our own translation, September 2007.

References

AFP (Online) (15 January 2008) 'Labour Unrest Growing in China: Activist', http://www.china-labour.org.hk:80/en/node/100193/

Andreas, J. (2008) 'Changing Colours in China', *New Left Review*, 54: 123–42.

Associated Press (19 October 2008) 'Factory Closure in China a Sign of Deeper Pain', http://ap.google.com/article/ALeqM5hkboG00r1GaStjjPcd6fXGEJV-tQD93TLTB80

Beijing Review (Online) (20 January 2009) 'Explosion in Disputes', http://www.bjreview.com.cn/nation/txt/2009-01/20/content_175296.htm#

Cai, Y. S. (2006) *State and Laid-off Workers in Reform China: the Silence and Collective Action of the Retrenched*, London: Routledge.

Chan, C. (2008a) 'Emerging Patterns of Workers' Protest in South China', *Peripherie*, Vol. 3 (in German); Centre for Comparative Labour Studies Working Papers (in English), University of Warwick.

Chan, C. (2008b) 'The Challenge of Labour in China: Strikes and the Changing Labour Regime in Global Factories', PhD thesis, Department of Sociology, University of Warwick.

Chan, C. (2009) 'Strike and Changing Workplace Relations in a Chinese Global Factory', *Industrial Relations Journal*, 40, 1: 60–77.

Chan, C. and Pun N. (2009) 'The Making of a New Working Class? A Study of Collective Actions of Migrant Workers in South China', *China Quarterly*, 198: 287–303.

Chan, J. (2005) 'The End of the Multi-Fiber Agreement and the Rising Tide of Labor Disputes in China', *CSR Asia Weekly*, 1, 11: 6–7 and 11.

Chan, J. (2006a) 'Chinese Women Workers Organize in the Export Zone', *New Labour Forum*, 15, 1: 19–27.

Chan, J. (2006b) 'The Labor Politics of Market Socialism: a Collective Action in a Global Workplace in South China', MPhil thesis, Department of Sociology, University of Hong Kong.

Chan, J. (2009) 'Meaningful Progress or Illusory Reform? Analysing China's Labour Contract Law', *New Labour Forum*, 18, 2: 43–51.

Chen, F. (2007) 'Individual Rights and Collective Rights: Labor's Predicament in China', *Communist and Post-Communist Studies*, 40, 1: 59–79.

China Daily (Online) (22 July 2008) 'Maneuver on Labor Law Faces Block', http://www.chinadaily.com.cn/china/2008-07/22/content_6865144.htm

China Daily (Online) (23 October 2008) 'Government Picks Up More than 24 Million Yuan Wage-bill', http://www.chinadaily.com.cn/bizchina/2008-10/23/content_7133662.htm

China Labour Statistical Yearbook (1995) 'Labour Disputes Accepted and Settled by Region', 491 (tables 8–11), Beijing: Beijing State Statistical Publishing House.

China Labour Statistical Yearbook (1996) 'Labour Disputes Accepted and Settled by Region', 423 (tables 8–9), Beijing: Beijing State Statistical Publishing House.

China Labour Statistical Yearbook (2004) 'Labour Disputes Accepted and Settled by Region', 518 (table 4), Beijing: Beijing State Statistical Publishing House.

China Labour Statistical Yearbook (2007) 'Labour Disputes Accepted and Settled by Region', 515–16 (table 9-1), Beijing: Beijing State Statistical Publishing House.

China News (Online) (15 March 2008) 'Vice-president of the All China Federation of Trade Unions: Over 80 per cent Have Concluded Labour Contracts' [in Chinese], http://www.chinanews.com.cn/cj/kong/news/2008/03-15/1192815.shtml

China's Ministry of Commerce (16 January 2003) 'Overseas Investment to China Reaches USD52.7 billion', http://english.mofcom.gov.cn/aarticle/newsrelease/commonnews/200301/20030100063506.html

China's Ministry of Commerce (12 June 2006) 'China's FDI in 2005 Revised to USD72.4 billion', http://english.mofcom.gov.cn/aarticle/counselorsreport/asiareport/200606/20060602423634.html

China's Ministry of Commerce (17 November 2008) 'China's Absorption of FDI, January–October 2008', http://english.mofcom.gov.cn/aarticle/newsrelease/significantnews/200811/20081105896381.html

China's Ministry of Labour and Social Security (2004) 'A Survey Report on Migrant Workers Shortage' [in Chinese], http://www.molss.gov.cn/news/2004/0908a.htm

China's State Council, Research Office Team (2006) *Research Report on China's Migrant Workers* [in Chinese], Beijing: Zhongguo Yanshi Publishing House.

Clarke, S., Lee, C. H. and Li, Q. (2004) 'Collective Consultation and Industrial Relations in China', *British Journal of Industrial Relations*, 42, 2: 255–81.

Davis, D. (ed.) (2000) *The Consumer Revolution in Urban China*, Berkeley: University of California Press.

Gaetano, A. M. and Jacka, T. (eds) (2004) *On the Move: Women in Rural-to-Urban Migration in Contemporary China*, New York: Columbia University Press.

Hershatter, G. (1986) *The Workers of Tianjin, 1900–1949*, Stanford: Stanford University Press.

Jacka, T. (2005) *Rural Women in Urban China: Gender, Migration and Social Change*, New York: M. E. Sharpe.

Kahn, A. and Riskin, C. (2005) 'China's Household Income and its Distribution, 1995 and 2002', *China Quarterly*, 182: 356–84.

Lee, C. K. (2004) 'Made in China: Labour as a Political Force?' Conference paper presented at the University of Montana, Missoula, 18–20 April.

Lee, C. K. (2007) *Against the Law: Labor Protests in China's Rustbelt and Sunbelt*, Berkeley: University of California Press

Leung, P. N. and Pun, N. (2009) 'The Radicalization of the New Working Class: the Collective Actions of Migrant Workers in South China', *Third World Quarterly*, 30, 3: 535–65.

Liebman, B. L. (2007) 'China's Courts: Restricted Reform', *China Quarterly*, 191: 620–38.

New York Times (20 January 2006) 'Pace and Scope of Protest in China Accelerated in 2005'.

Ngok, K. L. (2008) 'The Changes of Chinese Labor Policy and Labor Legislation in the Context of Market Transition', *International Labor and Working-Class History*, 73: 45–64.

Pei, M. (2003) 'Rights and Resistance: the Changing Contexts of the Dissident Movement', in E. Perry and M. Selden (eds), *Chinese Society: Change, Conflict, and Resistance*, London: RoutledgeCurzon.

Perry, E. (1993) *Shanghai on Strike: the Politics of Chinese Labor*, Stanford: Stanford University Press.

Pun, N. (1999) 'Becoming Dagongmei: the Politics of Identity and Difference in Reform China', *China Journal*, 42 (July): 1–19.

Pun, N. (2003) 'Subsumption or Consumption? The Phantom of Consumer Revolution in Globalizing China', *Cultural Anthropology*, 18, 4: 469–92.

Pun, N. (2005) *Made in China: Women Factory Workers in a Global Workplace*, Durham: Duke University Press.

Pun, N. and Lu, H. L. (2009) 'The Culture of Violence: the Labor Subcontract System and the Collective Action of Construction Workers in Post-Socialist China', working paper.

Pun, N. and Lu, H. L. (forthcoming) 'Incomplete Proletarianization: Self, Anger and Class Action of the Second Generation of Peasant-Workers in Reform China', *Modern China*.

Reed Electronics Research (2006) 'Emarketforecasts – China', http://www.rer.co.uk/emf/China04.shtml

Research and Markets (2008) 'China PCB Industry Report, 2008', http://www.researchandmarkets.com/research/b41e92/china_pcb_industry

Roberts, K., Connelly, R., Xie, Z. M. and Zheng, Z. Z. (2004) 'Patterns of Temporary Labor Migration of Rural Women from Anhui and Sichuan', *China Journal*, 52: 49–70.

Solinger, D. (1999) *Contesting Citizenship in Urban China: Peasant Migrants, the State, and the Logic of the Market*, Berkeley: University of California Press.

Southern Weekly (31 July 2008) 'Abide by the Labour Contact Law: Labour-Capital Negotiations' [in Chinese].

Taylor, B., Chang, K. and Li, Q. (2003) *Industrial Relations in China*, Cheltenham: Edward Elgar.

Walder, A. G. (1984) 'The Remaking of the Chinese Working Class: 1949–1981', *Modern China*, 10, 1: 3–48.

4
Globalization, Structural Reform and Labour Politics in China

Marc Blecher

> The cheap prices of commodities are the heavy artil-
> lery with which [capitalism] batters down all Chinese
> walls, with which it forces the barbarians' intensely
> obstinate hatred of foreigners to capitulate. It compels
> all nations, on pain of extinction, to adopt the bour-
> geois mode of production; it compels them to intro-
> duce what it calls civilization into their midst, i.e., to
> become bourgeois themselves. In one word, it creates
> a world after its own image.
>
> – Karl Marx and Friedrich Engels
> *The Communist Manifesto*

1. Introduction

Marx and Engels were right as far as they went, and they'd probably be
the first to welcome the criticism that their formulation did not fully
appreciate the power of the dialectic they hypothesized. When they
penned those words, Britons had literally battered down the walls militarily and politically; European and then American and Japanese merchants soon pried open the Chinese market with all manner of cheap
manufactures, and began setting up their own capitalist firms. Was the
country heading for 'underdevelopment'?

Here the masters would prove masterful with their resounding 'no':
China would be compelled to become bourgeois too. And so it did, taking its first steps on the long, convoluted road to capitalism with surprising celerity. By 1933, the new Chinese bourgeoisie owned 67 per cent
of the country's industrial factories, which employed 73 per cent of its

industrial labour. Rural handicraft production was not devastated the way it was in India (where it prompted Gandhi's iconic promotion of cotton spinning). In the 1930s, the volume of imported goods (other than textiles) that could compete with rural handicrafts was less than 5 per cent of the volume of handicraft production. China's capitalist road was blocked by the revolution and three decades of Maoist state socialism. But beginning tentatively in 1978, and going into high gear after 1992, national capitalism came roaring back. Completing the dialectic that Marx and Engels did not explicitly foresee, today China is battering down walls worldwide with its own cheap commodities. The clear beneficiaries have been the Chinese state and the renascent bourgeoisie. But what about the working class?

The Chinese proletariat's[1] political response to globalization has, on the whole, been broadly acquiescent in two senses. First, workers have almost never challenged the profound structural transformation from state socialism – under which they had achieved considerable power on the shop floor and material benefits – to capitalism that has deprived them of both and, indeed, driven millions into unemployment. This is all the more striking in view of the definite and often genuine radicalism of working-class politics in the Maoist period (Perry, 1994; Perry and Li, 1997; Wang, 1995). Second, while strikes and demonstrations have occurred, they have only involved a very small portion of the working class, and have almost never produced protest waves linking up workers beyond their factory walls. That said, the working class's response has modulated significantly in different areas. Comparative analysis can shed light both on the overall theme of proletarian accession as well as its variations.

Labour politics have diverged in three regions: the highly globalized south-east 'sunbelt', the relatively less 'reformed', barely globalized and decaying Manchurian rustbelt, and the broadly 'reformed' but only partially globalized and still largely domestically oriented areas that make up most of the rest of the country, represented in this chapter by the city of Tianjin, site of the author's field research. For each, we will identify key dimensions of labour politics. They are summarized in Table 4.1.

Taken together, this political configuration forms our *explanandum*. The next section fleshes it out region by region. The following section attempts to explain these salient similarities and differences, especially the key question of labour's level of resistance, in terms of the nature of the prevailing political economy, sociological factors such as generation and social space, and the role of the state.

66

Table 4.1 Labour politics by region

Regional political economy	Resistance/ quiescence	Participants	Locus	State presence	Size & cellularity	Dominant discourse
Globalized despotism (e.g. south-east)	Broadly quiescent with some resistance	Younger migrants	Factory	Lower	Smaller, mainly cellular	Wages and working conditions
Decaying rustbelt (e.g. north-east)	Broadly quiescent with some resistance	Older, laid-off and retired state sector workers	Government offices and public spaces	Higher	Larger, mainly cellular, tendency towards metastasis	Right to benefits; more politicized
Mixed, adaptive (e.g. Tianjin)	Broadly quiescent	–	–	Higher	–	–

2. Labour politics: three patterns

2.1 The south-east: globalized despotism

In the vast majority of export-oriented firms of south-east China, there is labour peace. Most of the workers are young rural migrants, many female. They tend to come from poorer villages and towns where little gainful employment is available. The modal pattern is that they stay for a few years after leaving middle school, remitting income home. When the time comes to marry, they often return home, since it is difficult to find a spouse in the city. Generally these late teenagers and early twenty-somethings are (ware)housed in dormitories on factory grounds. They often work long shifts of ten or twelve hours a day, six or seven days a week. Most of the factories do not have branches of the state-run All-China Federation of Trade Unions (ACFTU), Communist Party committees, or worker representative assemblies – the standard complement of political institutions in state- and collective-sector firms.

The regime of accumulation is the despotic capitalism resembling in many respects that of Marx's day. Firms operate within a highly competitive, largely unregulated environment. They are pressurized by ease and low costs of entry, 'just in time' technology, rapidly shifting demand, and intense pressures from buyers, including monopsonistic ones like Wal-Mart. This induces a draconian shop-floor regime of sweated labour, as capital struggles for every possible quantum of surplus value. Piece-rate and overtime wage systems are carefully calibrated. Tight discipline is maintained through the dormitory system, intensive surveillance on the shop floor, strict regulation of bathroom and meal breaks, and the like. Workers are often required to put down hiring deposits in order to minimize turnover. Safety takes a back seat. Factory doors are kept locked, which has caused significant casualties from fire.[2]

When it occurs, labour conflict here is generally focused on the material struggle over pay and labour process, i.e. between labour and capital over surplus value. Protest has often taken legal forms such as mediation, arbitration and litigation (Ching, 2007: 176–91). But it has also turned into contentious wildcat strikes, which of course are illegal. These normally occur in a cellular fashion, factory by factory, though there have been a small number of incidents in which workers in nearby factories demonstrate briefly in solidarity. Only rarely have they become politicized in the sense of expanding their terrain, much less their target, to the local government. In one typical case, management instituted a new time card system to help advance its position in the struggle within the economy of labour time by requiring workers to punch out and in at lunch time. This cost workers a precious ten minutes on either end of what had only been a thirty-minute break, essentially reducing their free time by two-thirds to a mere ten minutes. So they struck, demanding their time back and then expanding their agenda to a demand that the firm also observe minimum wage and overtime laws. Thousands of workers were involved, the strike lasted five days, at one point the manager was nearly beaten, and several strikers were arrested. In another case, in 2005 and 2006 management responded to successive rises in government-set minimum wage by jacking up production quotas, taxing workers beyond human endurance limits. When in 2007 the government again did not raise the minimum wage, and workers did not receive their expected annual raise, they struck in their thousands (King-Chi Chan and Ngai, 2009).

2.2 The decaying north-east

Manchuria was China's first heavy industrial heartland. The Maoist state continued to build it up, featuring two of its enterprises – the Anshan Steel Works and the Daqing Oilfield – as national models. Under the structural reforms, gargantuan state enterprises such as these did not fare well. In the 1980s their management and supervising ministries, ambivalent about the radical changes being mooted, and continuing to face only timid economic incentives and, in terms of the all-important price structure, actual disincentives to transform themselves, were slow to adapt. They also continued to maintain the Maoist period's relatively thick presence of party and neighbourhood committees, union offices and worker representative assemblies. By the 1990s, when globalization of the Chinese economy took off, most were not in a position either to attract significant foreign investment or to produce exportable products (such as the high-tech speciality steels rolling out of South Korea). As cheap input prices set in the Maoist period to promote heavy industry were gradually freed to market levels, as government subsidies for their losses dried up, and as these firms continued to struggle under the weight of providing extensive social welfare benefits for their ageing workforce, they began to shed labour through layoffs and early retirement buyouts.[3] Downsizing and bankruptcies became rife. Some managers, seeing the writing on the wall, quietly stripped their enterprises' assets and salted away or made away with the proceeds.

This toxic mix of a dying industrial heartland that was once the pride of the country, and the incompetence, laziness or dishonesty of its bloated management and political apparatus, has produced among workers both overarching despair leading to grudging silence, but also fury that has fuelled the largest and most politicized proletarian protests in China in recent years, and the only ones that seriously threatened to metastasize into potentially destabilizing protest waves. In March 2002, when China's National People's Congress was holding its annual session, tens of thousands of laid-off workers in Heilongjiang Province's Daqing, the oilfield that was the Maoist-era model of industrial development from which the whole country was exhorted to learn, protested arbitrary cutbacks in their already paltry severance packages. They blocked a railway and laid siege to the PetroChina headquarters. Unprecedented solidarity demonstrations were held at the Liaohe Oilfield in neighbouring Liaoning Province, but also much further afield at the almost equally famous Shengli Oilfield in Shandong and clear across the country in Xinjiang. An alarmed government called in not just the armed police but a proper army tank regiment.

Simultaneously, next door in Liaoning Province over 10,000 workers of the Liaoyang Ferro-Alloy Factory took to the streets and public squares demonstrating against wage arrears and benefit shortfalls resulting from alleged management misappropriation of funds that had led to the plant's bankruptcy. They were soon joined by thousands of workers from several other failing Liaoyang plants, another largely unprecedented and, for the government, dangerous development. Moreover, the protests went beyond original demonstrations' economic demands by becoming overtly political, demanding the dismissal of Gong Shangwu, the former Liaoyang mayor and Party secretary who was at that very moment representing the city at the National People's Congress in the capital. Even after the large initial protests were brought to an end with a combination of carrot and stick – specifically, economic concessions plus arrest of the protest leaders – significant protests dragged on for months demanding the release of the imprisoned workers. In the successive weeks, thousands of miners in Fushun and Fuxin, also in Liaoning, threatened to block railway lines in protest of the terms of their forced retirements. The government turned out the armed police in both cities (Blecher, forthcoming; Lee, 2007: Part II).

2.3 Adaptive Tianjin and beyond

Tianjin is broadly similar to many other parts of China in which much of the old state socialist sector has managed to adapt to the structural reforms through managerial and technological upgrading and the formation of joint ventures with foreign firms. New private or mixed-ownership enterprises, some Chinese and some foreign-invested, have also developed. Foreign investment has focused on production for

China's internal market as well as for export. That helps make the economic environment for capital – and therefore for labour – less intensely competitive and pressurized than in the south-east. To be sure, economic restructuring has led to layoffs, early retirement buyouts, and factory closures or consolidations. But on the whole the economy has been buoyant enough to provide a way out for many affected workers. Some have taken jobs in the expanding private or foreign sector, while others have become self-employed. Indeed, workers in state-run firms that have got into economic difficulty due to the structural reforms generally see globalization as holding out hope for a foreign investor to save their plant. Older laid-off or prematurely retired state sector workers who have been unable to find work have usually managed to scrape by, often by relying on help from grown children, who are, in turn, generally earning enough in the growing economy to support them. Moreover, the city government has had sufficient resources to support the cost of benefits promised to such people. For all these reasons, the level of labour protest in Tianjin and places like it is lower than in the north-east or the south-east (Blecher, forthcoming).

3. Labour's responses to structural reform and globalization: three patterns

Overall, then, the Chinese structural reforms have produced distinct patterns of capitalist development, which have in turn shaped different labour responses. The level of globalization appears to be a major *explanans* but in fact may not be the most important one. First, a highly globalized, export-oriented, hyper-competitive economy, centred in the south-east has produced a despotic labour regime relying on migrant labour. In turn workers have responded with broad quiescence punctuated by legal measures as well as mainly cellular, enterprise-based strikes and protests focusing on bread-and-butter issues and discourse. This complex concatenation can be encapsulated by the shorthand 'despotism'. Second, in what might be called 'decay', a failing state-run, import-substituting, heavy industrial sector, characteristic of the north-east, has left a labour force of younger, middle-aged and older workers facing unemployment and the prospect of surviving primarily on meagre state benefits. This too has produced broad quiescence alongside occasional large, more politicized, and, briefly, metastatic protest when jobs were lost or unemployment benefits reduced. Third is an 'adaptive' pattern. Here a mixed economy of state and collective enterprises that have managed to adjust to the new market forces on the one hand,

and newer private or joint-venture enterprises, some Chinese and some foreign-funded, on the other, has developed. It relies both on internal and export markets. In places like Tianjin, it has produced solid growth without the cut-throat competition driving capitalists to sweat labour. Workers have enjoyed a smoother transition, avoiding both being abused and cast aside. The adaptive pattern has therefore engendered a lower level of labour protest than despotism or decay.

Put this way, the analysis is in danger of excessive, potentially vulgar materialist explanation. In fact, a complex set of not just economic but also social and political *explanans* are also at work in producing the *explanandum* of labour's response.

3.1 Economic factors

3.1.1 Despotism

Labour has responded simultaneously in three apparently contradictory ways to globalization-driven despotism in China. Workers have lapped it up, as millions upon millions of rural migrants have streamed into the urban export platforms clamouring for work. They have for the most part endured the drudgery and degradation of the work with grudging though generally uncomplaining acquiescence. And they have occasionally fought back, and even sometimes lashed out, in a small number of cases of egregious abuse. Most generally and abstractly, the theory of exploitation explains why workers submit 'freely' to 'wage slavery'. First, they are driven into the wage relationship by economic compulsion, and then the fact that exploitation takes place in a 'hidden abode' helps obfuscate the asymmetry between labour and capital. What they see is, as the neoliberals emphasize, their higher incomes. What neither they nor the neoliberals see nearly as clearly, if at all, is the surplus value appropriated from them. This helps explain why Chinese migrants have flocked into the draconian world of despotic capitalism and suffered there mostly in silence.

What Marx was perhaps less good at grasping was the conditions under which workers actually would resist. He seemed to think opposition would emerge organically out of the dialectic of the capitalist labour process (which forces workers to cooperate the factory, leading to wider cooperation), the homogenization of social life, and capitalist crisis. What is implicit but perhaps not sufficiently explicit in Marx's theory is the proposition that working-class resistance requires that the process of exploitation, which is normally opaque, become transparent. In Chinese despotic, globalized capitalism, what has set off resistance is not the quotidian misery of factory life itself, but a series of events that drag exploitation from its 'hidden abode' out into the open. In the first case discussed above, workers who did not resist the appropriation of surplus value day in, day out nonetheless rose to their feet and found their voice when, in the usually obfuscated struggle over labour time, they lost twenty out of thirty minutes they had previously had. In the second case, they became incensed when management took advantage of changes in minimum wage regulations to end its brief practice sharing with the workers some of the increasing surplus value it was appropriating from them, leaving them with a precisely measurable decline in their expected income. It is only at that point that workers can take advantage of the way the labour process and the social and cultural spaces created by despotic capitalism enables workers to act collectively. Put the other way around, unless the exploitation were made transparent, the highly exploited migrant workers of Shenzhen would in general continue quietly to turn out masses of surplus value. The corollary for globalization is that it will produce resistance only in so far as it produces intense levels of competition that induce capital to take despotic measures on the shop floor that bring exploitation into the open.

3.1.2 Decay

The material basis of working-class protest under conditions of economic decay is utterly different. Like workers everywhere living amidst rapid economic decline, the Manchurian proletariat would love to be exploited in regular work, and those who manage to cling to the opportunity are generally uncomplaining about it. Resistance has occurred mainly when work has disappeared and workers have had to settle for state-provided subsistence which was then withdrawn.

Here moral economy has more explanatory power than Marxist political economy (Scott, 1976; Thompson, 1966). State socialism guaranteed the working class employment and the modest wages and comprehensive benefits that came with it. With the advent of the structural reforms, they had little or no way to provide for themselves without such employment. This can help explain why the protests occurred at a moment when the last vestiges of these state socialist rights were being withdrawn, and also why they so quickly reached a high dudgeon of moral and political fury not seen in the strikes in despotic southern factories. It can help explain the higher level of politicization of protest. In the decaying north-east, the moral and political right to stable employment and livelihood was created by the revolution and the socialist state, and thus could only be withdrawn by that state. And in material terms, even former workers depended on the state for their retirement or unemployment benefits, housing, health care and education for their children or grandchildren. Finally, this theory sheds light on the metastatic tendency of protest under decay. Since the moral and political right and set of material benefits had been provided to all workers and former workers, its withdrawal affected a broader swath of the local working class.

Decaying areas like China's north-east are only weakly linked at best to the international economy. Here globalization can be responsible for the situation only at several removes: once the Chinese economy opened to the world, much of its former state socialist sector could not compete; or it could only compete by abrogating the state socialist labour regime of guaranteed employment and benefits. In China, labour market reform was pioneered by foreign-invested firms (Gallagher, 2005). But globalization is only one factor responsible for the decay of former state-owned industry. These firms proved unable to adapt to the new marketizing environment introduced around 1980, long before they actually began to face direct global competition. And even if they had been healthy and efficient, in the 1990s they still would have laid off workers whether they needed to or not: in a stunning example of the stubborn commandist bureaucratism that still plagues China, in recent years profitable, prosperous state-owned enterprises in China's central coast have followed orders to lay off workers even if they did not have labour surpluses (Hurst, 2009: 55–6). In Chinese industry layoffs and restructuring more generally often have their own inner origins that are not attributable to globalization, or even for that matter to economic forces.

3.1.3 Adaptation

In places like Tianjin, the lower level of labour resistance to globalization and to structural reform more generally is due, as we have seen, in part to the capacity of the economy to generate enough alternative employment and modalities for taking care of the unemployed. But there is something deeper and more structural as well. Many former employees of state enterprises actually experienced their layoffs positively. They appreciated the opportunity to choose their own work. Some welcomed the tradeoff of working in a globalized firm, with its more arduous pace and even draconian shop floor regime, in return for higher pay. Others appreciated the existential benefits of self-employment, even if that meant just driving a taxi.[4] For them, resistance was the furthest thing from their minds.

3.2 Social factors

3.2.1 *Generation*

The young migrants employed in south-eastern despotism were born in the 1980s, when the 'iron rice bowl' of guaranteed employment and social welfare was already being consigned to the scrap heap of history. They lack any appreciation of what it meant, much less any sense of loss of such proletarian rights. For them there is little if any 'radiant past' (Burawoy and Lukács, 1992). Instead, their world is one of purer economic calculus, to which they react, as we have seen, with a mixture of acquiescence and occasional protest, both of which are grounded in the wage relationship.

By contrast, there most certainly is a 'radiant past' for the cashiered workers of the decaying north-east who find both themselves and their iron rice bowls in history's dustbin. Indeed, in a world that has become utterly devoid of the work, livelihood, routines, cultural values, social solidarities and political triumphs and struggles of their formative years, these workers have little left but the past. Little wonder, then, that they react strongly and politically when its last remnant – a miserable severance package – is pilfered.

The younger workers in adaptive political economies have a similar existential outlook to their generational cohort in the south-east. What they have much less of is the despotism to drive them from acquiescence to protest. Older workers who experienced the proletarian rights of state socialism may look back longingly for their iron rice bowls; they are less likely than their Manchurian cohort to have lost it utterly. Moreover, they are, if necessary, more likely to be able to fall back on the support of their own grown children, which is much more difficult in the decaying areas where their progeny are also having trouble making ends meet.

3.2.2 Danwei *(work units) and social space*

The Maoist-era *danwei*, in which the state organized the urban population into work-based communities that provided employment, social services, welfare, social life and political supervision and organization, proved to be a double-edged sword. It enabled the state to supervise the population and keep them dependent, which promoted political acquiescence and often even loyalty. But at moments of crisis the *danwei* also provided a ready source of solidarity that could fuel protest while also rendering it cellular. Whether during the Cultural Revolution, the 1989 anti-government protests, or the 1999 anti-American protests against the bombing of China's Belgrade Embassy, protesters tended to march under banners of their work units.

In the despotic factories of China's globalized south-east, work units are gone, but they have been replaced by enterprises in which workers are often required to live in dormitories and eat in factory canteens. And while the Maoist *danwei* combined political appeals and mobilization as well as surveillance and control, factory managers, concerned almost exclusively with economic control of their workforce, do not maintain such a political apparatus. In comparison with the Maoist-era *danwei*, the social space of the despotic factory dormitory and refectory may be more likely to promote the development of protest when the right catalyst – which, after all, affects all firm employees in the community equally – comes along (Lee, 2007: 192).[5]

In the decaying north-east, especially the company towns like Daqing, cashiered workers generally still huddle together with their former fellow workers in their old enterprise-supplied housing. Some of the old *danwei* apparatus, such as clinics and dining halls, have fallen into disuse or gone commercial. And while the political apparatus of neighbourhood committees often still functions, under the general depoliticization they exercise much less control and engage in less mobilization than they did in their glory days. In functional terms, the situation is broadly similar to that of the despotic dorms: people with identical relationships to the political economy are concentrated in tight, exclusive social spaces where state political surveillance and control are somewhat loose. And the potential implications for facilitating protest are congruent as well.

In adaptive settings like Tianjin, the old *danwei* have been more thoroughly eliminated. Much enterprise housing has been privatized or demolished. As a result, most people no longer live surrounded by their present or former co-workers. Of course such a situation is much less conducive to the development of collective resistance.

3.3 Political factors

Here just a few well-known points can be noted. The market Leninist state's ongoing monopoly of all political space – its strict prohibition against any self-organization of civil society – both hinders collective resistance and, when protest does occur, leaves it leaderless and disorganized while also driving it into the pervasive cellular pattern. Where, as in the decaying Manchurian towns in 2002, spontaneous resistance nonetheless threatens to metastasize, the state acts quickly and firmly, putting thick force on the ground. These are formidable obstacles indeed to labour protest.

All that notwithstanding, the state has also taken a somewhat measured approach to most protests. The vast majority of striking or demonstrating workers are not arrested or called in for political questioning – only their more obstreperous leaders are. And the government generally also responds with material emollients to meet at least some of the protesters' demands. This of course tends to encourage protest. A new ditty has arisen among disgruntled workers: 'If you make a small ruckus, you'll get small result; make a big ruckus and you'll get a big one.' But the state's approach also discourages protest leadership, further driving resistance into the familiar wildcat, spontaneous pattern that quickly burns itself out. The state has shrewdly calculated that it is better off allowing protest that it can manage than trying to stop it altogether with hard repression and tight surveillance. The latter might well be impossible, and would run the risk of producing a broad backlash. Moreover, allowing protest provides the state with a way of learning about egregious hotspots so it can cope with them by rooting out avaricious or ineffective leaders while also providing aggrieved citizens with some mollifying resources.

4. State reactions

In addition to tolerating protest, the state has tried with some success to embed labour relations in a framework of legislation. And it has also lately begun to try to control the situation through expansion and reinvigoration of China's moribund state-run labour union.

The legislative approach began in 1995 with a comprehensive labour law. It stipulated all manner of regulations on working conditions, hours and overtime, while also assigning to the ACFTU the responsibility of reaching collective contracts between employers and employees (of which more anon). To this it added mediation and arbitration channels that have seen increasing uptake from aggrieved workers. From 2003 to 2006, the number of disputes settled by arbitration increased from 95,800 to 141,500, while the number settled by mediation rose from 67,800 to 104,000.[6] In 2004 the National People's Congress passed the country's first minimum wage law. And in 2008 it introduced a controversial Labour Contract Law, opposed by many employers, including international firms, who lobbied against it because it gave workers rights to longer-term contracts and protections against arbitrary dismissal. Even some academics who claimed to have workers' interests at heart opposed it, arguing that it would only benefit the better-off workers who didn't need such protection anyway, while endangering the less skilled whom employers were now more likely to fire just before they reached eligibility for protection.

The rise of legalism in labour relations has had several purposes. It is a genuine attempt to rein in the most egregious labour practices, thereby pre-empting serious disputes, normalizing factory life, and proclaiming to workers that the government is looking out for their interests. It has also been intended, with some success, to canalize and individualize disputation – to drive it from strikes and demonstrations in the factory and streets towards arbitration and mediation in government meeting rooms. It has inadvertently functioned to provide angry workers with an organizing and legitimating tool. By citing the law, they become more convinced that they are justified, more able to persuade others, more confident, and thus bolder. Yet legalism also sets up the protagonists in a way favourable to the state, as workers cite central government documents as weapons against their managers and local government officials, focusing their ire on the latter rather than Beijing. The legalistic approach has its dangers for the state, however. The laws are rarely enforced, which is bound to shake workers' views of the whole project and, possibly, begin to undermine the state's increasingly legalistic claim to legitimacy.[7]

More recently, beginning in 2006, the government seemed poised to wake up its trade union federation, Rip van Winkle-like, from a long sleep.[8] A 'mass organization' of the Leninist state, it has not played any significant role in mediating, much less advocating for or fomenting, labour protest under structural reform. In most cases, workers with grievances serious enough to send them into mediation, arbitration, strikes or the streets have not even bothered to seek support from their labour union branches along the way. In so far as the union makes any systematic effort to prevent, pre-empt or canalize conflict, it is only in arranging and administering collective contracts between workers and employer. The union's other major role vis-à-vis labour politics is to monitor it, which it discharges through surveys of workers' opinions and writing reports when problems flare up. And of course there are the quaint functions, left over from Maoist days, of organizing leisure activities and minuscule welfare funds for injured workers, holiday parties and the like.

In much of the export-oriented sector, unions still do not even exist. The ACFTU has had difficulty keeping up with the efflorescence of new industrial enterprises since the start of the structural reforms in 1978, and especially since the Chinese economy and transition to capitalism, including labour market 'reform', took off in 1993.[9] Foreign firms that employ Chinese labour either directly in their own firms or indirectly through Chinese firms with which they contract divide into two broad categories in their approach to this situation. Those from countries with despotic systems of labour relations – which tend to include those from Hong Kong, South Korea and Taiwan – naturally welcome it. The absence of genuine labour union organization was often a significant consideration in their decision to come to China in the first place. Some South Korean firms in particular did so in part to escape an environment of increasing challenges from their working class at home. On the other hand, for firms accustomed to dealing with labour unions in their home countries – which tend to be those from the West and even Japan with its enterprise unionism – Chinese unions serve the valuable role of streamlining and regularizing labour relations. They find that collective contracting through the ACFTU saves them the administrative trouble of offering, inking and implementing contracts with each individual worker. It can also help them receive social accountability certifications such as SA 8000, which are required by some major Western retailers (Pun Ngai, 2005: 111). It is all the more beneficial for such employers that Chinese unions generally do little or nothing to enforce those contracts.

The new leadership that came to power in 2002 and 2003 under President Hu Jintao and Premier Wen Jiabao placed more emphasis than Jiang Zemin had in the 1990s on the growing inequalities and irritants that have caused a rising drumbeat of protest during China's transition to capitalism. Their ideological mantra has been the creation of a 'harmonious society'. They thought that resuscitation of the country's trade unions, especially in the foreign-invested sector, would help stabilize and monitor labour relations. But if it was intended to provide a counterweight to the most exploitative labour practices there, they began in the wrong place by taking on major international corporations, who were generally China's best foreign employers. In October 2004, the ACFTU published a 'blacklist' of global corporations – including Wal-Mart, Dell, Eastman Kodak, McDonald's and Samsung – that forbade the establishment of unions. It quickly lighted on Wal-Mart, the international paragon of anti-unionism, as its first victim. After a long and complex battle, in which the ACFTU deployed mass mobilization tactics that the Communist Party had not used since the revolution, identifying pugnacious Wal-Mart employees and encouraging them to take the lead, by autumn 2007 all Wal-Mart stores in China had union branches. In September 2008 it announced a further campaign to replicate the feat in all factories of Fortune 500 companies in China within the space of one month. The latter programme fizzled, a victim of excessive goal setting and, no doubt, the worsening worldwide depression.

Perhaps the ACFTU started (or was tasked by the government with starting) with the biggest and best foreign employers because they were low-hanging fruit. At least some such firms had experience at home working with labour unions, though that was surely not the case with Wal-Mart. Perhaps the ACFTU counted on the fact that these companies, aware that they were already relatively good employers by Chinese standards, would not feel they had much to lose. Perhaps it was just looking to score some cheap propaganda points that would win favour with the Chinese people, to whom it was increasingly appealing for legitimacy on nationalistic grounds.[10] To be sure, going after these gargantuan firms would be a great deal easier than tackling the thousands upon thousands of smaller manufacturers in the export sector, many of whom were cosseting or were cosseted by local government officials. The union could well have strategized that starting with the great firms would make going after the others easier – in Chinese parlance, 'killing the chicken to scare the monkey'.

In the event, both the chicken and the monkey emerged unscathed; the only victim was the Chinese working class. The Wal-Mart unionization drive may have appeared to introduce something new and volatile: the mobilization of genuine worker militancy by the state. But the reality proved all too depressingly familiar. Within months, most Wal-Mart union branches came to be dominated by management, its objective ally in the local Party branches, or both. Some dispirited worker activists cried out in their blogs to 'save the Wal-Mart union!' Others accused their democratically elected union branch leaders of corruption, authoritarianism and sloth. As early as March 2008, Han Dongfang, a leading advocate for workers' rights, was driven to abandon his earlier hopes, arguing that the Wal-Mart unions were mere window dressing. In the Nanchang Bayi Wal-Mart, Gao Haitao, an ordinary worker and elected union committee member, began militating when Wal-Mart shifted the cost of New Year bonuses to the union and treated its required contribution to the union of 2 per cent of the payroll as a loan. Wal-Mart pressured the Nanchang city-level union office to silence Gao, and also tried to create an alternative union committee under its control. Gao beat them back with his self-taught knowledge of the law and support he enlisted from the central union offices in Beijing. Membership in the Nanchang Bayi union soared, and workers began to organize their own fund to defend Gao and their union. Wal-Mart outfoxed Gao, though. In July 2008, it concluded its first collective contract with the local in

Shenyang in north-east China, an area where workers were likely to be more compliant and the party apparatus more conservative and in firm control. It provided for a 9 per cent wage increase to come into effect only a year hence, at a time when foodstuff inflation in China was running between 20 and 30 per cent and urban wages were rising an average of 18 per cent. Wal-Mart then sought to impose this contract on all its workers. Gao Haitao fought this move, but Wal-Mart bypassed him, getting a union chair from another store to sign the contract with Gao's local. Gao has resigned his union chair in disgust.[11] As noted above, in China law serves to control the working class and strengthen the position of the state, not to provide an objective set of rules or level playing field for sorting out conflicts between the state and society, and certainly not between labour and capital.

5. Conclusion

Globalization has comprised only one aspect of the Chinese structural reforms. As such, its effect on labour is difficult to separate analytically from that of the sweeping wider changes. Moreover, globalization has been unevenly distributed over the Chinese landscape. It has alighted with a wallop along the southern and central coasts, had much more muted and attenuated effects on the old north-eastern industrial heartland and much of the hinterland, and left many other places with consequences somewhere in between. Finally, even in its areas of greatest impact, the many aspects of the labour regimes that have arisen – such as the dormitory system – have not been imposed directly by international firms or globalization's pressures on Chinese enterprises. Rather, they are Chinese adaptations to the new economic institutions, opportunities and pressures. Thus it would be problematic to argue that the despotic capitalism that has emerged in hyper-globalized south-east China is a simple or pure product of globalization.

We have identified three patterns of political economy under structural reform, each of which involves a distinct impact of globalization and specific effects on labour. In the south-east, a highly competitive form of breathlessly burgeoning export-oriented capitalism has produced a despotic labour regime. In the much less globalized north-east, a decaying economy has put a large part of the Maoist-era industrial working class out of work and left it dependent on meagre handouts from the state. And in other areas such as Tianjin, economic development has been solid and only partly driven by globalization, enabling a smoother transition for labour.

Though labour has been broadly acquiescent in all of these new political economies, its pattern of resistance has varied. Under despotism protest has tended to be cellular and oriented to the nuts-and-bolts battle over surplus value on the shop floor and in the pay packet. Under decay, resistance has been more oriented to the preservation of the last remaining shreds of labour rights created by state socialism, which have occasionally fuelled metastatic protest across enterprise and geographic boundaries. In the adaptive pattern, there has been relatively less protest. While the specific economic relations have been major structural determinants of these differential labour responses, social factors (such as generation and social space) and political ones (such as the state's monopoly of organization and its carrot-and-stick policy towards protesters) have also shaped the various patterns of protest.

Finally, in the face of such protest, the state has adopted a three-pronged strategy. First, it treats outbursts with a carefully modulated combination of harshness towards protest leaders and tolerance and even reward towards the majority of protesters. Second, it has erected a legal superstructure to canalize protest and attempt to pre-empt it in the first place by reining in the worst employer practices. Third, it has reinvigorated state-run unionism for the selfsame purposes.

On the whole this strategy has worked. Within a very short period of time starting in earnest in the early 1990s, China has pulled off a profound transformation in the structure of its labour relations from state socialism to the capitalist wage. A working class that more than once undertook significant, and sometimes even furious, outbursts in defence of its interests, rights and privileges under Maoist state socialism has on the whole gone quietly into this new world. Along the way many of the victims of structural reform of the state socialist political economy have actually welcomed globalization in the form of foreign investment that creates jobs, despite the often draconian terms of such employment.

The political economy of Chinese market Leninism faced the depression of 2008–9 with some important assets. The government could tap ample amounts of cash, some earned from trade surpluses and some from the country's extraordinarily high savings rate. The latter is a reminder that the country has a massive internal market the potential of which has only begun to be developed. While there were fears that its 2008 growth rate would dip to 5 per cent – well under the 7 per cent needed to maintain its employment rate – in the end it racked up 9 per cent. Its financial system is not drowning in red ink (as so many pundits predicted it would several years ago), and large numbers of its people are not facing foreclosures and the disappearance of their life savings. Its working class has already endured structural changes far more profound than a small uptick in unemployment. Despite the pressures that globalization and the even larger domestic aspects of the country's transition to capitalism place on its proletariat, China's globalized market Leninism proved better positioned to survive the 2008–9 depression than Western neoliberalism.

Notes

1. Of course the Chinese working class, like classes everywhere, is highly differentiated. Indeed, this chapter fleshes out many of the important differences. At this most general level of abstraction, it simply includes those who do industrial work under any sort of wage relationship.
2. For more details, see Chan (2001).
3. William Hurst (2009) has shown that even economically viable state-run firms in the rustbelt came under political pressure to lay off workers.
4. Author's interviews, Tianjin, 1995–9. Subsequent visits and discussions with social scientists there confirm that the situation remains the same if not even more pronounced a decade on.
5. Of course factory-based dormitory housing is not a necessary feature of globalized despotism. Managers could just as easily not provide it and allow their workers to live off-site, assuming that the housing market would deliver appropriate supply (which it surely would – and often does – in China where the demand from workers exists). It is an interesting question, though, whether such off-site housing would be more or less conducive to collective mobilization.
6. *China Statistical Yearbook* (Beijing: China Statistics Press, various years).
7. On this whole complicated question, see Lee (2007).
8. Some of the following discussion draws upon Blecher (2008).
9. According to official statistics, the number of trade union branches in China declined from 627,000 in 1993 to 509,000 in 1999 (*Statistical Yearbook of China 2003*, tables 23–4). Figures for subsequent years gyrate wildly, and are highly suspect. The source contains a footnote referring to the need for statistical adjustment in 2003. The figures on union staff are steadier and, accordingly, more credible. They dropped from 554,000 in 1993 to 465,000 in 2003.
10. Witness its support for 2005 anti-Japanese demonstrations, the Tibet crackdown of 2008, and, of course, the Olympics.
11. 'Promising Wal-Mart Trade Union Chair Resigns Over Collective Contract Negotiations', *China Labour News Translations*, September 2008.

References

Blecher, M. (2008) 'When Wal-Mart Wimped Out', *Critical Asian Studies*, 40, 2: 263–76.
Blecher, M. (forthcoming) *A World to Lose: Working Class Formation in Twentieth-Century China*.
Burawoy, M. and János Lukács (1992) *The Radiant Past*, Chicago: University of Chicago Press.

Chan, A. (2001) *China's Workers Under Assault*, Armonk, NY: M. E. Sharpe.

China Statistical Yearbook (Beijing: China Statistics Press, various years).

Gallagher, M. (2005) *Contagious Capitalism: Globalization and the Politics of Labor in China*, Princeton: Princeton University Press.

Hurst, W. (2009) *The Chinese Worker After Socialism*, Cambridge: Cambridge University Press.

King-Chi Chan, C. and Ngai, P. (2009) 'The Making of a New Working Class? A Study of Collective Actions of Migrant Workers in South China', *China Quarterly*, 198: 293–6.

Lee, C. K. (2007) *Against the Law: Labor Protests in China's Rustbelt and Sunbelt*, Berkeley: University of California Press.

Ngai, P. (2005) 'Global Production, Company Codes of Conduct, and Labor Conditions in China: a Case Study of Two Factories', *China Journal*, 54: 101–13.

Perry, E. (1994) 'Shanghai's Strike Wave of 1957', *China Quarterly*, 137: 1–27.

Perry, E. and Xun, L. (1997) *Proletarian Power: Shanghai in the Cultural Revolution*, Boulder: Westview.

Scott, J. (1976) *The Moral Economy of the Peasant*, New Haven: Yale University Press.

Thompson, E. P. (1966) *The Making of the English Working Class*, New York: Vintage.

Wang, S. (1995) *Failure of Charisma: the Cultural Revolution in Wuhan*, Hong Kong: Oxford University Press.

5
China's New Labour Contract Law: Is China Moving Towards Increased Power for Workers?

Haiyan Wang, Richard P. Appelbaum, Francesca Degiuli and Nelson Lichtenstein

1. Introduction

Labour relations in modern China have long been unbalanced. During the Mao era, all workers were supposed to contribute their labour without reservation to the state-owned employing 'units', which were responsible for setting wages, as well as providing health care, housing, children's education, and even arranging marriages. Beginning with Deng Xiaoping's reforms in the 1980s, many state-owned enterprises were transformed into private businesses, but the organizational style – absolute power concentrated at the top of the enterprise – had not changed significantly. However, with the opening of China's economy to outside investment and enterprises, labour–management relations characteristic of the rest of East Asia, as well as other non-communist nations, have increasingly replaced the older Maoist style relationship between enterprise and individual. Of course this shift to an overtly capitalist brand of labour relations has not by itself done anything to ameliorate the hierarchy and authoritarianism endemic to the Chinese workplace. Commissar or capitalist, management in modern China has too often ruled with an iron fist.

Labour laws designed to protect the interests of workers have been put in place by the party-state since the revolution of 1949, but those statutes have largely gone unenforced, especially in recent years. The reason for the low level of enforcement lies, according to Lee (2007), in 'the central authority's strategy of decentralization, entailing the devolution of both fiscal authority and welfare responsibility'. Enforcement is therefore left to the local authorities – province governors, municipal officials, factory managers themselves – the same officials who are also responsible for the creation of a business environment that will sustain

84

2

foreign investment and generate high levels of economic growth in their quasi-autonomous regions. Workers' interests, including enforcement of the existing labour law, have therefore been of little concern among local political and commercial elites.

Indeed, strikes, protests, marches and various forms of self-organization have been strongly discouraged by China's government-sponsored trade unions, in the interest of promoting social stability and what China's leaders call a 'harmonious society' (see Ho, 2003: 228). Although an elaborate arbitration and mediation system has been on the books for years, it has been ineffective in resolving labour-related disputes. The Chinese labour law was a vague and ambiguous set of statutes, of which most workers knew little, thus giving employers significant latitude to interpret the law and explain regulations in ways that served their self-interest (ibid.: Chapter 4). These conditions, needless to say, increasingly aggravated labour–capital relations, especially in the costal provinces where tens of thousands of export-oriented factories have been situated. Given the seemingly endless labour supply from China's rural areas, workers who complained about wages or working conditions ran the risk of losing their jobs to others who were more compliant.

Guangdong province in the south of China has become one of the key nodes of the global economy, thanks to the combined interests of retailers like Wal-Mart and brand-defined companies like Nike, Mattel and Eileen Fisher. Since the early 1980s this Chinese province has become a virtual free trade zone, attracting a wide range of manufacturers in search of low corporate taxes, lax environmental/planning regulations, and a workforce thought to be both compliant and cheap. During the past decade Guangdong's economy has grown more than 14 per cent per year, accounting for about half of China's total GDP growth. Guangdong has been a magnet for tens of millions of labourers from rural provinces, where limited educational opportunities, a lack of village employment prospects, and low prices for agricultural products have pushed the young, women especially, out of their home villages. Some rural women also aspire to escape arranged marriages, familial conflicts and patriarchal oppression, while others want to widen their horizons and to experience modern urban life. Thus the coastal provinces of China, including Guangdong, have emerged as the workshop of the world, a new Manchester where seemingly powerless workers labour in abysmal and degrading conditions. Worker passivity is said to result from the presumed cultural docility of the largely female factory workforce, along with a repressive government more concerned with attracting foreign investment than with the welfare of its own people. Reinforcing these conditions is the virtually limitless reserve army of hundreds of millions of impoverished Chinese, whose competition for jobs, shelter and favour keeps wages low and workers in fear.

But a dramatic transformation in Chinese law and economy has made this construct, whatever its past merits, increasingly untenable. While working conditions are often extremely exploitative, the migrant workers who flock to urban China are hardly docile or passive. During much of the last decade, at least before the onset of the global financial crisis in 2008, labour shortages in the booming south – driven by the exploding demand for workers and a lower birth rate in the countryside – gave workers more bargaining power. Some left Guangdong Province for better-paid work in factories in the Yangtze River Delta near Shanghai, or elsewhere in large interior cities. Thanks to mobile phones and instant messaging, workers have been able to communicate easily with friends and relatives who are working elsewhere in China, comparing wages and working conditions, and to move to a new city or a new factory if they are dissatisfied with their current job (French, 2004: A4; Yardley and Barboza, 2005: 1). Workers have also put up picket lines, organized demonstrations or gone on strike. Such labour discontent, combined with rising wages and an appreciating renminbi have even led multinationals to look to Vietnam and other Asian countries for a new cohort of low-wage, first-generation industrial workers.

All this turmoil provided the context for the Chinese government's implementation of a new Labour Contract Law in early 2008. It formalizes workers' rights on a series of tension-generating issues, including the requirement that employers sign written contracts with every employee, limit overtime hours, and offer a greater role for the trade unions. 'The government is concerned because social turmoil can happen at any moment', argued Liu Cheng, a legal adviser to the authorities on the labour law. 'The government stresses social stability, so it needs to solve existing problems in the society.' Most controversially, the law gives long-service employees protection against dismissal. After two contract renewals – six to ten years – workers automatically earn the right to work for the employer indefinitely, barring dismissal for clear cause (Barboza, 2006: A1).

China has promulgated fine sounding labour laws before, but this one seems to have some bite. Before passage by the national legislature in 2007, a vigorous public debate erupted among those most impacted by the new law. 'I've never seen a law attract so much public attention', said one well-placed western observer. 'At the factory level people are talking about it everywhere' (Adams, 2008). The government-controlled All-China Federation of Trade Unions (ACFTU) thought the new law would enable it to make some long-delayed inroads among workers in the export industries. However, the Shanghai-based American Chamber of Commerce lobbied hard against the employment security provisions in the proposed law and won some last-minute concessions (Costello et al., 2006). But these were not enough, according to some employers, to prevent a wave of factory closures and threats of more among the most labour-intensive manufacturers of Guangdong Province. By one account a thousand footwear and accessory producers had reduced output or closed up shop. Some moved to the Chinese hinterland, others to Vietnam and Myanmar, where labour was cheaper and legally defenceless (Chung, 2008). Even Wal-Mart sought to evade the impact of the new law; more than a hundred employees who worked in the company's procurement offices were dismissed during the autumn of 2007, about 40 in Shanghai and 60 in Shenzhen. Although relatively small in number, these white-collar layoffs by such a high-profile company created an uproar among advocates of the new law. The company claimed that shifts in the nature of Wal-Mart's global sourcing mandated the layoffs, but it seems almost certain that top management in China wanted to get rid of those long-service employees who would soon be covered by the employment guarantees legalized in the new labour law (IHLO, 2007).

This chapter will examine the ways in which China has responded to these changing conditions – both in the form of worker resistance and public response. We will focus especially on the sources, impacts and response to China's newly adopted Labour Contract Law, which took effect on 1 January 2008. Finally, the significance of economic changes in coastal China during the period up to the global financial crisis – rising wages, growing labour scarcity and reported capital flight to Vietnam and other low-wage Asian countries – will be analysed, with particular reference to their impact on efforts to organize labour.

2. China's rapidly changing socio-economic conditions

In October 2006, the 6th Plenum of the 16th Central Committee of the Chinese Communist Party passed a detailed resolution seeking to resolve 'major issues concerning the building of a socialist harmonious society' (Ma, 2005). Statistics from the Ministry of Public Security showed that the number of public protests has risen dramatically – from 15,000 in

1990 to 74,000 in 2007.[1] The Communist Party therefore sought to shift national economic policy away from GDP growth and towards a broader effort to improve social welfare, resolve worker–management tensions, and even allow wages to rise. By 2020 the Chinese Communist Party (CCP) hoped to legitimize and codify the legal system, narrow the development gap between urban and rural regions, reduce income inequality and increase household wealth. At the 17th Party Congress held in October 2007, Premier Hu Jintao's vision of a 'harmonious society', along with his call for 'scientific development', was officially added to the new Party Charter.

While Hu's vision is officially intended to resolve many of China's endemic social conflicts, it also serves to recentralize government power. Under the rubric of a 'harmonious society', the Hu leadership has installed more centralized macroeconomic control mechanisms, especially with regard to fiscal matters. This, in turn, is intended to strengthen the control of the central government, as it gains more power over provincial and local administrations. Moreover, a nationwide anti-corruption campaign, not unlike Maoist purges of the past, has given the Bejing leadership an opportunity to deal with factional rivals and advance the careers of younger government officials. Likewise, the new Labour Contract Law, enacted immediately before the 2008 Olympics, is also a manifestation of the Party's desire to create a body of legal protections necessary for stable economic growth.

The central government's concern with social inequality was by no means a new policy innovation. For twenty years, Beijing has experimented with programmes designed to ameliorate the inequalities characteristic of recent Chinese economic transformations. Both the 8th and 9th Five Year Plans (1991–5, 1996–2000) were at least partially designed to pull millions of rural people out of their deep poverty, and in 1999 China's government launched a new programme of 'western development' in support of China's most economically backward and underdeveloped areas. These programmes, however, focused mainly on regional or rural–urban imbalances; less effort was made to address workers' rights, since such an attempt might threaten the foreign investment that fuelled China's economic boom.

By the turn of the millennium, however, China's leaders were no longer satisfied with a prosperity that depended on low-tech export manufacturing. Premier Zhu Rongji signalled the shift in a high-profile speech delivered at China's 1999 International Trade Fair, where he pressed China's state-run enterprises and research institutes to develop more high-end/high-tech products (*People's Daily*, 1999). This was a theme that became a constant throughout the next decade. 'China should take substantive measures to shift its focus from pursuing speed to improving the quality and efficiency of economic growth', said President Hu Jintao at the Central Economic Work Conference of 2006.[2] In the same conference, the target of China's economic development was adjusted from 'fast and good' to 'good and fast', a switch that revealed China's restructuring of its economic development model. While this shift towards a new economic structure does not end China's huge demand for cheap labour, it does privilege higher income and more consumption relative to traditional investment goals. This created additional space for the birth of the Labour Contract Law, which – in the process of protecting workers' rights and thereby reducing potential conflict – would raise wages, boost domestic consumption, and thereby reduce reliance on foreign investment as the sole source of China's economic growth. In view of the global economic slowdown that began in the fourth quarter of 2008, this move may prove to be prescient.

3. China's new Labour Contract Law

The new labour law is focused on 'improving and perfecting the labour contract system'[3] so as to make explicit the rights and obligations of both employees and employers. Although existing laws required employers to have labour contracts with their workers, less than a fifth complied.[4] Many contracts were highly informal, with labourers' basic rights – such as minimum wages, working conditions, working hours and social insurance – vaguely stated; employers' obligations were usually nowhere to be found. An increasing number of labour contracts in China were being signed on a 'short-term' or 'temporary' base, putting workers in a highly disadvantageous position.

To deal with these problems, the 2008 Labour Contract Law introduced the following provisions:

- A requirement that a written labour contract be concluded within one month after the date the employer starts using the labourer,[5] with the additional provision that if the employer fails to do so, it shall 'pay the labourer twice the amount of due remuneration for his/her labour'.[6] If the employer fails to conclude a contract within one year, the worker will be automatically entitled to a contract in which no termination date is stipulated (a so-called 'non-fixed-term labour contract').[7]

- A limitation on the use of 'short-term' or 'temporary' contracts, by requiring that non-fixed-term contracts be automatically provided if the worker has been employed by a firm for at least ten consecutive years, the worker is less than ten years away from his or her statutory retirement age, or the contract renewal occurs after the consecutive conclusion of two fixed-term labour contracts.
- Encouragement of collective bargaining by providing trade unions with new powers. According to Article 51, a collective contract – one applying to all the workers in an enterprise – can be signed by the labour union after 'bargaining on an equal basis with the employer'.[8] Moreover, the law introduces the concept of 'Specialized Collective Contracts' addressing certain specific issues, such as labour safety and hygiene, the protection of the rights and interests of female workers, as well as wage adjustment mechanisms. Such collective agreements are also signed between the labour union on one side, and the employers on the other.[9]
- The regulation and limitation of part-time work, 'dispatch contracting' (outsourcing), overtime and other special forms of work.[10]

The dramatic impact of the Labour Contract Law became clear even before it was promulgated. For much of 2006 and 2007 the text of the law was posted on a government website in order to solicit public comments. While this was not the first time that China's government had called for non-party input on pending legislation, the response from the public was substantially larger – and reportedly more seriously considered – than ever before. Nearly 200,000 comments flowed in during the first month, an unprecedented number. Two-thirds came from ordinary workers, while the rest came from employers, social organizations and academia; almost all were submitted online.[11] Based on public feedback, the new Labour Contract Law was revised three times (December 2006, April and June 2007), and was eventually passed on 29 June 2007 at the 28th Session of the 10th Standing Committee of the NPC.[12] By the time it took effect on 1 January 2008, suggestions from the public had proved instrumental in extending it to labour dispatch (contracted) workers and part-time labour, including students and farm labour. A provision was added under article 17 that called for setting detailed clauses regarding social insurance, while article 14 called for labour contracts to be signed for certain forms of non-fixed-term labour. Special provision was also added to the text of the law making it possible to address the rights and interests of female workers, along with setting more detailed standards for their compensation.

4. How effective is the new law?

Despite the new law's considerable political and public support, employer resistance has become increasingly manifest. There are also indications that the implementation of the law tends to be weak and varies widely across different regions of China (Maquila Solidarity Network (MSN), 2008). A research report released in May 2008 by the Dagongzhe Migrant Workers' Centre and the Hong Kong-based organization Worker Empowerment provides cause for concern (Migrant Workers' Centre, 2008). The report, based on a questionnaire survey of 320 workers in Shenzhen and nine in-depth interviews, collected during the first four months of the law's enactment, shows that employers have already devised multiple ways to sidestep the provisions of the law or to ignore them altogether. The report highlights that '64% of the time, workers reported that the hours they worked did not correspond to the hours specified in their contract and 28% of workers earned less than the legal minimum' (MSN, 2008: 4). Furthermore, while the majority of the workers had signed contracts '33.4 per cent said that they were forced to sign "blank or incomplete contracts" – without specifying the name of the employer, work position, wages, working hours, social insurance and benefits, and the terms for changes, renewal, and termination of the contract' (Chan, forthcoming: 4). In some cases workers were even asked to sign contracts written in English, a language few could read (IHLO, 2008; MSN, 2008).

Furthermore, in order to avoid minimum wage provisions employers are increasing the dormitory and canteen prices in order to offset wages. The survey shows that 22.2 per cent of the workers suffered from such increases, while 22.3 per cent of the workers complained about an increase in employees' fines for any number of insubordinations (MSN, 2008). Mr Sun (Worker Empowerment, 2008: 3), a worker in a metal factory clarifies:

> Our factory regulation says 50 yuan for a minor mistake, which includes being late for work for a minute or verbal argument with supervisors. For major mistakes, like arguing with the manager, the fine goes up to 200 yuan. The factory often sends us warning letters and each warning letter costs us 50 yuan. The second letter means dismissal.

Similar findings were reported by the Hong Kong Liaison Office (IHLO, 2008) of the international trade union movement in Hong Kong which studied standard labour contracts published online for employers in Beijing, Shanghai, Guangdong, Shenzhen and Suzhou (ibid.). The IHLO noted that while an increasing number of employers provide contracts for their employees to sign, most of them are not necessarily effective or even legal. The organization reported that employers often download from the internet sample contracts from bigger, labour-intensive cities, and then revise them to fit their needs, inserting paragraphs that look official but have no legal standing. They then present them to the workers as the 'official contract', tricking them into thinking that they are signing a routine legal document (ibid.: 4).

Still, judging from the upsurge in litigation on the part of workers, as well as reaction from Chinese and foreign businesses, the new law is being taken most seriously inside China and outside. One immediate result is that workers who believe their rights have been violated are much more likely to seek arbitration under the new law, than they were under the much weaker labour law enacted in 1995. The story of one migrant worker, who had been employed by a Xi'an musical instrument factory for nineteen years without a contract, is illustrative. Li Hao was fired shortly after the law took effect in January 2008. He brought charges against his former employer under the newly added article 14 of the law, according to which fixed-term contracts are required – if requested by the employee – when the worker has been employed in the same enterprise for at least ten years. Based upon this new regulation, the Labour Disputes Arbitration supported Li's plea and a similar finding restored employment for at least one other worker in the same enterprise.

The new law has resulted in a significant increase in the number of labour disputes following its implementation, particularly in the growth poles around Shanghai and throughout Guangdong Province. The labour courts in Dongguan, Shenzhen and Guangzhou accepted more than 10,000 cases[13] during the first quarter of 2008 alone, double the number over the same period in the year before.[14] The Yangtze River Delta near Shanghai experienced a comparable growth in the number of disputes: in Nanjing labour cases were filed five times more frequently than half a decade before (De, 2008).

Employers, on the other hand, have responded with efforts to circumvent the law. Since the statute provides greater support for workers defending their rights, employers are pushed into what they regard as a difficult situation: it has become harder for them to hire cheap labour without signing an official, legal contract – one that includes provisions for social insurance, overtime remuneration and employment guarantees for long-term workers. Employers face potentially costly lawsuits if sued by their labourers, in keeping with the Chinese proverb that holds, 'Wherever there are policies from top-down, there are counter-policies from bottom-up'.

Because 'coercive terminations' had become more difficult, many employers found innovative ways to pressure workers to 'voluntarily' dissolve their contracts. Indeed, as the new law came into effect, many companies had inaugurated a series of mass layoffs. According to the Labour Department of Nanjing, nearly 100,000 labour contracts were dissolved in the first half of 2008 alone, which tripled the number over the same time period during the previous year (Du and Bo, 2008). The case of Huawei Technologies Co. Ltd., a private high-tech enterprise located in Shenzhen provides a graphic example. Employing 83,000 workers, Huawei was one of the largest telecommunication and networking suppliers in mainland China. On 17 October 2007 – three months after the publication of the new Labour Contract Law – Ren Zhengfei, the founder and CEO of Huawei submitted his resignation. On the same day, all the employees who had worked for Huawei for eight years or more were also asked to terminate their contracts (Qui, 2007). Xiao Qin (alias)[15] was one of them. He was a 32-year-old middle manager at the time, and had worked for Huawei since he graduated from Zhongshan University in 1999. 'It was the morning of October 22', said Xiao, 'my director called me into his office and told me that I would have to submit the resignation as soon as possible. "Don't worry. We're just going through a certain process", the director gave me a pat on the back, "you know, Mr Ren has already resigned earlier this week, and me too. Actually all the old employees will do the same thing within the following two months. You'll need to reapply for your post. But I think you will get a new contract from the company very soon. And of course", the director added, "we will have a very generous compensation package for you".' When Xiao asked why, he was simply told '"We need a thorough reshuffle from top down so as to keep our company alive".'

Together with 7,000 of his colleagues, Xiao Qin eventually resigned and reapplied, receiving a new three-year contract and a compensation package, based on previous pay and years of service, totalling 160,000 RMB (US$23,400), equivalent to about two-thirds of his annual income.[16] According to Huawei's official spokesman,[17] the 7,000 resignations submitted at the end of 2007 were signed on a voluntary and negotiable basis, and cost Huawei more than 1 billion RMB (US$146 million).[18] This costly process received widespread attention in the

Chinese media, where it was viewed with great scepticism. According to one non-scientific online survey[19] conducted by SINA.com (the largest Chinese-language infotainment portal), three-fifths of the 91,000 respondents believed that Huawei was seeking to evade its responsibilities under the new law, since all of the employees who resigned had been working for Huawei for at least eight years (recall that after ten years they would have been granted non-fixed-term, open-ended appointments). By breaking their consecutive working years before the new law took effect, the company avoided having to sign open-ended contracts with most of its workers. Moreover, 500 of those who resigned were not granted new contracts at all. Since the resignations occurred immediately before the new law took effect, Huawei avoided having to pay the double compensation it mandated for unilateral firings. Huawei's model was quickly copied throughout Guangdong Province. On 21 November 2007, *Nanfang Daily* reported that Dayawan Huili Daily Products Co. Ltd. forced half of its 2,000 employees to terminate their old contracts and sign a new one. In the same month, more than 2,000 employees in Henan Zhengzhou Transport Company experienced the same situation.[20]

Early resignations and rehiring have not been the only countermeasure that employers have used to evade their responsibilities under the new law. The use of labour dispatching agencies provides another loophole. These agencies are a relatively new form of hiring in China, similar to temp agencies in the US and Europe: the workers are under contract with the dispatching agency, which in turn contracts with enterprises for the use of the workers. Normally the dispatched labours are hired for short-term positions. To avoid the requirements of the new law, however, many employers reportedly terminated their contracts with long-term employees, requiring them to sign contracts with a designated dispatching agency, which then leased them back to the employer in what has come to be called 'reverse dispatch' (Zhang, 2007). According to an investigation conducted by *Outlook Weekly* in January 2008, some employers purposely put their ageing workers into physically demanding jobs. Others transferred their senior managers to entry-level posts.[21] Xiong Xinyuan, for example, had been working for the Dongguan Curtain Co. Ltd. as a chef since 1995. Since his seniority was long enough to ask for an open-ended contract by the end of 2007, it was not easy for the employer to fire him without violating the new Labour Contract Law. In January 2008, the company transferred him to the wood workshop, which was physically overwhelming for a 53-year-old worker who had suffered from serious back pains for many years. Two months later Xiong quit the company 'voluntarily'.[22] Shao Zhenghua, 35 years old, had worked for nine years in a toy plant, where he was the section manager. In November 2007 he and other workers were pressured to resign and be rehired when they were demoted to the paint workshop as ordinary painters.[23] Fang Hongbing, a 33-year-old clothing factory worker in Qingpu, suddenly found that his firm had moved to Fengxian and changed its name, legal representative and stockholders. All the old contracts had become invalid overnight. 'I signed a new contract with a "new" company', said Fang. 'Of course my work years went back to zero.'[24]

5. Problems and disputes

As we have seen, workers complained about reprisals on the part of their employers; as a driver in Sichuan Province posted on Tianya.com, one of the largest public forums in China, 'the damned new law made my boss fire me on Christmas of 2007'. Other workers expressed their disappointment after suffering through various counter-measures.[25] 'The employers are always the dominant side', said Liaoyang (alias), 'since we workers have nothing to fight with their tricks anyway. I'd rather there were no such a law at all.'[26] But the employers were the ones who raised the greatest concerns. One common complaint – voiced on China's biggest Human Resources (HR) online forum – was that the new law's provisions were unfair or unbalanced, favouring workers over businesses.[27] For example, the provision that requires an employer to pay double wages if a contract is not signed within a month of employment could be invoked if the delay occurred because the worker refused to sign. As Zhang Yuanyuan, a 43-year-old HR manager of a toy factory in Shanghai explained:

> In January, five of our lathemen refused to sign labour contracts with the company. At that time we were desperately in need of experienced lathemen and had to start the labour relationships with those workers without a written contract. In March, these five lathemen came to me and asked for a double pay . . . Are we going back to the age of 'iron rice bowl' in the 30th year after Deng Xiaoping's reform in 1978? While the labourers get increasing legal support from the new Labour Law, we employers are facing more and more pressures. This is not only a problem of cost or creativity. People always consider the 'labourers' as a weak group, therefore needing more protection. However, when the workers gain enough advantages from the

law, conversely we employers can be the victims of the tendentious provisions also.[28]

Employers also expressed considerable concern over the definition of 'labour' under the new law, which included professional managers and technical staff as well as blue-collar workers. Managers viewed this as a problem because the law gives workers substantial freedom to dissolve their contracts: those who are on probation can do so at any time, while workers under contract only need give 30-day notice.[29] While blue-collar workers are presumably easily replaceable, technical and professional people are not. As Xia Shang, the head of a shipping company complained on an online posting, 'To cultivate a qualified ship pilot is not as easy as to train an automobile driver. We spend so much on them every year. And now the new law allows them to leave whenever they like!'[30]

6. Responses from the ACFTU

The ACFTU has tried to capitalize on the energies released by the new labour law, although the organization's status – as the official bridge between the Chinese Communist Party and the nation's burgeoning proletariat – has often made this work difficult and self-defeating. Ever since the establishment of the People's Republic of China in 1949, the ACFTU, now claiming to represent 120 million members, has been the largest (and only) government-designated organization that advocates for workers' rights. However, the ACFTU's presence in the export industries of Guangdong and other coastal provinces has been nominal. The ACFTU collects 2 per cent of payroll as member 'dues' while union representatives in such enterprises are often management figures as well. Given the explosive character of Chinese labour–capital relationships, the ACFTU's close identification with both autocratic local officials and industry management threatens to make the institution irrelevant. This is a situation it seeks to rectify, if only to ensure its legitimacy and institutional integrity.

On 5 December 2007, the ACFTU held a press conference in Beijing to broadcast the newly published Labour Contract Law. At the press conference, Liu Jichen, Minister of the Department of Legal Work of the ACFTU, criticized some typical counter-measures against the new law, such as coerced resignation, large-scale layoffs and reverse dispatch. Liu urged local trade unions to counter widespread violations of the new law[31] and report them to the ACFTU Labour Administrative Department. He also urged local unionists to keep a record of emerging problems, controversial issues and special cases, reporting them to the relevant governmental departments.

The ACFTU therefore responded quickly, if not all that effectively, when managers at firms like Huawei sought to circumvent the new labour law. On 9 November 2007, upon the request of the ACFTU, the Federation of Trade Unions in Guangdong Province sent a single delegate to negotiate with the Senior Vice-President of Huawei on the recent 'resignation storm'.[32] The delegate raised three points during the negotiations. First, the ACFTU supported the company's right to make any reforms that might inspire its employees' enthusiasm and creative vitality, as long as these reforms did not harm the employees' basic rights and interests. Second, before Huawei would enact, amend or make decisions directly related to labour's vital interests, the company should listen to the employees, and then make decisions in consultation with the trade unions. As for the 'resignation case', the company was told to hold a Workers' Congress and discuss the feasibility of this reform with employees and union representatives. Third, the ACFTU suggested that the company consult with its trade union on labour remuneration, working hours, vacation, labour safety and hygiene, and insurance benefits. The ACFTU urged the company to sign a collective bargaining contract with its local union so as to build a set of harmonious and stable labour relations. According to one worker, Huawei did hold a Workers' Congress in January 2008, but 'no one has heard anything about the collective contracts'.[33]

7. Responses from labour rights activists and NGOs

Labour rights advocates and activists, often organized into an influential set of transnational non-governmental organizations, have responded to China's new Labour Contract Law with a certain ambiguity. While quite willing and happy to add a new legal tool in their kit designed to assert workers' rights, they nevertheless remain sceptical of the larger implications inherent in the legalistic regime promoted by the central government, one ultimately designed to contain dissent and promote a party/state definition of the 'harmonious society'. At the base of this ambiguity lies the historical tension between the push for local economic accumulation and the felt need for some kind of legalistic legitimacy, a conflict highlighted by both activists and scholars (Chan, forthcoming; Lee, 2007).

Most labour rights advocates agree that the current Labour Contract Law, and the less-advertised new Arbitration Law enacted on 1 May 2008, offer two important tools in the struggle to promote workers' rights. One of the first outcomes of the new law is that most workers have become aware of the importance of obtaining a contract and becoming familiar with the provisions of the new legal regime. According to Manfred Elfstrom from the International Labour Rights Forum, NGOs on the mainland 'saw a tremendous spike in attendance at their legal training classes (almost double previous attendance) right after the Labour Contract Law went into effect in January'.

These attempts to educate workers, however, have generated a sometimes violent backlash from employers and local officials. Physical assaults against labour rights advocates trying to educate workers are not uncommon, according to Citizens Rights and Livelihood Watch (MSN, 2008: 18–19). Thus in November 2007, unknown assailants beat up Chinese labour rights advocate Huang Qingnan, after which the Dagongzhe Migrant Worker Centre closed its doors for several days (Clean Clothes, 2008). Despite this danger, worker advocates agree that education is key to promoting a new regime of labour rights. From the bottom up, cross-border labour NGOs strive to use the law to educate workers about their rights. SACOM and Worker Empowerment, for example, exposed the gap between the entitlement of rights and the delivery of legal protection through media campaigns (SACOM, 2008). Parallel to advocacy, frontline NGO organizers also raise workers' awareness by distributing simplified pamphlets of the Labour Contract Law in industrial districts in the Pearl River Delta (PRD), and, wherever appropriate, support aggrieved workers to make claims for rightful compensation through arbitration and litigation. An increasing number of worker protests may also result in stronger law enforcement.

8. Conclusion: accommodation or crisis in Chinese class relations?

The 2008 Labour Contract Law represents a wager by China's governmental elite. Although classic – and classless – Maoism has long since been replaced as a legitimating ideology by a new discourse that privileges national development and personal enrichment, the growth of social unrest in the Chinese export sector reached alarming proportions in the first decade of the twenty-first century. This was not merely a question of worker militancy itself, but also reflected labour shortages, high rates of turnover and unpredictable wage hikes. Exports still boomed, but scandal after scandal in the export sector – deadly fires, tainted products, exposés of exploitative working conditions – threatened the long-term viability of China's hyper-growth strategy. The new labour law is therefore part of a larger government strategy designed both to defuse social conflict and shift Chinese growth along a Keynesian pathway that emphasizes higher domestic living standards, technologically upscale production, and a greater balance between the impoverished country-side and the rapidly urbanizing coastal provinces.

But the success of this reform, in both the economic and political realms, is far from certain. Capital, both Chinese and otherwise, sees the new Labour Contract Law as a burdensome regulation that threatens to erode the price advantage that products assembled on the mainland have enjoyed in international markets. Before its promulgation, the Shanghai-based American Chamber of Commerce lobbied hard against the employment security provisions in the proposed labour law and won some last-minute concessions. We have also seen the degree to which many companies, foreign as well as domestic, have sought to subvert the employment guarantees in the labour law by coercing mass resignations and then rehiring employees on a contingent basis. And most importantly, employers have demonstrated their distaste for the law by deploying one of global capital's most frequently used weapons: flight to a country or region with cheaper labour and a more inviting set of laws governing the exploitation of that vital commodity.

Although it is difficult to disentangle the impact of the labour law from that of the general rise in production costs or the economy-wide slowdown generated by the world recession, thousands of factories, most often in the toy, shoe and apparel sectors, have closed in Guangdong Province during the last year. As early as the winter of 2008, 300 of some 1,000 shoe factories shut their doors, while as many as half of all toy exporters – 3,600 companies – were driven out of the market in the first seven months after passage of the Labour Contract Law (Chung, 2008). Looking forward a year or two, Guangdong business groups forecast a truly alarming scenario, with as many as one-third of all factories idle resulting in more than 2.7 million new job losses. Almost all of the companies that have closed are labour-intensive manufacturers head-quartered in Hong Kong, Taiwan or South Korea. Some moved to the Chinese hinterland, others to Vietnam, Bangladesh, or Myanmar, where labour was cheaper and legally defenceless (AP, 2008; Shirouzu, 2008).

In the West, such a slowdown would be sure to chill labour militancy and bolster the appeal of a management-oriented set of economic poli-cies. But the political and social dynamic in China is different. Economic growth and foreign investment continue, and at a level that would still be considered a boom in Europe or North America. More importantly, the new Labour Contract Law, as well as the drumbeat of criticism that both the central government and the ACFTU have directed against corrupt or oppressive employers, has generated a rights consciousness within the working class that exists independently of their employment prospects. This has been manifest in the continuing set of demonstrations and strikes, even at companies that have closed down. In October 2008 thousands of unemployed workers protested outside a Guangdong toy factory that closed abruptly, while the next month 200 workers showed up outside a Chang'an factory to demand from the government severance payments ranging from $1,500 to $3,700 each. A more orderly sort of rights protest may well be equally consequential as hundreds of thousands of workers take their grievances to the courts, flooding the dockets with individual labour cases. In less than a year labour disputes have increased in Beijing's Chaoyang District People's Court by 106 per cent, by 231 per cent in a similar Nanjing court, 126 per cent in Shenzhen, and 132 per cent in Dongguan (Harris and Luo, 2008).

To a large degree, the new labour law, created at the peak of domestic discontent, is an effort to harness conflict within a legal framework, thereby channelling anger away from direct labour militancy against the government. By providing favourable legal provisions for the most oppressed workers, the new law actually encourages them to channel the fight for their legal rights to their own employers – rather than merely rail against an 'unfair society'. But such individualized grievances, no matter how successful, are no substitute for collective organization within the Chinese working class. Hence the central role of the ACFTU, an immense, quasi-state organization that finds itself torn between its historic function as a Communist Party-controlled labour front and its desperate need to find a new source of institutional and ideological legitimacy. The ACFTU boasts that it has begun to use the new labour law to represent millions of workers in the export sector, but the quality of that representation is highly questionable given the corruption and collaborationist outlook of so many union officials at the level of the firm and province. But it would be a mistake to discount entirely the capacity of the ACFTU to reconfigure itself, especially given the dynamic sense of rights consciousness that China's new Labour Contract Law has engendered among so many of its constituents.

Notes

1. Available at http://www.mps.gov.cn/n16/n1237/n1432/index.html.
2. 'Comarade Hu Jintao's Important Speech at the Central Economic Work Conference', available at http://www.clxzfw.gov.cn/fb/show.asp?id=533.

3. Ibid.
4. As reported by the Judiciary Committee of the Standing Committee of the NPC. See Press Conference on the Feedback of the First Draft of the Labour Contract Law, 21 April 2006, released at http://www.gov.cn/xwfb/2006-04/21/content_260252.htm.
5. Labour Contract Law (2008), article 10.
6. Ibid., article 82.
7. Ibid., article 14.
8. Ibid., article 51.
9. Ibid., article 52.
10. Ibid., articles 57, 58, 68.
11. The exact number was 191,849, including 1,280 in letters and 145 in newspapers. Xin Chunyin, Vice Director of Judiciary Committee, Press Conference on the Feedback of the First Draft of the Labour Contract Law, 21 April 2006, released at http://www.gov.cn/xwfb/2006-04/21/content_260252.htm.
12. The full draft is available at Labour Law of the People's Republic of China (1995), http://www.cnfalv.com/a/ldf/; Labour Contract Law of the People's Republic of China (2008), http://www.ldht.org/Html/lifa/lfjc/038834.html. Various amendments to the different drafts are available at http://www.ldht.org/Html/lifa/lfjc/197985.html; http://www.ldht.org/Html/lifa/lfjc/633741746536.html; and http://www.ldht.org/Html/lifa/lfjc/7601997519036.html.
13. 4,347, 3,559 and 2,280 respectively.
14. 'Labour Disputes Multiplies in the Pearl River Delta', 3 June 2008, available at http://www.ldht.org/Html/news/news/244160889.html.
15. Phone interview with Xiao Qin (alias), Employee of Huawei Co. Ltd., conducted by the author, on 19 July 2008.
16. Under the new law, required compensation is calculated on the basis of one month's wages for every year worked in the enterprise; for unilateral firings, this amount is doubled. The previous law (1995) contained a similar formula, but without the doubling requirement. As we have noted above, the previous law was widely ignored as well.
17. Sina.net, 'Huawei claims that all the resignations were voluntary', 5 November 2007, http://tech.sina.com.cn/t/2007-11-05/00141831426.shtml.
18. 'Huawei spent 1 billion RMB in encouraging its old employees to resign', *Southern Municipal Daily*, 2 November 2007, http://news.xinhuanet.com/employment/2007-11/02/content_6996878.htm.
19. Survey on Huawei's Resignation Case, *Sina.net*, available at http://survey.news.sina.com.cn/voteresult.php?pid=19642. Data collected on 3 September 2008.
20. See http://cache.tianya.cn/publicforum/content/no20/1/141709.shtml.
21. 'New Labor-Capital Games with the New Labor Contract Law', *Outlook Weekly*, 23 January 2008.
22. Ibid.
23. Ibid.
24. Phone interview with Fang Hongbing (alias), former employee of an unnamed cloth factory in suburb Shanghai, conducted by the author on 31 July 2008.
25. See http://cache.tianya.cn/publicforum/content/free/1/1086175.shtml; http://cache.tianya.cn/publicforum/content/no20/1/156566.shtml; and http://cache.tianya.cn/publicforum/content/free/1/1082962.shtml.
26. Ibid.

27. VIPHR, http://www.viphr.net/bbs/index.asp.
28. Interview with Zhang Yuanyuan, Human Resource Manager of an unnamed toy company in Shanghai, conducted by the author on 19 August 2008.
29. Article 37.
30. See http://www.cnr.cn/xmfw/xwpd/zjxm/200802/t20080220_504709621.html.
31. 'ACFTU: Conference on the New Labour Contract Law', 5 December 2007, available at http://acftu.people.com.cn/GB/6616351.html.
32. 'ACFTU: Huawei's Resignation Issue Has Left Negative Effects', *Xinhua Press*, 10 November 2007, available at http://tech.163.com/07/1110/22/3SVIETFF000915BE.html.
33. Phone interview with Xiao Qin (alias), employee of Huawei Co. Ltd., conducted by the author on 19 July 2008.

References

Adams, J. (2008) 'New Labor Regulations Designed to Protect China's Workers are Already Having an Impact', *Newsweek*, 14 February, at www.newsweek.com.
AP (2008) 'Rising Costs Squeeze Chinese Factories; Some Companies Look to Cheaper Markets', *International Herald Tribune*, 22 February.
Barboza, D. (2006) 'China Drafts Law to Empower Unions and End Labor Abuse', *New York Times*, 13 October.
Chan, J. L. (forthcoming) 'Legalization of Labour Relations in China: the Labour Contract Law as a Double-Edged Sword'.
Chung, O. (2008) 'Last Call for Guangdong Shoemakers', *China Business*, 5 February.
Clean Clothes (2008) 'Chinese Activist Attacked', *Clean Clothes Newsletter*, 25: 18–19, at http://www.cleanclothes.org/ftp/ccc_newsletter_25.pdf, accessed 12 August 2008.
Costello, T., Smith, B. and Brecher, J. (2006) 'Labour Rights in China', *Foreign Policy in Focus*, 21 December, at www.fpif.org.
De, Jiang (2008) 'Four Months After Labor Contract Law Came into Effect, Employing Units Taste the Bitter Fruit for Evading the New Law', *Legal Daily*, 10 May, at http://www.legaldaily.com.cn/0705/2008-05/10/content_848607.htm.
Du Yiwen and Bo Yaoyao (2008) '100 Thousand People Dissolved Their Labor Contracts in Nanjing Since the New Labor Contract Law Took Effect', *Modern Express*, 19 June, available at http://www.ldht.org/Html/news/news/320059867.html.
French, H. (2004) 'Workers Demand Union at Wal-Mart Supplier in China', *New York Times*, 16 December.
Harris, D. and Luo, B. (2008) 'The Impact of China's Labour Contract Law', China Law Blog, at www.chinalawblog,com, 15 September.
Ho, V. H. (2003) *Labor Dispute Resolution in China: Implications for Labor Rights and Legal Reform*, China Research Monographs, no. 59, Berkeley: Institute of East Asian Studies.
IHLO (2007) 'Sackings at Wal-Mart: Global Restructuring or Avoiding the New Contract Law?' December, at www.ihlo.org.
IHLO (2008) 'New Labour Contract Law: Myth and Reality Six Months after Implementation', at http://www.ihlo.org/LRC/WC/270608.html.

Lee, Ching Kwan (2007) *Against the Law: Labour Protests in China's Rustbelt and Sunbelt*, Berkeley and Los Angeles: University of California Press.

Ma, Baoping (2005) 'Issues Concerning the Building of a Socialist Harmonious Society', *Journal of Lanzhou Commercial College*, 5.

Migrant Workers' Centre (2008) 'A Survey on the Implementation of the New Labour Contract Law', 19 May, at hbrindle-khym@fairlabour.org.

MSN (Maquila Solidarity Network) (2008) 'Chinese Labour Contract Law', *Maquila Solidarity Update*, 13, 3.

People's Daily (1999) 'Premier Zhu Rongji's Speech at the Closing Session of the National Technological Innovation Conference', 26 August.

Qiu Huihui (2007) 'Huawei's Countermeasure against the New Law', *The 21st Century Economic Report*, 27 October, available at http://tech.sina.com. cn/t/2007-10-27/00181817070.shtml.

SACOM (Students and Scholars Against Corporate Misbehaviour) (2008) *Paper Money: the Exploitation of Chinese Workers of the Nine Dragons Paper Owned by the 'Richest Woman' Zhang Yin*, research report, available at http://www.sacom. hk (in both Chinese and English).

Shirouzu, N. (2008) 'Chinese Laborers Face Grim Job Search', *Wall Street Journal*, 10 November.

Worker Empowerment (2008) 'New Ongoing Violations After the Implementation of Labour Contract Law in China', translation of the original document by the Shenzhen Dagongzhe Migrant Workers' Centre, available in Chinese at http://www.ngocn.org/?11799.

Yardley, J. and Barboza, D. (2005) 'Help Wanted: China Finds Itself With a Labor Shortage', *New York Times*, 3 April.

Zhang, Xinguo (2007) 'Several Problems on Reverse Dispatch and Consequent Labour Disputes', *People's Court News*, 16 April, at http://www.lawyer-sh.com. cn/ReadNews.asp?NewsID=4832.

.

Part III
India: Impacts and Responses

6

The Impact of Liberalization and Globalization on India's Agrarian Economy

V. K. Ramachandran and Vikas Rawal

1. Introduction

This chapter analyses the impact of policies of so-called stabilization and structural adjustment, or liberalization and globalization, on the agrarian economy of India. These are policies that have been imposed, in differing degrees, on the people of the Third World by international capital and domestic bourgeoisies for more than two decades now, and we shall examine their specific form and impact on the Indian countryside.[1] In India, although there are continuities between the era of globalization and preceding periods, particularly after 1984, the sharp acceleration of the policies of neoliberal reform can be said to have occurred after 1991, when the Congress Government in which the present Prime Minister was first made Finance Minister came to power.

In order to understand the impact of globalization and liberalization in rural India, it is important to understand the nature of the agrarian question and, in turn, the class character of the state in India. Landlords are a constituent part of the state in India, and nothing in the present situation has undermined landlordism as a fundamental barrier to agrarian and general social progress. At the same time, the general class policies of the Indian state in the countryside, and, specifically, its collaboration with imperialism, have taken qualitatively new forms since 1991.

The chapter begins with a discussion of land reform and landlordism. We discuss the interconnections between landlordism, moneylender-merchant exploitation and caste and gender oppression in the countryside, and argue that neoliberalism has not lessened the tactical or strategic importance of addressing these issues.

Next, we show how state policy has acted as a vast depressor in the countryside, and we document the reversal of policies of administered

agricultural input costs and output prices, cutbacks in public investment in rural physical and social infrastructure, the dismantling of
the institutional structure of social and development banking, the
withdrawal of quantitative restrictions on the import of agricultural
products, cutbacks in the public distribution system, and the undermining of national systems of research, extension and the protection of
national plant and other biological wealth.

We use data from, first, the major sources of national-level official
data, and, secondly, primary data collected as part of a larger Project on
Agrarian Relations in India.

2. The reversal of land reform

Genuine agrarian reform alters class relations in favour of the working
people, frees demand constraints and opens up home markets in the
countryside, and provides a basis for broad-based productive investment. The promise of land reform was part of India's freedom movement, a promise betrayed in practice by the ruling classes in the years
following Independence.

In India today, however, land reform as conceived during the
Independence movement and in the first decades after Independence,
has been jettisoned by official policy, and reversed in certain areas
in favour of counter-reform.[2] Legislation is being considered and has
been passed that raises ceilings to levels that undermine the objectives
of land ceiling laws and make absentee farming by large owners and
corporations a certainty. Such policies reduce the extent of land for
redistribution, accelerate the loss of land by poor peasants and worsen
inequalities in the distribution of land.

One of the objectives of land reform is the destruction of landlordism. A major feature of landlordism is the concentration of ownership
of land and other assets in the hands of landlords, that is, of a class that
does not work on the major manual operations on the land and is a
historical participant in the land monopoly. The data are clear that the
state has not abandoned the slogan of land reform because this class –
and such concentration of wealth – has ceased to exist. On the contrary,
data from the National Sample Survey (Table 6.1) and from recent village studies show the continuation of very sharp inequality.

In Table 6.1, data from the National Sample Survey (NSS) indicate
that the degree of concentration in the distribution of operational and
ownership holdings of land has marginally *increased* over the last four
decades.[3]

Table 6.1 Gini coefficients for the distribution of operational and ownership holdings of land, India, 1960–1961 to 2003–2004

Type of holding	1960–1961	1970–1971	1980–1981	1990–1991	2003–2004
Operational holdings	0.58	0.59	0.63	0.64	0.62
Ownership holdings	0.73	0.71	0.71	0.71	0.74

Source: Data taken from National Sample Survey (NSS) Land and Livestock Surveys cited in Ramakumar (2000), Ramachandran and Ramakumar (2000), NSS Report Nos. 491 and 492.
Note: These are official estimates of Gini coefficients. Ownership holdings in these estimates refer to ownership of any type of land including homestead land. Gini coefficient of ownership of agricultural land in 2003–4 was about 0.76 (Rawal, 2008).

Data from different villages across India confirm the existence of high levels of inequality. The Project on Agrarian Relations in India surveyed villages across a variety of agrarian regimes – in surface-irrigated, lift-irrigated, and unirrigated tracts – across the country and shows that although there are differences of degree, sharp inequalities persist in respect of the ownership of land.[4]

With regard to the actual redistribution of land, an estimate from official data by a senior member of the All-India Kisan Sabha[5] illustrates the chasm between potential and performance in India. Working with a ceiling of 25 acres a household, 'no less than 63 million acres of land would have been available in the mid-1950s and early 1960s for distribution among landless and land-poor farmer households' (Mishra, 2007). The reality, according to the Annual Report of the Ministry of Rural Development 2006–7, is that only 4.89 million acres of land were distributed over the first sixty years of Independence (ibid.). A recent estimate based on the National Sample Survey Office's (NSSO) Survey on Land and Livestock Holdings (2002–3) suggests that the current extent of ceiling-surplus land is more than three times the extent of land that has ever been redistributed under land reform (Rawal, 2008).

3. Public investment in agriculture and rural infrastructure (particularly irrigation and roads) slowed down substantially

Economists are familiar with the concept of complementarity between public and private expenditure; when the state withdraws from investment in public works, infrastructure and programmes of mass employment, it robs the countryside of the foundations for growth and the means of poverty alleviation.

Fiscal contraction is at the core of current policy, and Table 6.2, which shows the trends in public investment in agriculture and allied activities, shows that the decline in public investment in agriculture started in the 1980s and accelerated further in the 1990s. By the end of the 1990s, public investment in agriculture and allied activities was only about 1.6 per cent of agricultural GDP and about 6.6 per cent of total gross capital formation in the public sector.

4. Financial liberalization after 1991 decimated the institutional structure of rural banking in India

Financial liberalization represented a clear and explicit reversal of the policy of social and development banking, such as it was, and contributed in no small way to the extreme deprivation and distress of which the rural poor have been victims since the early 1990s.

It is well known that the burden of indebtedness in rural India is very great, and that, despite major structural changes in credit institutions and forms of rural credit in the post-Independence period, the exploitation of the rural masses in the credit market is one of the most pervasive and persistent features of rural life in India.

Historically, there have been four major problems with respect to the supply of credit to the Indian countryside. First, the supply of formal credit to the countryside as a whole has been inadequate. Second, rural credit markets themselves have been imperfect and fragmented. Third, as the foregoing suggests, the distribution of formal credit has been unequal, particularly with respect to region and class, caste and gender in the countryside. Formal sector credit needs especially to reach backward areas, income-poor households, people of the oppressed castes and tribes, and women. Fourth, the major source of credit to rural households, particularly income-poor working households, has been the informal sector. Informal sector loans, typically, are advanced at very high rates of interest. Further, the terms and conditions attached to these loans have given rise to an elaborate structure of coercion – economic and extra-economic – in the countryside.

That these constitute what may be called the 'problem of rural credit' has been widely recognized; recognized, in fact, in official evaluations and scholarship since the end of the nineteenth century. Given the issues involved, the declared objectives of public policy with regard to rural credit in the post-Independence period were, in the words of a

Table 6.2 Gross capital formation in agriculture and allied activities as a proportion of agricultural GDP and as a proportion of gross capital formation in all activities (%)

Year	As a proportion of GDP from agriculture and allied activities	As a proportion of gross capital formation in all activities
1960–61	1.8	11.2
1965–66	2.1	10.5
1970–71	1.8	11.9
1979–80	4.2	13.9
1980–81	3.7	15.6
1981–82	3.6	12.0
1982–83	3.7	11.2
1983–84	3.4	11.6
1984–85	3.4	10.5
1985–86	3.3	9.4
1986–87	3.2	8.3
1987–88	3.3	9.8
1988–89	2.8	8.6
1989–90	2.5	7.2
1990–91	2.3	6.8
1991–92	2.0	6.3
1992–93	2.0	6.5
1993–94	2.0	6.9
1994–95	2.2	6.8
1995–96	2.2	7.4
1996–97	2.0	7.6
1997–98	1.8	6.9
1998–99	1.6	6.6
1999–00	1.9	6.0
2000–01	1.8	5.7
2001–02	2.1	6.6
2002–03	2.0	6.4
2003–04	2.3	7.0
2004–05	2.9	7.4
2005–06	3.4	7.6
2006–07	3.7	7.9

Source: Data taken from Thulasamma (2003); EPW Research Foundation (2002); *Agricultural Statistics at a Glance* (2007, 2008); and National Account Statistics (2008).

former Governor of the Reserve Bank of India, 'to ensure that sufficient and timely credit, at reasonable rates of interest, is made available to as large a segment of the rural population as possible' (Rangarajan, 1996). The policy instruments to achieve these objectives were to be: first, extending the geographical and functional reach of the formal sector; second, directed lending; and third, concessional or subsidized credit (ibid.). Public policy was thus aimed not only at meeting rural credit needs, but also at pushing out the informal sector and the exploitation to which it subjected borrowers. Rural credit policy in India envisaged the provision of a range of credit services, including long-term and short-term credit and large-scale and small-scale loans to rural households.

The period from 1969 to the present can be characterized as representing, broadly speaking, three phases in banking policy vis-à-vis the Indian countryside. The period immediately following bank nationalization was also the early phase of the 'green revolution' in rural India, and one of the objectives of the nationalization of banks was for the state to gain access to new liquidity, particularly among rich farmers, in the countryside. The declared objectives of the new policy with respect to rural banking – what came to be known as 'social and development banking' – were: (i) to provide banking services in previously unbanked or under-banked rural areas; (ii) to provide substantial credit to specific activities including agriculture and cottage industries; (iii) to provide credit to certain disadvantaged groups, such as for example, Dalit and scheduled tribe households.

The second phase, which began in the late 1970s and early 1980s, was a period when the rhetoric of land reform was finally discarded by the ruling classes themselves, and when the major instruments of official anti-poverty policy were programmes for the creation of employment. Two strategies for employment generation were envisaged, namely wage employment through state-sponsored rural employment schemes and self-employment by means of loans-cum-subsidy schemes targeted at the rural poor. Thus began a period of directed credit, during which credit was to be directed towards 'the weaker sections' of society.

The third and current phase, which began in 1991, is that of liberalization. There has been much recent research on financial liberalization and rural credit in India.[6] The main features of the post-liberalization phase are the following:

• Social and development banking ceased to be official policy. The policy objectives of this phase are encapsulated in the *Report of the*

Committee on the Financial System, a committee appointed by the Reserve Bank of India, which called for 'a vibrant and competitive financial system . . . to sustain the ongoing reform in the structural aspects of the economy'. The committee said that redistributive objectives 'should use the instrumentality of the fiscal rather than the credit system' and, accordingly, that 'directed credit programmes should be phased out'. It also recommended that interest rates be deregulated, that capital adequacy norms be changed (to 'compete with banks globally'), that branch licensing policy be revoked, that a new institutional structure that is 'market-driven and based on profitability' be created, and that the part played by private Indian and foreign banks be enlarged.

- The expansion of public-sector rural banking was ended, and a large number of rural branches of commercial banks were actually shut down after 1995 (see Table 6.3).
- The credit/deposit ratios of rural commercial bank branches fell sharply between 1991 and 2004 from 61 per cent to 44 per cent.
- Inter-state inequalities in rural banking increased, and regions where banking has historically been underdeveloped suffered the worst.[7]
- Priority-sector advances fell, and, with that, so did the shares of credit to agriculture, to cultivators owning two hectares or less, and to Dalit and Adivasi households (Tables 6.4 and 6.5) (see Chavan, 2007).
- The share of informal-sector credit in the principal borrowed by rural households is very high, typically in the range of 66–80 per cent, and has increased over the liberalization phase.

There was a partial recovery in provision of formal-sector credit to rural areas after 2001. While the supply of rural credit started to increase in 2001, the major expansion in provision of rural credit, and a clear break from the earlier policy of withdrawal of formal-sector banking from rural areas, took place from 2004. It is noteworthy that, by 2008, the credit-deposit ratio of rural branches of scheduled commercial banks went back to the level in 1991. Table 6.2, on trends in public investment, shows that the share of agriculture and allied activities in total public investment also started to increase in 2004–5. Reversal of trends in rural credit and public investment was made possible because of the space opened by dependence of the UPA government on the left parties for its survival.[8] The left, in its demands, identified collapse of rural credit and decline in public investment as major causes of rural distress and actively lobbied for expansion of provision of formal-sector credit to rural areas and public investment in agriculture.

Table 6.3 Number of rural branches of scheduled commercial banks, India, 1978–2007

Year	Branches
1980	14,171
1985	25,541
1990	33,572
1991	34,867
1992	35,216
1993	35,218
1994	35,301
1995	35,379
1996	35,008
1997	33,092
1998	32,909
1999	32,854
2000	32,734
2001	32,640
2002	32,443
2003	32,283
2004	32,107
2005	31,967
2006	30,610
2007	30,393

Note: As has been pointed out by Ramakumar (2009), bank branches were classified into rural, semi-urban and urban until 1994 using the 1981 Census, between 1994 and 2005 using the 1991 Census, and from 2006 onwards using the 2001 Census. He shows that, because of these revisions in the classification of branches, the numbers are not strictly comparable across these sub-periods. However, despite this problem, the overall trends – of increase in number of rural branches until 1994 and a decline thereafter – are clearly seen in the data.
Source: Data taken from *Banking Statistics* and *Basic Statistical Returns of Scheduled Commercial Banks in India*, various issues.

5. The peasantry faces a two-pronged attack – from falling commodity prices and rising input costs

It is now impossible to ensure adequate incomes among the peasantry if they are not protected from the ravages of adverse product and input markets. Most peasants are net buyers of food grain, and thus victims of inflation in food prices as well. The costs of cultivation have risen steeply, particularly in the 1990s and early 2000s. The rise in the costs of seed, fertilizer, irrigation and the use of machinery has been particularly steep in the recent period.

Table 6.4 Share of priority sector and agricultural loans in outstanding credit (%)

Year	Priority sector	Agriculture
1981	36	17
1985	40	17
1986	41	17
1988	44	17
1991	38	15
1995	34	11
1996	33	11
1997	35	11
1998	35	11
1999	35	10
2000	37	10
2001	33	10
2002	33	10
2003	32	11
2004	35	11
2005	36	11
2006	36	13
2007	36	13

Source: Data taken from *Statistical Tables Relating to Banks in India*, Reserve Bank of India, various issues.

Table 6.5 Share of advances to 'weaker sections' in net bank credit of public and private sector banks, 1991–2008 (%)

Year	Public sector banks	Private sector banks	All banks
1991	10	5	10
1992	10	5	9
1993	9	4	9
1994	9	3	9
1995	8	3	8
1996	8	2	8
2001	7	2	6
2002	7	2	7
2003	7	2	6
2004	7	1	6
2005	9	1	7
2006	8	2	7
2007	7	2	6
2008	9	2	8

Source: Data taken from Chavan (2007), and *Trends and Progress of Banking in India*, Reserve Bank of India, various issues.

As a consequence of India's joining the World Trade Organization, Indian agriculture has been exposed, in a new and unprecedented way, to volatility in the international prices of food and non-food crops and, in the case of several commodities, prolonged periods of steep declines in prices (see, for instance, Ghosh, 2005). The most important policies of the Government of India in this regard are, of course, the removal of quantitative restrictions on the import and export of a very wide range of agricultural commodities, including wheat and wheat products, rice, pulses, edible oils and agricultural seeds, and substantial cuts in import tariffs on crops. New incentives and support to exports of agricultural commodities will inevitably have an impact on land use and cropping pattern, as will the decision to 'decanalize' and allow and encourage private agencies in the agricultural export sector.

In addition, the Minimum Support Prices (MSP) announced by the government to ensure remunerative prices have not compensated for the actual costs of production per unit of output for most crops in a majority of states. Further, the very policy of MSP has not been implemented in most states.

This problem of peasant incomes is particularly intense in the present context of the removal of quantitative restrictions on the import of agricultural products, the emphasis on export-oriented production, and the fall in the prices of primary commodities internationally. It is not fortuitous that the 1990s, the first decade of accelerated liberalization, was also the first period since the beginning of the 'green revolution' in which the rate of growth of food grain production was lower than the rate of growth of population in India.

The left in India has demanded that the government ensure that the costs of all inputs be controlled; that the system of MSP cover all twenty-six crops covered by the Commission on Agricultural Costs and Prices; that fair and remunerative prices be offered through a country-wide crop procurement system; that a universal public distribution system be established; and that the government reverse the abolition of quantitative restrictions and raise tariffs on the import of agricultural and agriculture-related products. In the context of widespread crop damage, low yields and the ruin of vulnerable cultivators, a new demand is that a Farm Income Insurance Scheme be implemented rapidly in all disaster areas and subsequently be extended to all districts of the country and to all crops.

Our survey data from Andhra Pradesh, Uttar Pradesh and Maharashtra indicate the near-impossibility, in the present circumstances, of peasant households with two hectares of operational holdings or less earning an income high enough for family survival.

Table 6.6   Median per capita household annual and daily incomes, PARI villages, 2005–2006 (rupees)

Village, region	Median per capita household income	
	per year	per day
Ananthavaram, Guntur district, south coastal Andhra Pradesh	7,465	20
Bukkacherla, Anantapur district, Rayalaseema region, south-west Andhra Pradesh	5,968	16
Kothapalle, Karimnagar district, North Telangana region, north Andhra Pradesh	5,669	15
Harevli, Bijnaur district, Western Uttar Pradesh	4,690	13
Mahatwar, Ballia district, Eastern Uttar Pradesh	3,164	9
Warwat Khanderao, Buldhana district, Vidarbha region, Maharashtra	7,248	20
Nimshirgaon, Kolhapur district, southern Maharashtra	8,792	24

Source: Survey data, Foundation for Agrarian Studies.

The daily per capita median income in the village with the highest median income was about Rs 24 (see Table 6.6). The net annual incomes of a substantial section of the poor and middle peasantry from crop production are negative. The data in Table 6.7 are new and truly alarming; it shows that over 30 per cent of cultivator-households in each of the three Andhra Pradesh households, 19 per cent of cultivator-households in Nimshirgaon (a village in Kolhapur district), 18 per cent of cultivator-households in Mahatwar (a village in eastern UP), 14 per cent of cultivator-households in Harevli (a village in Bijnaur district in western UP) and 5 per cent of cultivator-households in Warwat Khaderao (a village in Vidarbha) had negative net incomes from crop production.

Food self-sufficiency has been a key component of India's national sovereignty, and the new trends in the agrarian regime have very serious implications for land use, cropping patterns and the future of self-sufficiency in food in India.

6. The depressor-effect on rural employment

As is clear from the foregoing, liberalization and globalization imply the imposition of deflationary policies on the countryside; their

Table 6.7 Proportion of cultivator-households in individual size-classes of net annual income from crop production, Andhra Pradesh villages, 2005–2006 (%)

Size-classes of incomes from crop production	Ananthavaram, Guntur district, south coastal Andhra Pradesh	Bukkacherla, Anantapur district, Rayalaseema region, south-west Andhra Pradesh	Kothapalle, Karimnagar district, North Telangana region, north Andhra Pradesh	Harevli, Bijnaur district, Western Uttar Pradesh	Mahatwar, Ballia district, Eastern Uttar Pradesh	Warwat Khanderao, Buldhana district, Vidarbha region, Maharashtra	Nimshirgaon, Kolhapur district, southern Maharashtra
Less than 0	30	36	30	14	18	5	19
0–4,000	28	8	10	28	58	15	13
4,000–8,000	11	15	20	7	10	15	10
8,000–16,000	12	14	27	12	6	15	12
16,000–24,000	3	7	9	6	2	13	8
24,000–50,000	8	10	5	4	4	18	19
>50,000	10	8	0	29	1	19	19
All cultivator households	100	100	100	100	100	100	100

Source: Survey data, Foundation for Agrarian Studies.

depressor-effect on rural manual employment has been profound. The decline of public investment in agriculture, the decline in direct agricultural extension and information dissemination, and the consequent decline in agriculture itself have had a direct impact on the number of days of employment that a hired worker in rural India receives.[9]

There are insufficient macro-data on the number of days of employment, agricultural and non-agricultural, per worker per year in India. However, not only do the data from the Rural Labour Enquiries appear intuitively to be incorrect, but it is also well recognized that employment data from micro-studies show consistently lower volumes of employment than Rural Labour Enquiry data. There are, of course, major conceptual, definitional and methodological reasons for this divergence. This latter observation is as true now as it was twenty years ago.

The village data from Andhra Pradesh illustrate the scarcity of the means of employment available today to a hired rural manual worker (Table 6.8). The *prospects* for employment are disturbing indeed. Let us examine some factors that traditionally have influenced the volume of employment available to a rural manual worker.

6.1 Labour absorption in rice and wheat cultivation

The issues with regard to labour absorption have been summarized in Ramachandran and Swaminathan (2005). The main conclusions of that paper are that, with respect to wheat, mechanization has caused a secular decline in labour absorption. With regard to the cultivation of paddy, there has been, first, a decline in the employment of labour power per hectare. Secondly, female employment has been particularly affected by the decline in labour absorption. Thirdly, and as important, there are no viable technologies on offer today that involve higher levels of labour power input per hectare in the irrigated cultivation of high-yielding rice.

6.2 Irrigation

Much has been written on the causal links between an expansion of irrigation and an expansion of agricultural employment. It is entirely possible that irrigated area (groundwater- and surface-irrigated) may expand in certain regions and watersheds. Nevertheless, the question remains: given the nature of policies of so-called structural adjustment, is it likely that, in the aggregate, the rate of growth of either (i) direct or complementary investment necessary for the expansion of groundwater irrigation, or (ii) direct public investment necessary for the expansion of surface irrigation (large, medium or small scale), will rise to levels that are necessary to meet

Table 6.8 Average days of employment by type of employment, manual labour households, Andhra Pradesh villages, 2005–2006

Village	Male workers			Female workers		
	Agriculture	Non-agriculture	Total	Agriculture	Non-agriculture	Total
Ananthavaram, Guntur district, south coastal Andhra Pradesh	64	42	106	65	0	65
Bukkacherla, Anantapur district, Rayalaseema region, south-west Andhra Pradesh	53	5	58	67	1	68
Kothapalle, Karimnagar district, North Telangana region, north Andhra Pradesh	44	69	113	73	20	93

Source: Survey data, Foundation for Agrarian Studies.

the demand for irrigation (or provide for sustained increase in employment) in rural India? In an earlier period in India's development history, the answer may have been a qualified 'yes'. Given the record of sharp decline in public investment in agriculture since 1991 (see Table 6.2), the answer now is 'not under the present neoliberal regime'.

6.3 Non-agricultural employment

An important lesson from rural development experience in India and elsewhere in the less developed countries is that schemes for large-scale employment of hired manual workers or large-scale schemes for self-employment are necessarily *state-driven* and *state-financed*. The withdrawal of the state from state-sponsored employment schemes through the 1990s and early years of this decade is clear from Table 6.9.

The major change in this regard came after the passage, under pressure from the left, of the National Rural Employment Guarantee Act (NREGA) by the 2004–9 Parliament. The NREGA seeks to provide a guarantee of up to 100 days of employment per household. The scheme was introduced in 200 districts of India in 2005–6. In April 2008, the programme was extended to the rural areas of all districts in the country. The most important difference between the NREGA and previous

Table 6.9 Person days of employment created through wage employment schemes in rural areas, 1990–1991 to 2001–2002, selected years

Year	Person days of employment under different wage employment schemes	
	(in millions)	Index
1990–91	874	100
1996–97	804	92
2002–03	748	86
2003–04	856	98
2004–05	912	104
2005–06	1,116	128
2006–07	905	104
2007–08	1,437	164

Source: Data taken from *Economic Survey*, different years and Mehrotra (2008).
Notes: In 1990, the main wage employment schemes were the National Rural Employment Programme (NREP) and the Rural Landless Employment Guarantee Programme (RLEGP). These were combined to form the Jawahar Rozgar Yojana (JRY). Later the Employment Assurance Scheme was introduced. In 2001, the JRY was modified to the Jawahar Rozgar Gram Sidhi Yojana (JRGSY). In April 2002, all wage employment schemes were combined into the SGRY (Sampoorna Grameen Rozgar Yojana).

wage employment programmes is that the NREGA seeks to provide a *guarantee* of 100 days of employment per household to *any* rural household that demands it. Where employment is not provided within 15 days of a demand for employment, the scheme provides for an unemployment allowance to be paid to the household that demanded work.

Data show that in 2007–8, the second full year of the NREGA, about 1,400 million person-days of work were generated in the 330 districts in which it was in operation in the year (Table 6.9). This was much higher than the work generated under previous wage employment programmes. Data also show that, in 2007–8, on average, about 43 days of work were provided to households that participated in the programme. The evidence suggests that in many areas where the NREGA has been operational, the prospect of employment-generation under the scheme helped raise agricultural wage rates (Dreze and Khera, 2009; Mehrotra, 2008). It is also noteworthy that of the total employment generated under the programme, the share of employment gained by women was 48 per cent, by Dalit workers 31 per cent, and by Scheduled Tribe workers 24 per cent.

Although NREGA represents an important gain for the rural workforce, we must also remember that the programme provides a very limited guarantee of employment, and that it has been marred by serious obstacles and problems (Gupta, 2007; Karat, 2005). The implementation agencies, for example, have a restricted portfolio of works that can be undertaken under the scheme (Karat, 2008). Banks have been reluctant to open zero-balance accounts for workers who participate in the NREGA. In many cases, the piece-rates under the programme are low and, as a result, most workers are unable to do enough work on a sustained basis to earn the statutory minimum wage (Karat, 2008). The nature of work provided and the Schedule of Rates are such that they typically discriminate against women workers who, on average, earn substantially lower wages than male workers (ISWSD, 2007; Karat, 2008). The unemployment allowance is seldom paid and therefore the goal of providing a guarantee of 100 days of work per household has not been achieved in practice. Evaluations have pointed out that, in most states, implementation of the scheme is fraught with problems such as delays in the payment of wages, a lack of work-site facilities (particularly for women), and corruption in the execution of work and maintenance of records (Dreze and Khera, 2009; ISWSD, 2007).

6.4 Leaving land fallow

In situations characterized by rising costs, falling harvest-time prices, the absence of information through extension services on alternative crop-cultivation opportunities, and cutbacks in formal sector credit, cultivators may decide simply to leave land fallow. We have some documented cases of such shutdown in the *boro* season in West Bengal in 2002 (see Rawal, Swaminathan and Ramachandran, 2002), in Rayalaseema in Andhra Pradesh in 2005–6 and large tracts of land left fallow even in the Gang canal region of North West Rajasthan in 2007. This decision to leave land fallow was a direct consequence of the adverse impact of current policies on cultivators of different classes.

6.5 Land use and cropping pattern

It is entirely possible that cropping pattern in some areas may change, in the short or medium term, towards crops that are more labour-absorbent per hectare than crops currently grown. Such changes in cropping patterns may be a result of spontaneous forces of commercialization and crop diversification; in future, however, they may increasingly be responses to niche-market and export demand, and controlled directly by Indian or multinational corporate interests. Such changes in cropping pattern must be evaluated not only with respect to their immediate impact on employment and farm incomes but from a broader perspective on land use, food security and the preservation of biodiversity. Thus, if over a large tract (part of a block or sub-district, say), the cultivation of gherkins or cherry tomatoes replaces food grain or a diverse range of other crops, that change must be evaluated in terms not only of short-term gains in income and employment, but also in terms of its impact on land use, food self-sufficiency and the environment and biodiversity.

7. International corporations and Indian agriculture

The new trade and patent regime leaves the field of agricultural research at the mercy of multinational corporations, thus weakening public-sector national agricultural research systems and open-access international research institutions. Further, this regime infringes the rights of farmers and indigenous plant breeders and threatens to lead, in the words of India's leading agricultural scientist, 'from biodiversity to genetic slavery'.

A significant new aspect of globalization and the agrarian economy is the new intervention by US corporations in agricultural policy and policy-making institutions. The new Knowledge Initiative on Agriculture (KIA), formally called the 'US–India Knowledge Initiative on Agricultural Education, Teaching, Research, Service, and Commercial Linkages', seeks to tie the agrarian economy of India to US corporate interests.[10] The KIA is to support certain activities related to agricultural research, education and extension that will help bring an 'evergreen revolution' based on 'environmentally sustainable and market-oriented agriculture'. Specifically, the KIA focuses on 'capacity-building' for education (including curriculum revision), food processing, biotechnology (particularly aimed at making transgenic crops the focus of Indian agricultural research) and water management (with emphasis on precision and high-tech agriculture).

The agreement does not cover any funding for agricultural research and education by the US government. In fact, while the Government of India has already pledged Rs 3,500 million for the activities proposed, there has been no commitment from the United States. Documents available in the public domain make it clear that private funding from agribusiness corporations for research in public institutions in India will be linked to patent rights and licences on products that emerge from such research.

India's agricultural research infrastructure and institutional setup expanded greatly in the post-Independence period and is unmatched across most less-developed countries. In additional to a number of central institutions under the umbrella of the Indian Council for Agricultural Research (ICAR), there are a large number of state agricultural universities, colleges and other institutions of higher learning. India has more than 7,000 agricultural scientists and more than 40,000 agricultural extension workers. One aspect of the KIA is that it is to be a means by which US agribusiness corporations gain access to this institutional setup and pool of scientists and technological personnel.

The KIA is to be designed and monitored by a governing board that has, as members, representatives of major US agribusiness and retail firms. The US side includes, among its eight members, representatives from Monsanto and Wal-Mart and other business organizations.

It is clear that an important objective of the KIA is to bring a patent-protected regime of commercial agriculture to India that will, first, attempt to meet the demand for tropical agricultural products in the developed world, and second, to ensure large returns to multinational agribusiness firms through patent rights on biochemical farm inputs.

8. The public food-distribution system has been set back by decades

As a result of economic liberalization, major programmes of food security were reversed.[11] Three key objectives of economic reforms – and these are stated explicitly in many policy documents including different

Economic Surveys – have been to reduce food subsidies, to leave distribution to the market and to restrict public systems for food distribution by means of policies of narrow targeting.

Specifically, the central government introduced a policy of narrow targeting of the public distribution system (PDS), one of the pillars of food security policy in India. The PDS is a rationing mechanism that entitles households to specified quantities of selected commodities at subsidized prices. In most parts of the country, up to 1997, the PDS was universal and all households with a registered residential address, rural and urban, were entitled to rations. In 1996–7, a new system, the Targeted PDS, was introduced.

The implementation of the Targeted PDS led to the large-scale exclusion of genuinely needy persons from the PDS. Recent evidence from the 61st Round of the National Sample Survey, conducted in 2004–5, makes it clear that a large proportion of agricultural labour and other worker households, of households belonging to the Scheduled Castes and Tribes, of landless and near-landless households, and households in the lowest expenditure classes, are excluded from the PDS today. Swaminathan (2008a) defines households without a ration card or with an APL (Above Poverty Line) card as those effectively excluded from the PDS and those with a BPL (Below Poverty Line) card or an Antyodaya ('poorest of the poor') card as those effectively included in the PDS.[12] By this definition, the data show that there were only four states out of 27 (Tamil Nadu excluded) in which two-thirds or more of agricultural labour households were effectively included and 33 per cent or less were effectively excluded from the PDS. These states were Andhra Pradesh, Karnataka, Jammu and Kashmir and Tripura. *The all-India data indicate that 52 per cent of agricultural worker households were effectively excluded from the PDS.* The effective exclusion was 71 per cent in Bihar and 73 per cent in Uttar Pradesh.

While the size of subsidies – including food subsidies – is frequently criticized by the 'reformers', in reality, aggregate food subsidy has declined in recent years. The food subsidy, as defined in the Government of India's budget (the operational deficit of the Food Corporation of India), remained at an average of 0.6 per cent of GDP from the mid-1960s to the end of the 1990s. Between 2002–3 and 2006–7, the food subsidy bill shrunk in absolute terms, from Rs 24,176 crores in 2002–3 to Rs 23,828 crores in 2006–7 at current prices. As a share of GDP, food subsidies fell from 0.99 per cent in 2002–3 to 0.5 per cent in 2007–8.

In recent months, the situation has changed; stocks of food grain with the government have risen. In December 2008, rice and wheat stocks with the Government of India were 29.8 million tonnes against a buffer stock requirement of 16.2 million tonnes, that is, a surplus of 84 per cent. The rise in stocks is the combined outcome of increased procurement and reduced distribution.

After the recent general elections, the Government of India announced that it would draft a new National Food Security Act. The Government of India's proposal for legislation as elaborated in a note circulated to all state governments has been criticized by the left opposition in the Parliament as continuing the policy of exclusion and narrow targeting, of over-centralizing policy decisions with regard to food, and of allocating insufficient grain through the public distribution system.

The policies of large-scale exclusion of households from the PDS and continued cuts in allocation of food grain to states thus remain unchanged. It is clear that the objective of ensuring food security to all continues to be off the agenda of the central government.

9. The impact of the left on national rural policy over the past four and a half years has been limited, but significant and distinct

Firstly, continuous agitations by the left in Parliament and by means of direct action slowed down the sharp decline in public expenditure and the rapid dismantling of the structure of public banking.

Secondly, the most important nationwide development intervention of the present government, the National Rural Employment Guarantee Programme, was directly the result of left intervention and pressure.

Thirdly, the most important legislation directly affecting the right to livelihood of the Adivasi people, the Scheduled Tribe and Other Forest Dwellers (Recognition of Forest Rights) Act, was spearheaded by the left in Parliament, and would never have become law without the attention to detail of the left MPs, and without the struggles for forest rights of left-led mass organizations.

10. Some concluding notes

In conclusion, there are three features of the current situation that we shall highlight. First, the major force on the left in India considers the Indian state to be the organ of the class rule of the bourgeoisie *and landlords*, led by the big bourgeoisie, who are in increasing collaboration – as a junior partner or *subordinate ally* – of imperialism. This is the view of the state that informs this chapter, and we cannot emphasize enough that nothing in the present situation has undone *landlordism* as a fundamental barrier to agrarian and general social progress. By this view, the agrarian question has been, since Independence, and remains, the major national question in India. Any resolution of the agrarian question requires revolutionary change, including agrarian reform that targets landlordism, moneylender-merchant exploitation and caste and gender oppression in the countryside. Neoliberalism has not lessened the tactical or strategic importance of this contradiction; recent developments have sharpened the contradiction rather than blunted it.

Secondly, since 1991, state intervention and the part played by imperialism in the countryside – that is, the class policies of the state in rural India – have taken qualitatively new forms. As we have seen, state policy has acted as a vast depressor, reversing policies of administered agricultural input costs and output prices, scaling down public investment in rural physical and social infrastructure, dismantling the institutional structure of social and development banking, withdrawing quantitative restrictions on the import of agricultural products, restricting the public distribution system, and undermining national systems of research, extension and the protection of national plant and other biological wealth.

Thirdly, globalization does not flatten out all local landscapes – the problems of the uneven development of capitalism have been *accentuated* under neoliberalism. In the present situation, we need to study the common features of imperialist globalization and the transformation of rural societies – including the impact of globalization and liberalization – in *specific* situations.[13]

The current situation thus raises a crucial issue for those involved in the movement for radical, progressive rural change in less developed countries. The solution to the agrarian question involves both direct class struggle in the diverse conditions of the Third World countryside (in the Indian context, it involves the struggle against landlordism, moneylender-merchant exploitation and caste and gender oppression) *as well as* the struggle against the new onslaught by imperialism and domestic bourgeoisies. How the links are to be made between the different aspects of the struggle for agrarian change is a crucial issue of theory and practice for the future of democratic movements in the Third World countryside.

Notes

We are grateful to John Harriss, Paul Bowles, other participants at the Conference on 'Globalization(s) and Labour: China, India and the West' organized by the University of Northern British Columbia and Simon Fraser University, and two referees, for comments, and to Madhura Swaminathan for data, comments and much help with this chapter.

1. Ramachandran and Swaminathan (2002).
2. A detailed evaluation of the legislation is in Ramachandran and Ramakumar (2000). See also Ramachandran and Swaminathan (2002).
3. For a discussion of the problems of the NSS database on ownership and operational holdings of land, see Rawal (2008) and Bakshi (2008).
4. See Ramachandran and Rawal (2010) for further details.
5. The All-India Kisan Sabha (or Peasant Union) is the largest organization of the peasantry in India. It has over 20 million members.
6. Ramachandran and Swaminathan (2005) and the references in Ramakumar and Chavan (2007).
7. See Ramakumar and Chavan (2007) and Ramachandran and Swaminathan (2005).
8. The following parties comprise the left in the two Houses of the Parliament: the Communist Party of India (Marxist), the Communist Party of India, the All India Forward Bloc, and the Revolutionary Socialist Party.
9. For a detailed discussion of neoliberal economic policy and rural employment, see Ramachandran and Swaminathan (2005).
10. On this, see Rawal (2006) and Purkayastha (2006).
11. For the data in this section, see Swaminathan (2008a); see also Swaminathan (2000).
12. In 1997, the Public Distribution System was changed to the Targeted Public Distribution System under which subsidized food grain is provided only to those households that are given BPL (Below Poverty Line) cards. Above Poverty Line households have a smaller entitlement and are provided food grain without any subsidy.
13. In an important paper, Byres (2002) has argued against 'determinism' with respect to globalization, which ignores (as did dependency theory in an earlier period) the 'specificities and substantive diversity' of capitalist development in specific areas.

References

Bakshi, Aparajita (2008) 'Social Inequality in Land Ownership in India: a Study with Particular Reference to West Bengal', *Social Scientist*, 39, 9–10: 95–116.

Byres, T. J. (2002) 'Paths of Capitalist Agrarian Transition in the Past and in the Contemporary World', in V. K. Ramachandran and Madhura Swaminathan (eds), *Agrarian Studies: Essays on Agrarian Relations in Less-Developed Countries*, New Delhi and London: Tulika and Zed Books, pp. 54–83.

Chavan, Pallavi (2007) 'Access to Bank Credit: Implications for Dalit Rural Households', *Economic and Political Weekly*, 42, 31: 3219–24.

Dreze, Jean and Khera, Reetika (2009) 'The Battle for Employment Guarantee', *Frontline*, 26, 1: 3–16.

EPW Research Foundation (2002) *National Account Statistics*, Mumbai: EPW Research Foundation.

Ghosh, Jayati (2005) 'Trade Liberalization in Agriculture: an Examination of Impact and Policy Strategies with Special Reference to India', Occasional Paper,

Human Development Report 2005, New York: United Nations Development Programme.

Government of India, Ministry of Agriculture and Cooperation (2007, 2008) *Agricultural Statistics at a Glance*, New Delhi.

Gupta, Smita (2007) 'The Significance and Limitations of India's National Rural Employment Guarantee Act in Addressing Rural Poverty', paper presented at the International Conference and Workshop on 'Policy Perspectives on Growth, Economic Structures and Poverty Reduction', Beijing, 3–9 June, http://www.networkideas.org/ideasact/Jun07/Beijing_Conference_07/Smita_Gupta.pdf, accessed 17 September 2009.

Indian School of Women's Studies and Development (ISWSD) (2007) 'Implementation of the National Rural Employment Guarantee Scheme: Submission to the Parliamentary Standing Committee on Rural Development', New Delhi.

Karat, Brinda (2005) 'Towards Implementing the Rural Employment Guarantee Act', *People's Democracy*, 29, 42 and 43, 16 and 23 October.

Karat, Brinda (2008) 'Stop Dilution of REGA', *People's Democracy*, 32, 20–21, 1 June–25 May.

Mehrotra, Santosh (2008) 'NREG Two Years On: Where Do We Go from Here?' *Economic and Political Weekly*, 2 August.

Mishra, Surjya Kanta (2007) 'On Agrarian Transition in West Bengal', *The Marxist*, 23, 2, April–June.

National Account Statistics (2008) Central Statistical Organization, Ministry of Statistics and Programme Implementation, Government of India, New Delhi.

Purkayastha, Prabir (2006) 'Indo-US Agricultural Initiative: Handing Indian Agriculture to Monsantos', *People's Democracy*, 30, 9, 26 February.

Ramachandran, V. K. and Ramakumar, R. (2000) 'Agrarian Reforms and Rural Development Policies in India: a Note', paper presented at the International Conference on Agrarian Reform and Rural Development organized by the Department of Agrarian Reform, Government of the Philippines and the Philippines Development Academy, Tagaytay City, 5–8 December.

Ramachandran, V. K. and Rawal, V. (2010) 'The Impact of Liberalization and Globalization on India's Agrarian Economy', *Global Labour Journal*, 1, 1: 56–91.

Ramachandran, V. K. and Swaminathan, Madhura (2002) 'Introduction', in V. K. Ramachandran and Madhura Swaminathan (eds), *Agrarian Studies: Essays on Agrarian Relations in Less-Developed Countries*, New Delhi and London: Tulika and Zed Books.

Ramachandran, V. K. and Swaminathan, Madhura (eds) (2005) *Financial Liberalization and Rural Credit in India*, New Delhi: Tulika Books.

Ramakumar, R. (2000) 'Magnitude and Terms of Tenancy in India: a State-wise Analysis of Changes, 1981–82 to 1991–92', *Indian Journal of Agricultural Economics*, 55.

Ramakumar, R. (2009) 'Declining Number of Rural Bank Branches in India', manuscript, Tata Institute of Social Sciences, Mumbai.

Ramakumar, R. and Chavan, Pallavi (2007) 'Revival of Agricultural Credit in the 2000s: an Explanation', *Economic and Political Weekly*, 42, 52: 955–65.

Rangarajan, C. (1996) 'Rural India: the Role of Credit', *Reserve Bank of India Bulletin*, May, Bombay: Reserve Bank of India.

Rawal, Vikas (2006), 'The Indo-US Knowledge Initiative on Agriculture: What Does it Have for Indian Farmers?', manuscript, Jawaharlal Nehru University, New Delhi.

Rawal, Vikas (2008) 'Ownership Holdings of Land in Rural India: Putting the Record Straight', *Economic and Political Weekly*, 43, 10: 43–7.

Rawal, Vikas, Swaminathan, Madhura and Ramachandran, V. K. (2002) 'Agriculture in West Bengal: Current Trends and Directions for Future Growth', Background paper for the West Bengal State Development Report, submitted to the West Bengal State Planning Board, Kolkata.

Swaminathan, Madhura (2000) *Weakening Welfare: the Public Distribution of Food in India*, Delhi: Leftword Books.

Swaminathan, Madhura (2008a) 'Programmes to Protect the Hungry: Lessons from India', DESA (Department of Economic and Social Analysis) Working Paper no. 70, New York: United Nations.

Swaminathan, Madhura (2008b) 'Public Distribution System and Social Exclusion', *The Hindu*, Chennai, 7 May.

Thulasamma, L. (2003) 'Investment in Agriculture: Trends and Issues', paper presented at the All-India Conference on Agriculture and Rural Society in Contemporary India, Barddhaman, 17–20 December.

7
Globalization, the Financial Crisis and Petty Commodity Production in India's Socially Regulated Informal Economy

Barbara Harriss-White[1]

1. Introduction

This chapter explores some theoretical and practical problems arising from the impact of liberalization/globalization and its latest crisis on India's informal economy – heavily populated by petty commodity producers and petty traders (henceforth pcp). Its theoretical focus is the distinctions between pcp and 'labour' more generally because it is now common practice theoretically to elide the two kinds of work.[2] Reviewing field material it focuses on two aspects of India's informal economy – the persistence of small firms and their regulation by social institutions rather than by the state. These social institutions express identity as well as class. The practical focus of this chapter is on the impact of globalization and the financial crisis on pcp in India.

India's informal economy includes entire industrial clusters making goods for export (metalware, machine tools, leatherware, textiles and garments, tools and equipment, and some IT services). In 1999, over 40 per cent of India's manufactured exports were estimated to have originated in unregistered workshops and 'gulleys' (Sinha et al., 1999). The informal economy includes the black economy, focused on retail inventory, construction and real estate, the film industry, precious metals and the products of tax evasion (Roy, 1996). Estimated at 40 per cent of GDP ten years ago (Kumar, 2005) and growing, India's black economy is not marginal or confined to socially excluded people; it is central and involves prominent and socially powerful people too. The informal economy is not confined to services, but includes production and property rights protection as well as informal institutions of economic/'social' security (provision of help in time of need) – formal responsibilities of the state which it has all too often honoured in the breach.

The scale of pcp in India is a well-established and comparatively well-studied phenomenon. Two-thirds of GDP comes from unregistered, informal activity. This proportion is growing rather than contracting, and accounts for over 90 per cent of India's livelihoods. More than half of these livelihoods come from self employment – as much as one-third of GDP – and 98 per cent of self-employed livelihoods are in the informal economy (Kannan, 2008: 8). The informal economy persists in the era of globalized and advanced capitalism; but its role changes, as do the roles of its key features of smallness of scale, and social – rather than state – regulation.[3] These shifts have to be appreciated if we are to understand the impact of globalization on an economy like India's. In order to examine the relationships between liberalization, globalization and crisis on the one hand and the persistent structure of socially regulated petty production in India's informal economy on the other, we use case studies and secondary literature.

2. Trade liberalization, globalization and petty production in India

India's engagement with globalization has encouraged export-led industrialization in certain manufactured goods and services which have also been stimulated by imported technological upgrades. Thirty-four sectors of India's import substituting core have been opened up in this way (Nath, 2008: 539). Less foreign capital and even less foreign direct investment (FDI) than was predicted has materialized – it is rather that some investment has been reallocated from the informal to the formal ('modern', 'tradable') part of the economy in which forces of centralization and concentration are operating (Ghose, 2008). Some fractions of Indian capital have embarked on mergers and acquisitions in Europe and the USA (Sardar, 2008). Simultaneously under liberalization, capital-biased technology in the formal sector displaces labour into the informal economy in which production is decentralized (Sinha and Adam, 2007). Nath notes UN agencies' dignifying this process by classifying informal workers as 'own account'/'independent producers' (2008: 539). As well as dignifying labour, they are trying to distinguish pcp from wage-work. In fact, these formal/informal, wage-work/pcp migrations put downward pressure on labour productivity and wages in the informal economy (where productivity is now a third that of formal sector workers). They stall the process of improvement of conditions of production (Ghose, 2008: 503–4).[4] The

2006 NCEUS report on *Social Security for Unorganised Workers* records that in 2005, nearly 80 per cent of workers subsisted on Rs 20 per day or less, without rights to work, at work or to social security.

What is happening? Official data on employment are often hard to interpret since a given task may occupy varying class and status positions and even vary in its classification (Huws, 2007). Scholars of globalization and employment/labour use official statistics which conflate wage-work and self-employment (occasionally expressing regret for doing so). They make theoretical arguments assuming that they are mutually substitutable. But the empirical case-study evidence we have shows that this assumption is wrong.

The case-study literature traces the emergence of global value chains (GVCs) which structure an ever more complex division of tasks and add stages and value to the production of raw materials in developing countries. GVCs also develop internationally from existing 'artisan' clusters. A variety of organizational technologies sit side by side in GVCs within a given sector (Vijay, 2008: 5–10). Both processes of emergence require the construction and exploitation of competitive advantages in labour costs. They replace horizontal competition in transactions at each link in the chain by tight vertical coordination in production. Multinational corporations (MNCs) redefine core competences to focus on innovation, product strategy, marketing and the highest value-creating processes in manufacturing and services. They divest direct ownership over non-core functions such as services and volume production. Codification, standardization and computer-aided design have enabled control over GVC logistics (Huws, 2007; Vijay, 2008). Tightly controlled 'network governance' requires shedding risk and cost wherever incentives to work can be self-driven – key to which is the shedding of wage-work, or attempting never to assume the costs of a wage-labour force in the first place.

The significance of the degrees of coercion, dependence, autonomy and freedom of pcp is debated. So are the legitimate and illegitimate reasons for the process of global informalization through layoffs and the extinction of formal employment in advanced capitalist countries, and in the formal sector of developing ones. Modes of exploitation are also seen to become more complex in GVCs. While in agricultural production, for instance, rent, surplus value, interest and exchange have always coexisted, now such 'horizontal' coexistence is complicated by the 'vertical' coexistence of multiple modes of appropriation of surplus.

In an era when 'human development' has regained currency as an end as well as a means, the value chains literature at least reasserts a concept of development as a process of industrialization (though a development model of industrialization for 'human development' remains unelaborated). The GVC literature, however, reduces development to the successful creation and protection of rents inside GVCs (Kaplinsky and Morris, 2000) or even to the mere integration of local production into GVCs (Mezzadri, 2008: 604). In this politically unimaginative 'developmental' process of incorporation, rent protection and non-competitive alliances or monopolies, distributive shares in value chains (the relation of wage shares – or returns to labour – to profit) are being tilted towards profit and away from 'labour'.[5] Human development suffers. Although increases in production can take place without great concentrations of capital, in the current era decentralized production clearly fulfils the accumulation objectives of large firms controlling the strategic GVC links. The collusion between pcp and wage labour that would be necessary to resist this shift is far easier said than done.[6]

2.1 Small size

In the National Sample Survey's (NSS) 61st round for 2004–5, two-thirds of jobs in India were found to be self-employment: 'One of the most significant employment trends is the rise in self employment ... (with) ... a surge in trade, commerce, private business, outsourcing, sub-contracting, home based working and provision of services' in sectors such as food processing, beverages, textiles, garments, footwear, catering, lace, embroidery, bidi and agarbathi making, street vending, transport and domestic services (Nath, 2008: 539). At the same time insecure contract labour has doubled from 12 per cent of employment in 1980 to 25 per cent in 2004, including in hi-tech science-based industries such as pharmaceuticals and chemicals – apparently displacing permanent salaried employment, rather than pcp (Neethi, 2008: 565). GVCs evidently incorporate both of the main categories of insecure labour in the informal economy: wage-work and pcp.

Two questions may be asked of this dual trend. First, how does pcp differ from casual wage labour in GVCs? There is no doubt a conceptual grey area between pcp and wage labour, since much wage-work requires the labourer to own certain equipment (e.g. head-loading baskets and hods in the construction industry, knives in forest work, mamoties/hoes for agricultural labour, needles and sewing machines for embroidery and garment making, etc.). There is certainly also some volatility and substitutability between the two forms of work. Pcp is distinguished by the combination of ownership of the means of production, self/family exploitation and exploitation through several markets other than that for labour. Singh and Sapra's multi-sited field research on the liberalization of garments GVCs provides empirical evidence for the following tentative conclusions about the distinguishing features of pcp in GVC: pcp reduces but does not shed all supervision or teleme-diation costs associated with wage labour management; it reduces fixed and variable costs of equipment and working capital; pcp may avoid the need for in-house vertical integration; it also enables production with non-written records and verbal contracts and so avoids the costs of scrutiny by the state; it reduces employers' needs for infrastructure; and it sheds statutory obligations to labour under the factories acts and exploits child labour (Singh and Sapra, 2007: 83–4; also confirmed by Jhabvala and Kanbur's gendered analysis, 2004: 304). All these repre-sent actual or potential cost advantages of pcp on own premises over casual wage labour using the equipment of others.

The second question is if pcp can cost even less than the wage labour it may contribute to subsidizing, why do wage labour and pcp coexist in the informal economy? Studies of the gendering of productivity in sex-sequenced and sex-segregated production suggest that to answer this question we should distinguish three kinds of coexistence in the rela-tions between pcp and wage labour. They are ignored or confused in the literature on GVCs, clusters and industrial districts. The first is 'process-sequential' in which pcp and wage are deployed at different *stages* in a GVC; the second is 'process-segregated' in which certain *sectors* of the informal economy are populated by pcp and others by wage-work; and the third is 'process-integrated' in which pcp and factory production using wage labour are *mixed at all stages* of a GVC.

Comparative field economic research on silk weaving and garment making suggests that conditions favouring *process sequence* include modularized stages of production where self-exploitation is possible without supervision, where equipment is not lumpy, where high skill/ craft apprenticeships are necessary to entry, where risks of opportunism (e.g. adulteration) are low, where production does not require unmedi-ated access to market information, where coordination costs are low and there is no need for continuous relationships with the next buyer, where reputation polices incentives and where the costs of codifica-tion and standardization argued necessary for decentralized production can be avoided. These conditions certainly characterize sari weaving, button-holing and stitching, dyeing, bleaching, label making and gem cutting[7] and are also found in transport and services such as cleaning. And while tiers of sub-contractors may be controlled by merchants/ commercial capital, large economic spaces also exist for the prolifera-tion of small intermediates, agents and traders.

Process segregation is found in social structures and sectors generating small capital sums, where firms are held tightly in exchange relations and/or regulative environments which prevent savings, investment and accumulation, and where occupations are regulated by social status groups and still firmly mapped onto either rural or urban sites. Process segregation is a common attribute of bespoke production and services. It is also compatible with seasonal non-farm production as income supplements in agrarian society and with short value chains for local demand. A case in point is the remote mountain state of Arunachal Pradesh, where the richly varied local craft production is done for use as well as exchange and in multi-skilled households not specialized in artisan occupation groups.[8] Small-scale businesses are commercializing craft under restricted economic citizenship and a subsistence-remittance economy.[9] By contrast, craft production and petty trade have all but vanished from the commercialized and remittance-based hill economy of the state of Uttarakhand, due north of New Delhi.

In *process-integrated* GVCs, pcp and wage labour *compete* at every stage of the value chain. This is the case in garment manufacturing in Tiruppur in South India. The type and quality of the finished product affords no sign of the conditions under which it was produced, and no variation in quality due to the organization of production. Sometimes there is even little difference in technology between the two forms of production. Economies of scale in Taylorist production coexist with no economies of scale, self-exploitation and – in some cases – the development of collective capabilities. Process integration is found under conditions of easy entry, versatile and unspecific assets, low fixed costs, wide variation in the conditions of finance and raw materials supply under which production is possible and variation in demand for specific processes and competences. Some pcp is of course spurious, where physical production units are decentralized but are masking a concentration of economic control. In such instances its 'development' is pre-emptive, to avoid the costs of regulatory enforcement. In the life-cycle of a product/commodity, pcp can perform a variety of roles in all three types of niched coexistence with wage labour. With these distinctions in mind, we can evaluate case material to trace the impact of globalization on pcp.

India's GVC for garments has never been a regulatory free-for-all, export production being regulated by the Apparel Export Promotion Council. From 1974 to 2005 the global Multi Fibre Agreement imposed quotas on exports and formalized informal GVCs in many developing countries, not least in India. From 1985 restrictions on the organization of the garment sector were formally removed so as to increase the flexibility of the 'labour market' (Singh and Sapra, 2007: 45). However, since in practice pre-liberalization production was structured pre-emptively around the formal exclusion of small-scale hand loom and power loom production from the provisions of the Factories Acts, the pressure of global regulative regimes on local liberalization merely intensified existing tendencies to outsource production to small firms. The Indian segments of these GVCs are 'layered and complex' (ibid.: 49). Quite commonly, owners of formal sector factories also own unregistered firms, split off to obtain benefits from small industry policy (ibid.: 83).

In the process-integrated knitwear cluster of Tiruppur, thousands of small workshops coexist with mechanized factories. Between 25 per cent and 100 per cent of factory production is outsourced. Knitwear and garments in Tiruppur are dominated by intertwined commercial and manufacturing capital that control a cluster of networked, flexibly specialized pcp. The process of labour-displacing mechanization coexists with labour-intensive resistance to technical change. Until now, this flexibility has been geared to the global expansion of markets and to increasing velocity in the peaks and troughs of fashion orders.

By contrast in 2005, the low-end garments clusters in and around Delhi are process-sequenced, providing about 250,000 livelihoods in a range of firm sizes. Over 80 per cent of the firms were unregistered, employing increasing numbers of male migrant wage-workers, 'in-contracted' as gangs organized by, and accountable to, a layer of contractors inside the factories who were also sub-contracting to pcp. In Mezzadri's account, sub-contracting is increasingly confined to the craft production of embroiderers in rural artisanal clusters at some distance from – but integrated with – the metropolitan industrial cluster. Pcp has proved unable to increase its productivity through upgrading technology. Globalization here is having an opposite impact on the organization of production from its effect in Tiruppur and pressure for cost-cutting with quality improvement in the low-price segment has resulted in a reduction in pcp and a shift to in-factory gangs of contract labour (Mezzadri, 2008; Singh and Sapra, 2007).

Meanwhile in the Moradabad metalwork cluster studied by Ruthven, several kinds of value chain for final markets in Europe have developed side by side, with wage-work interleaved with (sub-sub-contracted) outsourcing and even in-sourcing (involving workers' own machines resited inside factory premises). While most GVCs in Moradabad are process-sequenced, some are process-integrated. Pcp is valued by employers for its flexibility as a mechanism of cost minimization when orders are unpredictable and peaked. It is valued by workers for the social independence it provides, the opportunity it gives to express identity through values derived from religion, and the liberty to choose between several manufacturers and merchants rather than relying on a single employer. The struggle between forms of production is seen to be the product of institutions and relationships operating outside the workplace as well as in it. The household is a site of production for exchange as well as reproduction and production for use (Ruthven, 2008).

The case material shows that the impact of globalization on pcp is highly differentiated and specific to different GVCs. In GVCs, a given commodity may be produced under process-sequenced and process-integrated combinations of pcp and wage labour.

2.2 Social regulation

Social structure and relations based in identity which transcends the economy play fundamental regulatory roles in informal market exchange. Changes to their economic regulatory role may derive from agency or deviance outside the economy as well as inside it.

In Tiruppur for instance, sub-contracting relations are cemented through tight networks of caste. The local dominant agrarian caste has played a controlling role throughout the history of development of this cluster – sufficient to block outsiders from entry. The subordination of women means that even for similar tasks (tailoring and cutting) women earn less than men. Evidently wages are shaped by patriarchal norms rather than by gender differentials in productivity. Formal unions (once strong) have atrophied and been replaced by corporatized control over production conditions by business and caste associations (Singh and Sapra, 2007: 45, 92–7).

It is certainly possible for regional 'outsiders' to enter, but successful entrants have had to occupy particular niches – on a larger scale, with imported wage-labour forces and vertically integrated production processes. As 'deviants' they faced hostile opposition from an alliance of trade unions and local exporters and have had to cede to local informal labour contractors and use local casual labour.

The production of Delhi's low-value garments is regulated through groups of migrants recruited on the basis of region, age and domestic status (without families) and gender (men migrating without women). Work conditions are so poor that workshops are used as dormitories: productive and socially reproductive spaces are one and the same (Mezzadri, 2008: 612–13). The workings of these social institutions 'fill the regulatory gaps opened by neo-liberal policies', are incorporated into the cycle of capitalist production, and become necessary to global 'capitalist architecture' (ibid.: 603).

As well as being stratified by gender (women being secluded) and by Hindu/Muslim religious identities, the Moradabad metalwork cluster is regulated by the voluntary codes of conduct demanded by foreign buyers (and consumers). Imported from abroad, confined to organized manufacturing, and designed to improve working conditions, these codes have developed in India since the turn of this century. Ruthven finds them confined to suburban factories, and only where a third party audit or a company inspectorate is provided. Most suppliers seek to operate outside the new voluntary codes (Ruthven, 2008: ch. 3; see also Singh and Sapra, 2007: 71).

In the light of such social regulatory practices the common assumption by labour economists about the substitutability of pcp and wage labour is an open question.

In these case studies all four trajectories of institutional change (persistence, creation, destruction and adaptation) have been observed. Institutional continuity characterizes gender relations. Women are incorporated into the labour market on persistently disadvantageous terms. They are often reported to earn less than minimum wages, or their equivalent in returns to pcp. The lengthening of the working day, the absence of crèches or holidays, and the classification of women as trainees on lower pay (a trick not confined to women but very common for them) all attest to a prevalent deterioration in women's working conditions (Chatterjee, 2008; Unni, 2008). The field material also indicates a range of newly created institutions – in particular in new contractual forms such as in-sourcing, in-contracting and the rapid spread of casualized, piece-rate, contract labour. The operation of GVCs is evidently able to destroy established contractual forms such as permanent, salaried labour and to create conditions which threaten or destroy trade unions – in other words, to put the conventional sequence of 'development' into reverse. But older institutions are also reworked and adapted to suit the purposes of accumulation: caste is formalized into regulative trade associations; region of origin is important in the organization of both capital and labour. Instituted non-state behaviour also shows the capacity to police itself against deviance: outsiders to Tiruppur for instance had their labour relations policed into local conformity. In the material summarized here, both pcp and wage labour are regulated through identity. In the informal sector, the economics of identity slows class formation and fragments labour.

These different trajectories of institutional change reflect the reproduction of workers in oppressive conditions in the informal sector.
Sustaining this institutional restructuring is the state – operating beyond
its own direct reach. Its response to globalization has been described
by Ahluwalia (2008) as 'gradualist'.[10] Gradualism arrogates to the state
the power of selectivity in its welcome to FDI.[11] The state has created
the conditions in which capital is being concentrated but production
is being decentralized in the socially regulated informal economy. In so
doing the state is selectively not intervening as a matter of (undeclared)
policy.

3. The financial crisis and Indian petty production

At the time of writing (early–mid 2009), there were four reasons why
this part of the chapter is the most speculative. First, the financial
crisis was just developing in India and was expected by the Planning
Commission to hit the economy with full force only later in 2009–10.
Second, mainstream economics failed either to predict the crisis or to
understand its prime movers. An array of views has been tabled ranging
from – to name but a few – contagion from subprime lending, through
business cycle explanations, misconceived expectations, mismanage-
ment of reserves, Hayekian instability, to moral hazard in the financial
sector, incompetence and stupidity among policy-makers.[12] Third, the
science of economics has proved unable to ascertain either the likely
extent of the slowdown or its impact on labour, an outcome linked
to the failure to understand the dynamics of the informal economy.
Fourth, since the analyses of economists of labour do not generally
distinguish between wage labour and 'self-employment', pcp, the largest single employment category in the economy and the focus of this
chapter, goes almost entirely unnoticed.

Given the openly acknowledged failure of economics, we use the
explanation for the financial crisis given by the international political economist Peter Gowan (2009) as a backcloth to the analysis of its
impact on India's informal economy. Gowan situates the most destructive speculative bubble – in US housing – in a regular series that has
been necessary to the new Wall Street financial system. The latter is
dominated by an oligopoly of banks and their satellites which have
been permitted to speculate on future assets and collateralized debts.
Only a few Indian banks have been directly exposed to the financial
collapse triggered by the new Wall Street system and its satellites. But
while the Indian financial system is relatively well capitalized, it is

suffering from the seizure in lending, outflows from the stock market and shrunken flows of remittances.[13]

The major impact, however, is being felt in the real economy where oil and food price instability was already generating inflation and slowing corporate investment. The Planning Commission is rightly concerned with the fact that its predicted 9–11 per cent growth rate will be reduced down to 6 per cent or even 5 per cent in 2009–10.[14] This will 'hurt labour' but the extent, sectors, sequencing and duration of the damage are unknown. There is no theory of the likely impact on the unprotected informal economy where the reduction in growth rates means livelihood losses.

Demand for exports was predicted to drop by anywhere from 10–40 per cent during 2009 and information technology (IT) exports, already under pressure in 2008, were expected to be badly hit (CLSA, 2009). The manufacturing growth rate halved from November 2007 to 2008 (Government of India, 2009). Lack of export credit is regressively hitting the smallest export firms in a disproportionate way while the depreciation of the Rupee hits imported components. India's exports are relatively labour intensive (Sardar, 2008) – textiles, hand loom garments, leather, gems and jewellery, metalware, carpets, agricultural products (spices, basmati rice and seafood) together with IT/BPO (business process outsourcing) services. By December 2008, 100,000 jobs were known to have been lost in the diamond industry in Surat and 750,000 in power loom weaving (Alagh, 2008). A survey of eleven states in October–December 2008 recorded significant drops in capacity in the automobile, metals and export industries with about 500,000 job losses in the automobile, transport and gem/jewellery sectors. The rate of job losses in the informal sector ('contract work') is estimated to be six times greater than in the formal sector (Government of India, 2009). WIEGO's responsive research showed a rapid and dramatic drop in demand and prices for recyclable waste from the informal economy – metals, cloth, plastics and glass – more insecurity in contracts and greater delays in payment in informal textiles and garments production and reductions in days worked and wage rates in the construction industry.[15] Field research underway in Chennai shows that the multiplier of the decline in IT exports reduces demand and finance for construction, demand for auto- and domestic services, street vending, laundry and ready-made food supplies (Penny Vera Sanso, personal communication, 2009).

Earlier research already cited showed that the incorporation of pcp into GVC has not necessarily produced gains either for pcp or wage workers. There is also no single, let alone easily modelled way in which

GVCs have responded to previous changes in the market or the policy environment (Harriss-White and Sinha, 2007a: 7). So it is to be expected that a similar complexity – and ingenuity by both capital and labour – will characterize responses to the crisis.

What will be the role of pcp in this crisis? Small producers are easily disposed of by employers, but so too is casual labour, especially female casual labour.[16] The three modes of insertion of pcp identified earlier will structure the crisis relationship. Since process-segmented sectors of the economy (where pcp is prevalent) involve basic wage goods for which the demand is income-inelastic, pcp will survive there. In process-sequenced GVCs, both wage labour and pcp will be affected by reductions in foreign demand. But in process-mixed/integrated forms of GVCs, will wage labour be laid off first or pcp workers? Theoretically wage labour is less divisible than pcp – though recent changes in contracts aim to make it more flexibly exploitable (through piece rates and contract labour rather than time/day rates). That wage labour is more easily organized to resist layoffs than is scattered pcp will encourage employers to dismiss it earliest (Huws, 2003). Scale economies evaporate under reduced demand, whereas pcp does not depend on them. If, under pcp, 'super-efficient' labour works until its marginal product approaches zero, and 'super-exploited' labour intensifies its own oppression compared with wage labour, then reducing demand will first increase the marginal product of labour before lowering it, while total returns to the household of self-employed workers will drop throughout this process of contraction. Below the point where the marginal product of work is equal under both forms of production, wage-work will not be an alternative. So the informal economy might witness some reversion to non-market production logics. Further, since the mode of exploitation of pcp is not through the wage but through prices, rent and interest, exploitation can be intensified through exchange relations on several markets whereas labour is exploited only on one. These arguments suggest that pcp may well be more 'resilient' and able to 'bear shock' – and to be exploited in more oppressive ways – than wage labour.

Changes in the economy are bound to have far-reaching effects on social and political relations outside it.[17] Reduced returns and incomes will put stresses on household budgets and gendered relations of social reproduction. Women's unpaid work is certain to increase, as unemployment rises, household incomes fall and labour and production for use is substituted for purchased goods. The extent to which this substitution is possible also depends on the availability of free resources and common property rights to resources to gather and glean. This may be easier in rural sites than in urban ones. The retreat of the state has also triggered the substitution of private expenditure for former meagrely provided public goods and services such as education and health care. The state will struggle to maintain subsistence guarantees, the costs of which will rise. So households will be left with reduced incomes and greater expenditure needs; the impact will be greatest on the most vulnerable. In such conditions we can expect not just the persistence – even the proliferation – of pcp plus the persistence of decentralization by large firms (Vijay, 2008), but also the vigorous social policing of livelihoods in sectors producing basic wage goods; plus attempts to eject from such sectors workers who are recent entrants with 'deviant' social identities and a marked strengthening of identity as a regulator of the economy.

4. Pro-labour responses and their politics

This chapter has explored globalization and the persistence of what many consider to be 'pre-modern forms' of labour organization at the heart of the modern Indian informal economy. Self-employment/petty commodity production has been distinguished from wage-work on the one hand and petty capitalism on the other – with both of which pcp may elide. When it comes to the juggernaut of the responses of the state and organized labour, however, such distinctions are mostly ignored; and the argument that pcp is wage labour in disguise, or even 'disguisedly unemployed' and thus a reserve army of sorts[18] becomes the political basis for the state's reaction.

In this final section we first summarize the recent responses to globalization, and then the 'normative' responses to the economic crisis.

4.1 The current 'labourist' response to globalization

The return of Congress in 2004 testified to voters' dissatisfaction with both the politics of Hindu nationalism and the failure of the reforms to improve economic and social conditions in the informal economy. But rather than enforcing the enabling laws and existing legal structure protecting labour at work and rather than spreading basic social security,[19] a specific commitment was made to a new 'common minimum programme' for workers. Sufficient time has elapsed for its progress to be evaluated. According to the National Commission for Enterprises in the Unorganized Sector (NCEUS, 2008) its components have suffered systematic under-funding, delays and corruption: the historic achievement of the National Rural Employment Guarantee (in December 2005: 100 days' work per year for people below the poverty line) is performing 'well below entitlement'; the

Bharat Nirman project for rural infrastructure, irrigation and telephony suffers 'significant implementation lags'; rural electrification has 'major shortfalls'; water and drainage has used only 'half its budget'; and education, health and food supplied under the public distribution system are under-funded. The NCEUS (2006) proposed bills for a social security safety net for urban and rural informal sector workers below the poverty line. Estimated at 0.5 per cent GDP, they consisted of benefits for sickness, maternity, disability, breadwinner death and old age with a national fund to implement them. Two bills did indeed pass through Parliament, but in a watered-down form and a non-compulsory enabling idiom, with ad hoc schemes, no national fund and no enforcement powers.[20]

At the same time a surge of activism and public interest litigation has created conditions in which a labourist and petty bourgeois agenda is publicly debated, developed and attacked. Civil society has organized around rights to work and to food, and some financial think-tanks are mobilizing around the right to (micro)finance.

4.2 Responses to crisis: compounding the problem?

In Europe and North America as well as in India, the crisis has led to risky Keynesian fiscal expansion to stimulate the economy. Two kinds of response resonate to the tensions between social democracy and delinquent financial markets. The first involves a coordinated counter-cyclical expansion in state investment and expenditure to sustain the effective demand of victims of the crisis in the real economy, while the second is a fiscal expansion confined to underwriting finance capital.[21] Globally the drift is towards the latter. In India the contradiction between the demands of the markets and those of democratic politics is reflected in the economic stimulus proposed respectively by the Ministry of Finance (MoF) and the NCEUS. The MoF recommends pumping sufficient liquidity into the banking system to enable bank credit to meet the expanded requirements of the economy (keeping in mind the contraction in credit from non-bank sources). It suggests authorizing additional plan expenditure, reducing central VAT, facilitating housing loans though bank interest rate management, boosting infrastructure finance through public–private partnerships, and supporting the credit needs of small and medium enterprises (SMEs) through credit, etc. Banks are the key medium of implementation (Government of India, 2008b). But banks are risk-averse and favour securities over commercial lending. Investments have stalled on a massive scale. Disbursements to the informal sector under 'priority sector' norms have been egregiously neglected (EPW Research Foundation, 2009). Two recent government reports – the Raghuram Rajan Committee's on *Financial Sector Reforms* (2008) and the Reserve Bank of India's on the *Trend and Progress of Banking in India* (2007) confirm that 41 per cent of the adult Indian population live outside the ambit of banks altogether.

By contrast, the NCEUS (2008) documenting the mass poverty, low skills and negligible control over productive assets of informal sector workers – lumping pcp with wage-work – has clarified that it is those earning below Rs 20 per day who are rationed out of the banking sector, excluded from credit markets and thus untouched by the MoF's measures. The NCEUS stimulus (endorsed by the International Labour Organization (ILO)) would strengthen the National Rural Employment Programme, expand local control, urbanize it and link it with complementary projects of state governments, introduce universal social protection etc. It has been largely ignored. It is said that there is no 'Plan B',[22] but the NCEUS has a Plan B. Were it implemented, however, it would increase demand for wage goods, the production and prices of which have become unstable (Ghosh, 2009; Patnaik, 2007).

The supply side needs repair too. The NCEUS has proposed the creation of a national fund for the 'unorganized' sector, credit to small and marginal farmers and a massive infrastructure programme – rural and urban housing, water, watershed management, sanitation and waste management together with the under-funded 'human development trio' (food, education and health).

The NCEUS has attempted to outline a response specifically for pcp. This emphasizes the need to persevere with the improvement of industrial capabilities to respond innovatively as sectors are under threat and to resuscitate growth poles (NCEUS, 2009). Skills, technology, credit, services and human development, all currently restricted to the formal sector, need investment (Kannan, 2008).

5. Conclusion

The majority of Indian livelihoods take the form of petty production, trade and services. Pcp is theorized as disguised unemployment and the manifestation of the 'reserve army'. We have argued here that this is not generally correct, even if pcp may sometimes be performed under conditions of oppression and distress. Pcp is also understood as disguised wage labour, formally if not really subsumed to capital. But here we found that pcp differs from wage labour in crucial respects.

Pcp is neither free nor unfree. It is not separated from the means of production, nor is it free of the restraints of self-ownership, nor completely able to quit and seek alternatives. Pcp is a relation of exploitation on three markets: property, money and commodity markets, using a range of modes of extraction of surplus. By contrast, the wage-labour relation involves exploitation on one market.[23] At the same time petty producers and traders may move (seasonally) between pcp, wage work and petty capitalism (employing others) and in these practices they are not unfree. Even so, pcp is not, as Partha Chatterjee wrote of it (2008), free as 'subjects with consent'. While free from state regulation and protection, pcp is regulated instead by social institutions – forms of economic authority and domination made manifest through multiple social identities. Class politics is mediated through these institutions and also by corporatist guilds where it is often found that the interests of the smallest firms are pushed to the foot of the agenda. Social change takes three institutional forms: destruction, creation and adaptation – over and above persistence, which the evidence reveals rarely happens without a struggle between purposive action and punishable deviance.

In practice pcp is incorporated into global value chains in three ways: process segmentation, process sequence and process integration. Their existence conditions have been explored here. In process integration, pcp competes directly with wage labour, while throughout GVCs and because of its dispersed sites pcp is less easily organized than is wage labour. The distributive share in India's GVCs has moved towards profit and away from wages/returns to pcp.

Pcp survives not as a failure of capitalism to transform pre-capitalist forms, but as a success of capitalist exploitation. If its persistence is a form of failure, it is due to the selective failure of the state to enforce its own laws regulating markets.

The Indian state is devoid of a coherent project for the pcp which this capitalist transformation has produced. In official labour statistics, pcp is hard to detect. At one and the same time the state destroys pcp (through eviction and displacement), protects it (through infrastructural and welfarist projects directed to conditions of its social reproduction), promotes it (through experiments with micro-finance) and perpetuates it through its neglect (perpetuating oppressive and exploitative conditions in the informal economy which prevent differentiation and accumulation).

The state's response to the crisis has been to keep the leading (financial) market players afloat[24] at the expense of the vast impoverished majority in the informal sector – where the state does not distinguish pcp from wage labour. The conditions of both will deteriorate as growth decelerates.[25] The capacity of pcp for super-efficiency/super-exploitation will ensure it competes vigorously with both wage-work and capital-biased technology achieving scale economies.

More than ever before, the ILO's Decent Work Agenda needs to be a development objective (Nath, 2008). It needs extension to all sectors of the informal economy. Less than ever before do the international and domestic political conditions suggest it is anything but a remote goal.

Notes

1. Please see the version of this paper published in the *Global Labour Journal*, 1, 1 (2010): 151–76 for sincere acknowledgements.
2. See the review in Lerche (2010).
3. Other notable features not discussed in this chapter include lack of legal or social protection and vulnerability (Kannan, 2008: 5–8; see also Harriss-White, forthcoming).
4. See also Jhabwala and Kanbur (2004: 293–7, 311); Ghosh (2009); and Ghose et al. (2008), who corroborate this globally.
5. Auer and Jha (2008); Chatterjee (2008: 530); see Huws and Dahlmann (2007) generally.
6. In addition 'marginal work' and open unemployment have also increased significantly during the period 1999–2005, putting pressure on those with livelihoods (Auer and Jha, 2008).
7. See Roman (2008) for saris; Singh and Sapra (2007) for garments; and Kapadia (1999) for gems and rural industrialization generally in South India. There are also, of course, many explanations for pcp that do not rely on its superiority to wage labour in task-specific sequences: for example both may be used by employers for their flexible response to seasonality of demand in the non-farm economy (Singh and Sapra, 2007: 82–4).
8. See Harriss-White et al. (2009) for details.
9. While all non-locals require formal inner line permits to enter, even local tribal people are disenfranchised from economic citizenship under customary law outside their own territories. See Harriss-White et al. (2010).
10. In presentation at the conference 'Development, Freedom, Welfare', Cornell University and Institute of Human Development, New Delhi, December 2008 (henceforth 'Sen-conf').
11. A process not without opposition at the federal and state levels.
12. Respectively Bouchard (2008); Holland (2009); Soros (2008); Ackerman (2008); Edmund Phelps and Joseph Stiglitz (December 2008, presentations at the Sen-conf).
13. Asian Development Bank (2009).
14. Ahluwalia (Sen-conf).
15. WIEGO (2009). WIEGO does not distinguish pcp from labour.
16. Asian Development Bank (2009: 6).
17. The activist Aruna Roy predicts an upsurge in violence (Sen-conf).
18. Respectively Banaji (1977) and Kannan (2008: 22).
19. For which a legal template was adopted by central government as long ago as 1995.

20. The fault lines of the two bills concerned are agriculture and non-agriculture, not pcp and labour. The pension age threshold (60 years) resists revising downwards to be appropriate for landless labourers and construction workers who are frequently worn out by their late thirties (Penny Vera Sanso, personal communication, 2009).
21. In the absence of such coordination, national protectionism will trigger political conflicts.
22. For instance, by Lord Meghnad Desai (Sen-conf).
23. See Breman (2006) and Breman, Guerin and Prakash (2009), for the discussion of neo-bonded labour, which involves money plus labour markets.
24. Asian Development Bank (2009: 8).
25. International Labour Organization (2009).

References

Ackerman, F. (2008) 'The Economics of Collapsing Markets', *Real-world Economics Review*, 48: 279–90.

Alagh, Y. (2008) 'India and the World', plenary presentation to the conference 'Development, Freedom, Welfare', Cornell University and Institute of Human Development, New Delhi, December.

Asian Development Bank (ADB) (2009) *The Global Economic Crisis: Challenges for Developing Asia and ADB's Response*, Manila: ADB.

Auer, P. and Jha, P. (2008) 'Labour Market Reforms in India: Barking Up the Wrong Tree?' Plenary paper, Indian Society for Labour Economics, Golden Jubilee Conference, Giri Institute, Lucknow.

Banaji, J. (1977) 'Capitalist Domination and the Small Peasantry Deccan Districts in the Late 19th Century', *Economic and Political Weekly*, Special Number (August): 1375–1404.

Bouchaud, J. P. (2008) 'Economics Needs a Scientific Revolution', *Real-world Economics Review*, 48: 291–2.

Breman, J. (2006) *The Poverty Regime in Village India*, New Delhi: Oxford University Press.

Breman, J., Guerin, I. and Prakash, A. (eds) (2009) *India's Unfree Workforce: Old and New Practices of Labour Bondage*, New Delhi: Oxford University Press.

Chatterjee, B. (2008) 'Democracy and Economic Transformation in India', *Economic and Political Weekly*, 43, 16 (19 April).

Credit Lyonnais Securities Asia (CLSA) (2009) 'Asia-Pacific Market', *Triple: a Weekly Economic Commentary*, 3, 4: 1–9.

EPW Research Foundation (2009) 'Stimulus Packages Facing Institutional Constraints', *Economic and Political Weekly*, 44, 4: 23–9.

Ghose, A. K. (2008) 'Globalization and Employment in Developing Countries', *Indian Journal of Labour Economics*, 52, 4: 497–504.

Ghose, A. K., Majid, N. and Ernst, C. (2008) *The Global Employment Challenge*, Geneva: International Labour Office.

Ghosh, J. (2009) 'The Outcry is Muted but the Food Crisis is Getting Worse', *The Guardian*, 9 January, p. 34.

Gowan, P. (2009) 'Crisis in the Heartland', *New Left Review*, 55: 5–29.

Government of India (GoI) (2007) *Trend and Progress of Banking in India*, Reserve Bank of India, Mumbai.

Government of India (GoI) (2008a) *Financial Sector Reforms*, Planning Commission, New Delhi.

Government of India (GoI) (2008b) Memorandum on the Financial Crisis, Ministry of Finance.

Government of India (GoI) (2009) *Report on Effect of Economic Slowdown on Employment in India*, Ministry of Labour and Employment, Labour Bureau, Chandigarh.

Harriss-White, B. (2003) *India Working: Essays on Society and Economy*, Cambridge: Cambridge University Press.

Harriss-White, B. (Forthcoming) 'Work and Well-being in Informal Economies: the Regulative Roles of Institutions of Identity and the State', *World Development*.

Harriss-White, B. and Sinha, A. (2007a) 'Introduction', in B. Harriss-White and A. Sinha (eds), *Trade Liberalisation and India's Informal Economy*, New Delhi: Oxford University Press, pp. 1–14.

Harriss-White, B. and Sinha, A. (eds) (2007b) *Trade Liberalisation and India's Informal Economy*, New Delhi: Oxford University Press.

Harriss-White, B., Mishra, D. and Upadhyay, V. (2009) 'Institutional Diversity and Capitalist Transition: the Political Economy of Agrarian Change in Arunachal Pradesh', *Journal of Agrarian Change*, 9, 4: 230–66.

Harriss-White, B., Prakash, A. and Mishra, D. (2010) 'Globalization, Economic Citizenship and India's Inclusive Developmentalism', Workshop on Citizenship, Heidelberg University, South Asia Institute.

Holland, S. (2009) 'The World after Keynes', *Red Pepper*, 163: 22–4.

Huws, U. (2003) *The Making of the Cybertariat*, London: Merlin.

Huws, U. (2007) 'The Emergence of Emergence: the Challenge of Designed New Research on the New International Division of Labour', *Work Organization, Labour and Globalization*, 1, 2: 20–35.

Huws, U. and Dahlmann, S. (2007) 'Global Restructuring of Value Chains and Class Issues', *Proceedings of the ISA Conference: Work and Employment: New Challenges*, Montreal, August.

International Labour Organization (ILO) (2009) *Global Employment Trends*, Geneva: International Labour Office.

Jhabvala, R. and Kanbur, R. (2004) 'Globalization and Economic Reform as Seen from the Ground: SEWA's Experience in India', in K. Basu (ed.), *India's Emerging Economy: Performance and Prospects in the 1990s and Beyond*, Cambridge, MA: MIT Press, pp. 293–312.

Kannan, K. P. (2008) 'Dualism, Informality and Social Inequality', Presidential Address, Indian Society for Labour Economics, Golden Jubilee Conference, Giri Institute, Lucknow.

Kapadia, K. (1999) 'Gender Ideology and the Formation of Rural Industrial Classes in S. India Today', *Contributions to Indian Sociology*, 33, 1–2: 329–52.

Kaplinsky, R. and Morris, M. (2000) *A Handbook for Value Chain Research*, IDRC/ Institute of Development Studies, Sussex.

Kumar, A. (2005) *Black Economy in India*, New Delhi: Penguin Books.

Lerche, J. (2010) 'From "Rural Labour" to "Classes of Labour": Class Fragmentation, Caste and Class Struggle at the Bottom of the Indian Labour Hierarchy', in B. Harriss-White and J. Heyer (eds), *The Comparative Political Economy of Development: Africa and South Asia*, Oxford and New York: Routledge, pp. 64–85.

Mezzadri, A. (2008) 'The Rise of Neoliberal Globalization and the "New-Old" Social Regulation of Labour: a Case of the Delhi Garment Sector', *Indian Journal of Labour Economics*, 52, 4: 603–18.

Nath, G. B. (2008) 'Globalization and Growth of Precarious Jobs in the Indian Labour Market: Implication for Economic Policy', *Indian Journal of Labour Economics*, 52, 4: 533–44.

National Commission for Enterprises in the Unorganized Sector (NCEUS) (2006) *Social Security for Marginalised Workers*, New Delhi: NCEUS.

National Commission for Enterprises in the Unorganized Sector (NCEUS) (2008) *The Global Economic Crisis and the Informal Economy in India: Need for Urgent Measures and Fiscal Stimulus to Protect Incomes in the Informal Economy*, New Delhi: NCEUS.

National Commission for Enterprises in the Unorganized Sector (NCEUS) (2009) *Growth Pole Programme for Unorganised Sector Enterprise Development*, New Delhi: NCEUS.

Neethi, P. (2008) 'Contract Work in the Organised Manufacturing Sector: a Disaggregated Analysis of Trends and their Implications', *Indian Journal of Labour Economics*, 52, 4: 559–74.

Patnaik, U. (2007) *The Republic of Hunger and Other Essays*, London: Merlin.

Roman, C. (2008) 'Learning and Innovation in Clusters: Case Studies from the Indian Silk Industry', DPhil thesis, Oxford University.

Roy, R. (1996) 'State Failure: Political-Fiscal Implications of the Black Economy', *IDS Bulletin*, 27, 2: 22–31.

Ruthven, O. (2008) 'Value and Values in a North Indian Value Chain', unpublished DPhil thesis, Oxford University.

Sardar, S. I. (2008) 'The Indian Experience of Globalization: an Overview', *Regional Studies*, 26, 3: 83–110.

Singh, N. and Sapra, M. K. (2007) 'Liberalisation in Trade and Finance: India's Garment Sector', in B. Harriss-White and A. Sinha (eds), *Trade Liberalisation and India's Informal Economy*, New Delhi: Oxford University Press, pp. 42–127.

Sinha, A. and Adam, C. (2007) 'Modelling the Informal Economy in India: an Analysis of Trade Reforms', in B. Harriss-White and A. Sinha (eds), *Trade Liberalisation and India's Informal Economy*, New Delhi: Oxford University Press, pp. 307–64.

Sinha, A., Sangeeta, N. and Siddiqui, K. (1999) 'The Impact of Alternative Policies on the Economy with Special Reference to the Informal Sector: a Multisectoral Study', National Council for Applied Economic Research, New Delhi.

Soros, G. (2008) 'The Crisis and What to Do About It', *Real-world Economics Review*, 48: 312–18.

Unni, J. (2008) 'Women Workers in the New Economy', *Indian Journal of Labour Economics*, 52, 4: 657–74.

Vijay, G. (2008) 'De-fragmenting Approaches to the Global Disintegration of Value Creation: From Value Chains to Value Cycles', Department of Economics, University of Hyderabad, gudavarthyvijay@hotmail.com.

Women in the Informal Economy Globalizing and Organizing (WIEGO) (2009) 'Impact of the Global Recession on the Working Poor in the Informal Economy', http://wiego.org/about_ie/ie_news/EconomicCrises2009.php, accessed 11 June 2009.

8
Beyond the Factory: Globalization, Informalization of Production and the Changing Locations of Labour

Kalyan Sanyal and Rajesh Bhattacharya

1. Introduction

There are two contradictory views on the impact of globalization on labour activism. It is widely argued that globalization has considerably weakened labour movements all over the world. It is observed that, with labour tied to its specific geographical locations, increasingly footloose capital has made economies, especially the developing ones, vulnerable to capital strike – the threat of capital moving out to places more attractive in terms of wages and standards – unleashing a race to the bottom for developing countries. Labour, unlike in the second half of the twentieth century, now has passively to adapt to the terms dictated by mobile global capital.

This view, however, has not gone uncontested. There is also a counter-perspective in which it is asserted that while globalization has undoubtedly undermined the conditions that made traditional trade unionism associated with Fordist mass production possible, the forces of globalization themselves have opened up new terrain where radically new forms of labour activism can be imagined. Globalization may have created conditions that are debilitating for labour in the traditional sense of working-class power; but at the same time it has potentially empowered the working class in ways that the twentieth-century pre-globalized world did not allow. As Silver (2003) and Webster et al. (2008) argue, the complex global network of production – based on outsourcing and sub-contracting – is making global capital more vulnerable than before to disruptions in the global circuit of production and circulation, thus increasing the bargaining power of the working class.

In this otherwise illuminating debate, labour, it is to be noted, is characterized as wage labour, and employment as wage employment.

In other words, it focuses exclusively on employment based on capitalist production relations that are rooted in the separation of capital and labour. The reality of developing countries today, however, does not correspond with this characterization of labour. It is now a common observation that developing economies are marked by the existence of an overwhelmingly large volume of economic activities that fall within what is described as the 'informal sector'. It is an economic space in which workers engage in economic activities in ways that are very different from the capitalist organization of production. In particular, the prevalent form of labour in the informal sector is self-employment, which is different from the usual wage-based employment resting on the alienation of labour from capital.

Decades ago, Theodor Shanin, in introducing A. V. Chayanov's *The Theory of Peasant Economy*, wrote: 'while in the "developing societies" islands of pre-capitalism disappear, what comes instead is mostly not the industrial proletariat of Europe's nineteenth century but strata of plebian survivors – a mixture of increasingly mobile, half employed slum-dwellers, part farmers, lumpen traders, or pimps – another extra-capitalist pattern of social and economic existence under capitalism' (Chayanov, 1987: 23); and 'Chayanov's fundamental methods and insights may prove particularly enriching for worlds of fewer peasants as well as of fewer "classical" industrial proletarians while the subject of his actual concern, the Russian peasantry, has all but disappeared' (Chayanov, 1987: 24). The observation that nearly 50 per cent of the non-agricultural workers in the Indian economy do not have an employer corroborates Shanin's characterization of developing societies. In the capitalist economic formations of today's developing countries, the extra-capitalist space described by Shanin is increasingly visible. A large section of the population now reproduce the material conditions of their precarious existence by engaging in economic activities governed by a logic that is fundamentally different from the one that animates the world of capitalist production.

The purpose of this chapter is to foreground the phenomenon of informalized self-employment and explore its implications for the potentially new forms of labour activism. And in doing this we take particular note of the household as a site of commodity production, that is, of activities undertaken within the household in which marketable commodities are produced with family labour. Although our primary focus is on the urban informal sector, the analysis reaches out to rural non-farm employment as well.

2. Globalization and informalization

While the informal sector has always existed in developing economies, there is ample evidence that globalization has exacerbated the process of informalization, in two ways:

(a) The dismantling of barriers to trade and capital flows has made way for the unhindered mobility of commodities and capital across national boundaries. Faced with competition on the global level, firms in the formal sector of developing economies are engaged in a battle of competitive cost cutting. They are increasingly relying on outsourcing of production processes to informal units where wage costs and costs associated with complying with labour and environmental standards are considerably lower.

(b) The inflow of cheaper imports has caused a contraction of the import competing industries in the formal sector, but the expansion of the export sector has failed to generate sufficient employment to compensate for the loss. Moreover, global competition has forced domestic private as well as state enterprises to raise labour productivity and adopt lean production methods involving large-scale retrenchment of workers. Further, the neoliberal focus on fiscal discipline and inflation-targeting has eroded the power of the state to create employment. In other words, job destruction has dominated job creation in the formal sector, forcing those thrown out of employment to eke out a living in the informal sector.

These two types of informalization relate to two distinct spheres within the informal economy: (1) the first expands informal production activities *within* the circuit of capital, connected to the latter through a complex network of sub-contracting and outsourcing; (2) the second expands the economic space *outside* the circuit of capital. Thus, while both types of informalization constitute a reversal of Fordist capital–labour relations,[1] they have different implications for the labour force as it relates to capital. The heterogeneous locations of labour with respect to capital call for recognition of the plurality of contradictions that constitute capital–labour relations.

There is yet a third process, probably more significant even as it is less recognized, by which capital in the formal sector relates to the informal economy. The classic paradigm of economic growth in developing countries was based on the presupposition that the modern (capitalist)

economy will expand by breaking up traditional (pre-capitalist) economies, transferring both economic resources and labourers from the
traditional to the modern economy. Yet, the experience of economic
growth in developing countries shows that while the capitalist economy did expand by breaking up traditional economies, it did so by
transferring resources but not labourers. As a result, a 'surplus' labour
force emerged in developing countries consisting of dispossessed producers whose traditional livelihoods have been destroyed and yet who
were not absorbed in the modern sector. Wherever the 'surplus' labour
force settled, the following economic characteristics emerged – the clear
preponderance of self-employment largely assisted by family labour,
the household as a major site of commodity production particularly in
case of non-agricultural activities and community or kinship networks
involving trust and reciprocity in place of impersonal exchange relations.

Enterprises with these characteristics came to be referred to as
informal enterprises. The informal economy, i.e. the economy of the
'surplus' labour force, is a product of the process by which the capitalist economy secures its resources minus the people who traditionally
survived with them, a process that Sanyal (2007) refers to as *exclusion*.
A part of the informal economy is integrated to global or domestic capital via processes of sub-contracting and putting-out, but an even larger
part of it constitutes a non-capitalist production space.

Further, exclusion is a constitutive process of the capitalist economy
such that the reproduction and expansion of the latter involves
repeated invasion of resources which lie outside it. Globalization exac-
erbates the process by unleashing competitive pressure on capitalist
firms to expand at minimum cost, often by dismantling social barriers
to such dispossession. This low-cost expansion of the capitalist sector often involves a flow of economic assets – especially when they
are cheaply valued by the market – from the informal to the formal
economy either through coercion or compulsions of the market. This
is, for example, what happens when peasant landholdings are forci-
bly acquired for industrial projects by the invocation of the 'eminent
domain' clause, traditional economies are destroyed to make way for
large-scale infrastructure projects or hawkers are evicted for urban
renewal projects. However, for all the reasons mentioned before, the
rate of job creation in the formal sector remains low or even declines in
the neoliberal regime. Therefore, dispossessed producers who join the
labour force continue to find themselves in relative super-abundance
to labour demand in the formal sector enterprises. This understanding

of the informal economy as a product of exclusion places it right at the heart of capitalist development and *yet outside the circuit of capital* – an outside that is expanded along with and in proportion to capitalist accumulation.

The foregoing analysis brings a fresh perspective to the debate on globalization and its effects on labour. While the proponents of globalization argue that globalization opens up new opportunities for the informal economy to integrate with the more dynamic and productive part of the economy, detractors of globalization point to the subordinated nature of such integration as well as jobless growth under globalization. While each side of the debate picks up either aspect of the contradiction between globalized capital and its outside, *the very positing of the outside is a theoretical move largely absent in the ongoing debate.* Our conceptualization of the post-colonial economy as a contradictory totality constituted by capital and its outside (a) contests the 'oneness' of the economy that supporters of globalization believe in and at the same time (b) inscribes a radical discontinuity in the economy that is different from the traditional/modern or pre-capital/capital dichotomy in conventional dualistic theories of under-development. In our theorization, capital and its outside mutually constitute each other – and so capitalist development cannot dissolve such dualism. This is where we depart radically from standard models of the dual economy where dualism is fated to disappear with capitalist accumulation. We rather understand the informal producers as a 'surplus' labour force akin to what is known as the 'marginal mass' in Latin American theories (Nun, 2000; Quijano and Westwell, 1983): '[M]y marginal mass thesis was meant to question a left hyperfunctionalism, wherein even the last landless peasant in Latin America (or Africa) was considered to be functional to the reproduction of capitalist exploitation. On the contrary, I tried to show that in many places a surplus population was growing that in the best of cases was simply *irrelevant* to the hegemonic sector of the economy and in the worst of the cases endangered its stability. This presented the established order with the political problem of managing such nonfunctional surpluses to prevent them from being *dysfunctional*' (Nun, 2000: 12, emphasis added).

The 'redundant' labour force emerges as a product of exteriorization of labour by capital, the social outcome of the *exclusionary* expansion of capital that relegates the victims of its expansion – dispossessed informal producers, the *detritus* of modern capitalism – to a non-capitalist outside, thus reproducing a basic fault line running through the economy.

3. Characterizing the informal sector

This 'surplus' labour force is categorically distinguished from (a) wage-workers whom capital *exploits*, (b) the reserve army of labour which enables such exploitation to go on and (c) non-capitalist producers tied to capital via sub-contracting or outsourcing and from whom capital *extracts* surplus. As opposed to the relations of exploitation and extraction that lie at the heart of traditional labour movements, we posit a third relation, *exclusion*, to identify the 'surplus' labour force as a potential political force in the post-colonial social landscape.

The 'surplus' labour force presents the problem of livelihood on a scale that exceeds the redistributive capacity of most post-colonial nation-states. Hence, an economic space has to emerge which must function in such a way as to ensure economic survival of surplus labour. This economic space must be organized around the needs of the people and hence must constitute an outside to the space of capital where accumulation structures social outcomes. Sanyal (2007) refers to the space of capital as the 'accumulation-economy' and its outside as the 'need-economy'. The informal economy is that economic space where people innovate new forms of production, distribution and redistribution so as to accommodate the 'surplus' labour force at levels of economic subsistence.

To understand this 'need-economy', it is quite natural that social scientists have looked back to the peasant economy which has always been the traditional fall-back option for the outcast labourers under modern capitalism. Almost a century ago, in the Russian context, Chayanov presented a theory of peasant economy, holding that the peasant household takes its production decision on the basis of the needs of the household on the one hand and the drudgery of labour at the margin, on the other. The needs of the Chayanovian peasant household depend on the size of the family while only a sub-set of the family members can perform labour. The working members labour on land owned by the family to satisfy its needs. The amount of labour expended, and the output obtained, is determined by equating at the margin the utility derived from an additional unit of output to the drudgery of working an additional hour. The crucial point made by Chayanov is that the categories associated with capitalist production, such as revenues, wages and profits, have no place in the calculations on which the decisions regarding peasant production are based.

The difference between today's informal self-employment based activities and Chayanov's peasants is that urban petty producers do not belong to the 'natural economy'. While for Chayanov's peasants, there is unity of labour and the means of labour, this unity for urban petty producers is mediated by the market and hence dependent on credit. While the traditional peasant economy is characterized by production of use-values, the urban informal economy is dominated by production for the market. It is an economy fully entrenched in the system of money and exchange.

Yet this informal economy has instituted a social mechanism that mimics the classical solution to survival – sharing of income! It has been well recognized that the peasant economy accommodates the surplus labour force by maximizing income rather than profit and then distributing the average product to the family members irrespective of their contribution to income. The same phenomenon is also observed in more non-traditional forms of the informal economy.

We must hasten to add that 'need' and 'accumulation' are not to be treated as economic objectives of the informal and the formal enterprises in the way neoclassical economics endows an economic agent with an objective function. Marx made it abundantly clear that accumulation by the capitalist firm is a response to the economic forces of competition.[2] Similarly, 'external coercive laws' compel informal producers to organize the economic space so as to ensure their economic subsistence. The ceaseless reproduction of the surplus labour force – as a result of dispossession accompanying capitalist accumulation – requires that the informal economy accommodate the surplus labour force on a residual resource base. The informal economy responds to this social conjuncture by distributing the total income generated on the resource base as average product among its members. It is this mechanism in the informal economy that establishes 'need' as the organizing/structuring principle of the contemporary petty producers' economy. We call this space the 'Chayanovian outside of capital'.

Since the informal economy acts as a sponge that absorbs the surplus labour force, it is characterized by free entry – but only up to the point where average product is at the subsistence level. Further entry of labour jeopardizes the social reproduction of the informal economy itself. The contemporary crisis in Indian agriculture reflects such a turning point. As a result, another component of the 'need-economy' – the rural non-farm sector – expands to accommodate a part of the 'surplus' labour force, while the rest of it is absorbed mainly in the urban informal economy. Contemporary post-colonial capitalism is an endless reproduction of a complex of capital and its Chayanovian outsides.

4. Globalization and locations of labour in the Indian economy

We disaggregate the labour force to identify how globalization affects each location of labour in the Indian context. We use a three-tier classification: (a) direct wage-workers in capitalist production; (b) labour force in informal enterprises linked to the capitalist enterprises in the formal economy through sub-contracting and putting-out; and (c) labour force in informal enterprises outside the circuit of capital. Wage-workers in capitalist production relations consist of agricultural workers on capitalist farms, public sector employees and private sector non-agricultural workers. The second tier of the labour force consists mainly of those in non-agricultural informal enterprises linked to the capitalist economy via sub-contracting and the agricultural workforce tied to agro-business enterprises through contract-farming. The third tier of the labour force constitutes the surplus labour force and populates the Chayanovian *outside* of capital. It consists of the rural non-farm and urban informal labour force with no direct linkages with the formal economy.

Globalization has its particular impact on each of these three tiers of the labour force in the Indian context. For reasons already discussed, the forces of globalization have constrained employment growth in the first tier. Public sector employment has steadily declined over the period 1999–2005, from 190.58 lakhs in 1999 to 180.07 lakhs in 2005 (Ministry of Finance, *Economic Survey 2007–8*). Private enterprises in the formal sector have generated additional employment entirely in the category of unprotected regular, casual or contract wage-workers which constitutes informal employment *within* the formal sector. Most of the growing labour force is accommodated in the other two tiers. A part of the additional labour force has been accommodated via putting-out and sub-contracting. The growth in informal employment in the formal sector together with that of informal producers in sub-contracting relationships is often referred to as informalization of capitalist production and constitutes a reversal of Fordist capital–labour relations.

Yet, an overwhelming share of the growing labour force has been absorbed mainly as 'independent' self-employed producers in rural non-farm and urban informal activities. In our understanding, it animates a production space outside the circuit of capital. Agriculture, which has traditionally acted as the sponge of surplus labour, has finally hit its limits and is absorbing additional labour only at a sluggish rate. Manufacturing (wholesale and retail), trading and repairing activities are the areas where informal employment is predominantly generated (see Table 8.1).

Table 8.1 Employment (in millions) by type and sector

	1999–2000			2004–2005		
	Informal workers	Formal workers	Total workers	Informal workers	Formal workers	Total workers
Informal sector	341.3	1.4	342.6	393.5	1.4	394.9
Formal sector	20.5	33.7	54.1	29.1	33.4	62.6
Total	361.7	35	396.8	422.6	34.9	457.5

Source: Data taken from NCEUS (2007: 3).

Total employment in the Indian economy increased from 396.8 million in 1999–2000 to 457.5 million in 2004–5. The informal sector absorbed an additional 52.3 million labourers, 86 per cent of total employment generated between 1999–2000 and 2004–2005. The number of protected formal sector jobs declined marginally from 33.7 to 33.4 million while informal jobs in the formal sector – consisting of regular, casual and contract workers without any job security or social security benefits – increased by 8.5 million. Thus, while employment in the informal sector increased by 52.3 million, informal employment increased by 60.9 million. The distinction between *informal employment* and *employment in the informal sector* reflects the impact of globalization on the workforce. While the informal sector has always dominated employment in the Indian economy, globalization has led to growth of employment *within* the formal sector under conditions (casual and contract employment, regular employment without stipulated benefits) that approximate employment in the informal sector. In addition, there are homeworkers in the non-agricultural informal sector, who are often located in domestic or global value-chains (e.g. garments) through sub-contracting or putting-out relationships and are really 'disguised wage-workers'. Homeworkers (8.2 million) – included as informal 'self-employed' in the statistics – constituted 7.4 per cent of the non-agricultural informal labour force and 30 per cent of the informal manufacturing workforce in 1999–2000 (ibid.: 57). Sub-contracting from large firms to small firms has been increasing and consequently numbers of homeworkers, to whom small firms in turn sub-contract, are also increasing.

On the other hand, the growth in numbers of self-employed producers – minus the category of homeworkers – constitutes an expanding non-capitalist space in the Indian economy. Self-employed workers constituted 56 per cent of the total workforce – 64 per cent of the agricultural workforce and 46 per cent of the non-agricultural workforce in 2004–5 (ibid.: 49). In agriculture, farmers (self-employed in agriculture)[3] still dominate the agricultural workforce – their share in fact rising between 1999–2000 and 2004–5 after a steady decline in the 1990s, while the agricultural wage-labour force actually declined over the same period[4] (ibid.: 111).

Within the unorganized non-agricultural sector, there are two kinds of enterprises: (a) own-account enterprises (OAEs) where production is done by the owner-operator assisted by family labour and (b) establishments where production is done by the owner-operator along with family labour and 'hired labour'. OAEs constituted 87 per cent of all informal enterprises and accounted for 73 per cent of the informal non-agricultural workforce in 1999–2000 (ibid.: 51). A majority of the OAEs were engaged in manufacturing (31.83 per cent), repairing and (wholesale and retail) trading activities (39.67 per cent) in 1999–2000 (NSSO, 2001). The fact that only about 11 per cent of OAEs worked with any kind of contract with master-enterprises/contractors in 1999–2000 (ibid.) reflects the relatively 'independent' mode of petty production in the informal economy.

There is thus a growing informalization of the Indian economy with a clear trend towards self-employment as the main source of livelihood for the informal labour force. These developments within the labour force point out a basic feature of economic growth in the Indian economy under globalization: there is a decoupling of employment growth from output growth in the formal sector of the economy. As a document of the Ministry of Labour points out, throughout the period under globalization, 'self-employment and casual labour continued to play a pivotal role in rehabilitation of the unemployed'.[5]

5. Urbanization of poverty and the informal labourers

For half a century after Independence, agriculture as a whole has played the role of a Chayanovian outside to capitalist industrialization in India. In recent times, there are clear signs that this traditional 'sink' of surplus labour is overflowing. In the Indian economy, the expansion of the rural non-farm sector is largely distress-driven, for the era of globalization has seen poor agricultural output and employment growth. While the total workforce grew by 2.1 per cent between 1983 and 1994 and by 1.9 per cent between 1994 and 2005, the corresponding growth rates of agricultural workforce have been 1.4 and 0.8 per cent respectively (NCEUS, 2007: 116).

The rising share of farmers in the agricultural workforce is reflective of agricultural involution, where a growing part of the agricultural workforce is absorbed on the basis of fragmentation of land and sharing of work (ibid.). The proportion of rural households with marginal holdings increased from 59 per cent in 1999–2000 to 62 per cent in 2004–5 while that of households with small, medium and large holdings declined slightly over the same period. As a result, the average size of holdings decreased from 1.00 hectare in 1999–2000 to 0.8 hectare in 2004–5 (ibid.: 112). This pattern of change in the distribution of landholdings – the increasing share of marginal farms vis-à-vis all other categories of farms – has been a continuous process over the entire period since the 1950s. In 2002–3, marginal and small farmers constituted 86 per cent of all farmers and cultivated 43 per cent of land (ibid.: 113). This process underlies the classic mechanism by which agriculture absorbed the surplus labour through fragmentation of land and sharing of average product – the textbook example of disguised unemployment. A comparison between average monthly income and average monthly expenditure by farm size shows that for small and marginal farmers, per capita monthly income levels fall short of expenditure levels, so that these households have to borrow to meet their consumption needs (ibid.: 120).

The critical condition of agriculture in India is reflected in a steadily declining share of agricultural workers in the rural workforce (from 81.4 per cent in 1983 to 72.7 per cent in 2004–5) with clear signs of occupational diversification among the rural workers with people migrating out of agriculture. A significant number are absorbed in the rural non-farm sector, largely as informal self-employment in manufacture of apparel, retail trade, land transport, STD/ISD booths, maintenance and repair of motor vehicles and hotels and restaurants.

Rural–urban migration of course is the other great response to the exhaustion of agriculture. For the first time in history, urban population exceeds rural population. 'As rural areas lose their "storage capacity", slums take their place, and urban "involution" replaces rural involution as a sink for surplus labour which can only keep pace with subsistence by ever more heroic feats of self-exploitation and the further competitive subdivision of already densely filled survival niches' (Davis, 2004: 27).

Most of the urban OAEs in India operate with a very low average value of investment (Rs 70,000 in 1999–2000) in fixed assets,[6] most of them owned by the petty producer. Monthly gross value-added per urban informal own-account enterprise was Rs 2,175 on average in 1999–2000[7] (NCEUS, 2007: 52–3). The gross value-added per worker approximates the income of the petty producer who hires no labour and minimal capital. On average, therefore, urban petty production units operate at subsistence levels – implying that with projected levels of urbanization, the urban informal economy is going to replace the rural economy as the largest location of poverty in the world in the near future.

A significant part of non-agricultural informal activity takes place within the household using family labour. Self-employed production units involve the contribution of family members as 'helpers', the dwelling unit itself is used as the site of production, personal assets of family members like bicycles act as assets of the enterprise, durable assets of households act as fixed business investments and household expenditures and production expenditures overlap. It is thus difficult to separate household production of use-values for immediate consumption and production of commodities within the household. Production of commodities *within* household premises allows informal production units to supplement their scarce resources by drawing on household resources for consumption. The location of production within the household explains how informal production units with such low levels of fixed business investment manage to survive. This is particularly true for manufacturing enterprises. In 1999–2000, among manufacturing OAEs, 76 per cent of rural units and 63 per cent of urban units were located within household premises (ibid.: 265).

As the home and the workshop converge, the production of commodities is synchronized with reproduction of life. The inseparability of the *life process* and the *labour process* within the household is thus an emerging feature of the informal economy. This is a radical reversal of the general twentieth-century notion of labour where the worker works for eight hours within the factory gates, after which the worker reproduces his or her life within the family. The blurring of the distinction between the home and the workshop implies that labour activism must face up to the new conditions of labour that home-based production brings to the fore and the potentially new subjectivity of labour shaped by such conditions.

The urban slums are exemplary products of *homesteading* by the urban informal population. Slums are more than poor people's settlements – each slum literally is a production hub by itself. With close to a one billion-strong slum population in 2001 (UN-Habitat, 2003: 246), slums worldwide are emerging as poor people's Manchesters and Chicagos. The convergence of the home and the workshop takes place at the level of entire 'townships' which is what the mega-slums already are in urban metropolises. The unstoppable horizontal spread of Third World metropolises is fuelled by the explosive growth of slums. The horizontal sprawl of the slums reflects the demand for 'fungible' space – so essential to survival of the informal producers in the slums – that can function both as the site of production of commodities and reproduction of life. Mumbai's Dharavi is spread over 550 acres with the number of residents ranging from 700,000 to 1.2 million (Chatterji, 2005). No comprehensive survey of Dharavi exists, but Dharavi's annual turnover is estimated to lie between US$700 and $1 billion. There are at least 5,000 estimated industrial enterprises amid the cramped housing of Dharavi, producing textiles, pottery and leather, jewellery, food products etc. (Apte, 2008). At least 200,000 people are engaged in recycling (Ramchandran, 2008).

When an ambitious US$3 billion Dharavi Redevelopment Project was announced by the Maharashtra government in 2004, it immediately faced resistance from the Dharavi people. According to the plan, Dharavi residents were to be provided with 225 square foot of housing free of cost in high-rise buildings (Menon, 2008). Such small residential spaces cannot accommodate production units and the 'rise', by replacing the 'sprawl', destroys the fungibility of space required for informal home-based economic activities. The problem with the redevelopment plan is that it recognizes the 'residents' and not the 'producers' of Dharavi.[8]

The entire business district of Dharavi is under threat because most of the enterprises do not have licences and so cannot find any place in the new redeveloped Daharavi. The government has agreed to reha-bilitate industrial units within redeveloped Dharavi as long as these are 'non-hazardous and non-polluting'. But this will mean closure of Dharavi's most important businesses – pottery, leather goods and recycling. At the heart of resistance to the Dharavi plan, therefore, are the 'producers' rather than squatters.

6. The new forms of labour resistance

In our understanding, the Dharavi resistance qualifies more as a 'labour' mobilization than slum dwellers' resistance. It is symptomatic of an emerging terrain of 'labour' mobilization – outside the familiar space of proletarian resistance and peasant uprisings – originating in a new loca-tion of labour that is discernible as a theorized outside of capital. The 'outside' of capital brings forth new demonstrations of workers' power articulated differently, in style and content, from traditional working-class power.

The traditional power of the working class flows from its location within the capitalist class structure. Eric Olin Wright (2000) makes a distinction between *associational* and *structural* working-class power.

Structural power accrues to the working class by virtue of its location within the economic institutions of capitalism. The market bargaining power of workers depends on the level of unemployment as well as the presence of remunerative non-capitalist sources of livelihood. In the conditions of the Indian labour market, such power is almost entirely absent for unskilled workers. The other form of structural power emerges in the context of integrated production systems where localized resistance by labour (strikes, 'work to rule', etc.) is transmitted throughout the entire production chain. Associational power, on the other hand, originates in the formation of collective organizations of workers, such as trade unions and political parties.

Working-class power in the formal sector in India has historically taken the form of workplace structural power, usually backed by trade unions and political parties. Globalization has weakened this form of working-class power by informalization, though Silver (2003) argues that new deployments of working-class associational power are possible to counter this trend. Associational power has to be enhanced in order to make up for the loss of structural power. Textile workers, for example, 'have quite limited structural power, since production can be easily rerouted, and have therefore had to compensate by strengthening their associational power' (Webster et al., 2008: 11–12). Silver argues that such strengthening of associational power depends on community-based organization and involves new tactics of mobilization.

Webster et al. (2008: 12–13) extend Silver's argument by introducing the concepts of *symbolic* power and *logistical* power which are forms of associational and structural power respectively. Symbolic power 'draws its strength from taking moral claims in the workplace and articulating them as general social claims'. Logistical power is a kind of structural power that 'takes matters out of the workplace and onto the landscape where workplaces are located' by blocking transportation (roads) and communication (internet) lines essential to production. Both symbolic power and logistical power take resistance to capital outside the capital–labour relation itself and into the public domain (Fine, 2006).

We argue, however, that this deployment of the concepts of symbolic and logistical power revolves around *exploitation* of labour by capital. It is the articulation in the public domain of legitimate claims of the wage-labourer on the fruits of his or her labour – the moral right of the worker to the wealth produced by labour and appropriated by capital. Informalization of wage-labour creates conditions for an increase in the degree of exploitation of labour by enabling greater appropriation or extraction of surplus value from the wage-worker by the capitalist. It is this brazen exploitation that calls forth the deployment of symbolic and logistical power by the working class.

The informal petty producers, on the other hand, contest capital from outside. They are always on the boundary, pushing it back as they struggle to close the frontiers against encroaching capital. The legitimate claim of capital to valorize and reproduce itself – and it can do so only by 'accumulation by dispossession' (Harvey, 2005) – comes into conflict with the legitimate claim of petty producers to reproduce their subsistence. Here, two different economic systems are pitted against each other, each taking to the broader society its own moral claims – the capitalist economy representing itself as the vehicle of progress and development and the petty producers championing the inalienable right to survival.

Structural power of excluded labour emanates from its ability to encroach on the domain of capital; 'squatting' becomes the new form of resistance. Squatting has traditionally been the tactic resorted to by the urban poor for reproduction of their life processes. In an age when the life process and the labour process get so intricately enmeshed for a growing part of the labouring population, squatting provides the compelling image of resistance to capital. As capital invades, the dispossessed fight back through silent encroachment on property. Such encroachments may take the form of 'colonization' of public and private land by the migrants to the city and piracy of copyrights and trademarks by street vendors, etc. Associational power is raised to the level of entire communities – conjunctural or lasting – forged in opposition to capital and engaged in violent and periodic uprisings against eviction and dispossession. Such collective actions by 'informal' communities involve mobilizations which are defensive (holding on to the 'colonies') as well as aggressive (seeking redistribution of society's resources to improve life in the informal communities). Symbolic power in this case stems from pitting the 'ethics of the local' against the profit-calculus of global capital (Basu, 2007) and logistical power is exercised by taking the fight to the streets where the day-to-day life of the entire society is reproduced.

7. Conclusion

In this chapter, we have made an attempt to mark a new location of labour – independent petty production based on family labour and organized within the household. We do not deny other locations of labour that are emerging (the 'homeworkers' in the putting-out system of the global or domestic circuits of capital) or continue to be important (the regular as well as the casual wage-labour force). Instead, we offer a new topographical account of the labour force. New locations constitute new relations between labour and capital. Thus, while capital has always exploited wage-workers by appropriating surplus value from them, globalized capital raises exploitation to a higher degree by casualization of the wage-labour force. At the same time, informalization within circuits of capital – global as well as domestic – allows capital to extract surplus from petty producers within the putting-out system. Yet, in all of these relations, capital relates to labour as a source of surplus value or profit. The relation we emphasize and which defines the new location of labour is one in which the labourer is no longer a source of surplus, but rather the unwanted possessor or occupier of economic resources from which he or she must be divorced in order to free those resources for use in the circuit of capital. This process of dispossession without proletarianization or exploitation is what we refer to as exclusion. It is this picture of the labour force that presents a real problem for labour activism. The traditional contradiction between wage-labour and capital is overshadowed by the contradiction between capital and surplus labour force. Marxist class politics – traditionally focused on exploitation of wage-labour – must reinvent itself to address the other great political movement shaping up around the exclusion of labour.

The radical mobilizations against capitalist globalization that we have been witnessing all over the world – in the streets of Seattle, Prague, Washington, Genoa and elsewhere, the Zapatista movement in Mexico down to peasant resistance in Singur and Nandigram – are all largely mobilizations against dispossession and loss of livelihood rather than against exploitation by capital. In order to locate the agents of such mobilization, we have identified the informal petty producers' economy as a Chayanovian outside of capital. At the same time, we understand that the sociology and anthropology of the urban informal petty producer is different from that of traditional peasants. Thus, contemporary politics of the informals is shaped outside the narrative of transition.

Traditionally, post-colonial politics has been dominated by questions such as: What kind of class configurations are acting as the obstacle on the way to a full-scale capitalist transformation? Is there a national bourgeoisie capable of resisting imperialist domination and ushering in a national capitalist development? If the bourgeoisie is inadequate for that task, could an alliance of the working class and peasantry bring about a people's democratic revolution? The *politics of transition* was defined around these questions. This is still the dominant political language in which contemporary struggles are articulated. Take, for example, the case of Singur and Nandigram in West Bengal where the government's attempts to acquire agricultural land for proposed special economic zones (SEZs) and modern factories have caused intense political and social unrest. The ruling and the opposition parties have both engaged in a representation of the conflict as one between the traditional peasant economy and the capitalist economy. According to the ruling party, capitalist industrialization will transform the impoverished peasant economy, paving the way to an advanced and dynamic mode of production. On the other hand, for the opposition, the peasant community must resist alienation of its land. The arguments remind one of the Lenin–Narodnik debate.

In our understanding, the sociology of contemporary peasants in Singur and Nandigram is very different from that of nineteenth-century insurgent peasants in British India. What is at play here is not the political conflict over the process of transition from one mode of production to a higher one. Rather, at the heart of the conflict lies the recognition of the *impossibility* of transition itself – a recognition of the process of dispossession without proletarianization that leaves a majority of the labouring population outside the dynamics of the great transformation. The resistance in Singur drew much of its strength from the presence in the mobilization not only of landless agricultural labourers who were left out of the proposed compensation package but more importantly of people who, although without any ownership right, derived their livelihood from the acquired land in various forms of non-farm employment. To describe it merely as peasant resistance against big capital is misleading for such a description hides the fact that it is also the resistance of excluded labour, located outside the circuit of capital, defending subsistence-driven production activities against capitalist encroachment. In this sense, there is a thread of continuity running through the Dharavi resistance, the petty retailers' fight against department stores and shopping malls and the rural resistance in Singur and Nandigram.

The forces of globalization have brought about large changes in the structure of the production economy, resulting in the emergence of multiple locations of labour and, therefore, a plurality of labour–capital contradictions. While globalization has weakened the traditional forms of working-class power within the capitalist relations of production, in a double movement it has opened up new terrains of labour activism where labour, from its newly emergent locations, can confront capital from outside. The dismay over the loss of the traditional forms of labour activism should not be allowed to overshadow the potential of these new forms of resistance against capital.

Notes

1. In the pre-globalization era, Fordist capital–labour relations prevailed in developed economies and in certain 'enclaves' in developing economies, e.g. state enterprises and large corporate enterprises.
2. 'Moreover, the development of capitalist production makes it constantly necessary to keep increasing the amount of the capital laid out in a given industrial undertaking, and competition makes the immanent laws of capitalist production to be felt by each individual capitalist, as *external coercive laws*. It compels him to keep constantly expanding his capital, in order to preserve it, but extend it he cannot, except by means of progressive accumulation' (Marx, 1983: 555, my emphasis).
3. There is heterogeneity within the class of farmers. Indian agriculture is mainly a farmers' economy, with limited presence of large-scale capitalist farming. Medium and large farmers (with more than 2 hectares of land) are net employers of labour, while marginal (0.4–1 hectare of land) and small farmers (1–2 hectares of land) – constituting 86 per cent of the farmers – are subsistence farmers who often have to resort to wage-employment to supplement their income from land. In our understanding, small and marginal farmers truly constitute the self-exploitative peasant economy of India.
4. Farmers constituted 60.1 per cent of the agricultural workforce in 1993–1994, 57.8 per cent in 1999–2000 and 64.2 per cent in 2004–5 (NCEUS, 2007).
5. Employment and Unemployment Scenario in India, Directorate General of Employment and Training, Ministry of Labour, Government of India, http:// dget.nic.in/dex/empscenario.pdf.
6. Only 8 per cent of the OAEs had business fixed investment over 1 lakh and 37 per cent had average value of fixed assets less than Rs 5,000. Sixty per cent of urban informal OAEs did not hire any fixed assets in 1999–2000. Thus most of the non-agricultural OAEs mirror the scale of operation of small and marginal farmers in agriculture.
7. The average gross value-added per worker in the rural non-farm OAEs was Rs 1,167 in 1999–2000. Thus rural non-farm self-employment generated incomes that lie between that of marginal and small farmers.
8. 'Case studies all over the world have documented the inappropriateness of high-rise resettlement projects in poor areas. The social and economic networks which the poor rely on for subsistence can hardly be sustained in high-rise structures. These high-rise projects are not appropriate for home-based economic activities, which play a major role in Dharavi. The least that can be done in this redevelopment plan is to refurbish the work places of the existing industries within the residential areas and remodel this project by providing low-rise high-density row housing for existing families engaged in home-based occupations. This way, each house will have a ground floor and an additional story, as well as a terrace and a courtyard which can be used for these home-based business activities' (Apte, 2008).

References

Apte, P. (2008) *Dharavi: India's Model Slum*, http://www.planetizen.com/node/35269, accessed 12 March 2009.
Basu, P. K. (2007) 'The Politics of Land Grab', *Economic and Political Weekly*, 42, 14: 1281–7.

Chatterji, R. (2005) 'Plans, Habitation and Slum Redevelopment: the Production of Community in Dharavi, Mumbai', *Contributions to Indian Sociology*, 39: 197–218.

Chayanov, A. V. (1987) *The Theory of Peasant Economy*, New Delhi: Oxford University Press.

Davis, M. (2004) 'The Planet of Slums', *New Left Review*, 26 (March–April): 5–34.

Fine, J. (2006) *Workers Centres: Organizing Communities at the Edge of the Dream*, London: ILR Press.

Harvey, D. (2005) *The New Imperialism*, New York: Oxford University Press.

Marx, K. (1983) *Capital*, Vol. I, Moscow: Progress Publishers.

Menon, M. (2008) 'Supreme Court Order Cheers Dharavi Residents', *The Hindu*, 6 April 2008, Internet edition, accessed 12 March 2009, http://www.hindu.com/2008/04/06/stories/2008040659271100.htm

Ministry of Finance (2008) *Economic Survey 2007–2008*, New Delhi: Government of India.

National Commission for Enterprises in the Unorganized Sector (NCEUS) (2007) *Report on Conditions of Work and Promotion of Livelihoods in the Unorganized Sector*, August, New Delhi, Government of India.

NSSO (2001) 'Informal Sector in India: Salient Features: Employment–Unemployment Situation in India 1999–2000', 55th Round, Report No. 459(55/2.0/2), Ministry of Statistics and Programme Implementation, New Delhi, Government of India.

NSSO (2006) 'Employment–Unemployment Situation in India 2004–2005', 61st Round, Report No. 515(61/10/1), Part I, Ministry of Statistics and Programme Implementation, New Delhi, Government of India.

Nun, J. (2000) 'The End of Work and the Marginal Mass Thesis', *Latin American Perspectives*, 27, 1: 6–32.

Quijano, A. and Westwell, P. (1983) 'Imperialism and Marginality in Latin America', *Latin American Perspectives*, 10, 2–3: 76–85.

Ramachandran, S. (2008) 'Dharavi: Rising to a Foggy Dawn', http://dayafterindia.com/may208/states1.html, accessed 12 March 2009.

Sanyal, K. (2007) *Rethinking Capitalist Development: Primitive Accumulation, Governmentality and Post-Colonial Capitalism*, New Delhi: Routledge.

Silver, B. (2003) *Forces of Labour: Workers' Movements and Globalization Since 1870*, Cambridge: Cambridge University Press.

UN-Habitat (2003) *The Challenge of the Slums: Global Report on Human Settlements 2003*, London: United Nations Human Settlements Programme.

Webster, E., Lambert, R. and Bezuidenhout, A. (2008) *Grounding Globalization: Labour in the Age of Insecurity*, Oxford: Blackwell Publishers.

Wright, E. O. (2000) 'Working-Class Power, Capitalist-Class Interests, and Class Compromise', *American Journal of Sociology*, 105, 4 (January): 957–1002.

9
'Class' in Industrial Disputes: Case Studies from Bangalore

Supriya RoyChowdhury

1. Introduction: the relevance of industrial conflict

The decline of labour activism has been noted as a global phenomenon. One important reason for this decline has been said to be the change in the *structure* of labour. First, new labour practices – outsourcing and contract work – have meant that relatively smaller numbers of workers are now concentrated in single locations, in Fordist, assembly-line production centres. Secondly, as manufacturing units become capital intensive, and high technology driven, large numbers of semi-skilled or unskilled workers are replaced by a small, skilled workforce, frequently with highly specialized, individualized functions, and individual, rather than collective pay scales and benefits: all of this takes away the teeth of collective action within the factory in particular and in the workforce in general. Thus the classical management–labour conflict may no longer be so significant. Finally, as is well known, there has occurred a rapid expansion of the informal sector, and in the numbers of those who are self-employed, or employed in small and unregulated enterprises. In this domain industrial dispute has few overt or political manifestations. It is in this sense that industrial conflict is no longer seen to be a key to understanding political or social dynamics.

Have industrial conflicts disappeared? If not, what are the modalities through which they appear, and what is conveyed by the dynamics of industrial conflicts as they appear today? I suggest in this chapter that the decline of the political significance of industrial conflicts is less a result of the structural changes in management–labour relations, as is commonly thought, and more the result of the *politics* of labour. The nature of industrial relations reveals in fact that disputes within industry continue to be defined by classical management/capital–labour conflicts. Thus while labour practices may have changed to some extent in the directions indicated above, industrial disputes continue to occur around issues which have historically defined management–labour conflicts: over wages, hours of work, production targets and so on, which are underpinned by the structural relations of capitalist production where the margin of profit is determined by the extraction of surplus value. It is not so much that the structure of labour has changed so as to preclude labour politics; rather, in the current context, changes in employment practices wrought by globalization and technological advancements coexist with the enduring character of the labour–capital opposition in capitalist production. Though industrial relations are apparently different from the classical labour–capital conflict, more searching examination reveals that industrial relations continue to be defined by the capital/management–labour opposition.

If industrial relations do not translate into industrial conflicts, however, and are of declining social and political significance, we may well be looking at a situation where the incompatibilities of (globalizing) capitalism with the interests of the working classes have not generated an *appropriate agency and politics*. Precisely for these reasons it may be all the more important to turn our attention to the kinds of conflicts, contradictions and tensions that in fact characterize the industrial scenario. This may enable us to look at the gaps between the spaces in which industrial conflicts are occurring, and the dynamics of their articulation in the political arena.

Bangalore is a city that typifies rapid industrial transformation in a globalizing context. While a large public sector marked the city's development from the 1950s up until the 1980s, the city has seen the decline of this sector (Rajeev and DasGupta, 2003) and its gradual replacement with a pattern of industrial development driven by private capital, both domestic and international. This development has been symbolized by technologically cutting-edge sectors such as information technology (IT) and biotechnology (BT), and a large multinational presence in areas such as automobiles, on the one hand, and labour-intensive, export-oriented sectors such as ready-made garments, on the other, where a rapidly expanding number of domestic firms produce for international retailers.

What has been the impact of this development on industrial relations? The highly skilled and highly paid employees of the so-called knowledge industry – IT and BT – are removed from the world of unionization. In these sectors 'human resource development' has replaced 'industrial relations'. The city's industrial workers continue to be employed in the older industrial firms – public as well as private – in new multinational companies, in the rapidly expanding export sectors, as well as in the small-scale industry sector. In these sectors, employment practices vary, but the absence of unionized activism, and of collective bargaining processes, is a shared feature in different spheres of employment. Thus, within the formal sector itself, a certain rewriting of employment relations has taken place as a non-permanent (contractual) workforce exists alongside the steadily shrinking permanent workforce (RoyChowdhury, 2005a). Similarly, for the large numbers who work in the small-scale industries sector, the rapid decline of small enterprises, resulting in thousands of closures and loss of jobs, has happened in a context where there has been little recourse to union activities to ensure payment of compensation, social security and so on (Gayathri, 2002). Finally, to take the example of the newly emerging export sectors, Bangalore's nearly four lakh (400,000) women workers are employed in the ready-made garment sector where unionization is not permitted by employers (RoyChowdhury, 2005b).

Given this range, the city offers a meaningful context in which to address the questions raised at the outset in this chapter: what are the specific modalities through which industrial conflicts are articulated, and what is the impact of these modalities on the scale and significance of industrial conflicts? Section 2 fleshes out the argument outlined above that it is the politics of industrial disputes, rather than the structure of labour, that provides the clue to understanding the declining significance of industrial conflicts, both in the formal and informal sectors. Section 3 provides a brief overview of case studies of industrial disputes in five large private sector companies in Bangalore; section 4 attempts to place the issue of trade union power in the context of the history of trade union activism in the city; and section 5, in conclusion, touches upon certain theoretical dimensions of the questions raised earlier in the chapter.

2. The modalities of industrial conflicts

The spaces in which industrial disputes occur span the emerging export sectors as well as older industrial establishments. In the ready-made garments (RMG) sector, a large majority of firms in Bangalore produce almost exclusively for export. The relationship between global capital and domestic producers in this rapidly growing sector is determined by the availability of relatively cheap, non-unionized labour.

In Bangalore, the majority of workers in this industry are women. Employers do not allow the presence of unions within factory gates.

Recent unionization, initiated by outsiders, rather than by workers, has been confined to activities outside the factory. The methods of struggle are not marked by workers' assertive collective action (strikes), but more in the form of lobbying with multinational companies, which are buyers of apparel manufactured by this sector, to enforce implementation of labour codes by local manufacturers. The RMG sector, therefore – marked by the newness of fledgling unionization, non-traditional methods of activism, and the seeming apathy of governments towards regulation of wages and working conditions – falls in the grey area between the formal and the informal sectors. This political-institutional framework has set definite limits to union activism in the sector.

In the 'formal' manufacturing sector, political-institutional constraints upon union activities are highlighted even further. The cases of industrial disputes reviewed below involve firms in the formal manufacturing sector. The disputes were over issues of work and wage, productivity levels, retrenchment and layoffs, the legitimacy of strikes, and the status of *badli* ('substitute') workers. These issues relate to typical capital–labour conflicts, and at the same time obviously emerge from new currents in the broader political economy – changing economic policies and structures – which affect labour closely. While this sector has historically been unionized, the industrial disputes reviewed here suggest a pattern of declining bargaining leverage of labour vis-à-vis management. In situations of conflict, worker morale is low, the government's position ranges from neutral to unsympathetic, and managements are able to tilt the balance in their own favour. What is highlighted is that workers and unions have few *political resources* with which to influence government decisions.

The question of political resources is a function of the connectedness (or otherwise) of workers' issues to two levels. The first level relates to the links between trade unions and political parties. The turn towards economic liberalization and private sector-driven development has led to a certain loss of interest in the working class, and in worker-related issues, as far as political parties – across the left/centre-left spectrum – are concerned. This has to an extent led to the disappearance of a political/ideological anchoring for workers' movements.

Secondly, within the organized working class, there is now a trend towards independent, firm-based unions, not connected to central trade union federations. Even where unions are associated with the mainstream trade unions, these are seen to be concerned exclusively with firm level issues, which typically arise within the factory or the shopfloor, and not with broader issues related to wages and conditions of work. They thus typically embody a specific problem-solving orientation, rather than an ideological or political agenda. Firm level issues are taken up on an ad hoc basis, as and when they come up, lacking the conceptual/political anchoring from which these local issues might have been connected with broader policy issues.

The case studies presented below highlight this emerging trend wherein industrial disputes are isolated from the mainstream of political and policy context, both in terms of the conceptualization of the issues and because disputes occur as stand-alone events, unconnected to, and having little impact upon, related issues and constituencies. Thus, while the issues generating industrial disputes are about the structural opposition between the interests of labour and capital, the dynamics of the disputes are not articulated within this broader framework.

3. Industrial disputes in Bangalore: 1998–2003

This section reviews industrial disputes in five large-scale private sector units in different sectors of manufacturing. These companies are: Larsen and Toubro, Guest Keen Williams, WIDIA India Ltd., Kirloskar Electric and Binny Textiles. The first three are multinational companies, while the latter two are Indian firms. In the first three companies, industrial conflict manifested itself in the form of strikes. In the last two, worker–management conflict was referred to the Labour Commissioner's office and thereafter to the Labour Tribunal, for adjudication. The selected enterprises thus provide a variation in products, in ownership and in the modalities of conflict.

3.1 Larsen and Toubro Komatsu Ltd.[1]

Larsen and Toubro is an old and established engineering company, the head office being located in Mumbai. The annual turnover of the company is over Rs 250 crores (US$54 million at 2009 exchange rates). The Bangalore unit, set up in 1975, began a collaboration with Komatsu of Japan in 1997. The Bangalore unit has witnessed three major strikes, the first in 1994, lasting 120 days, the second in 1997, lasting 99 days, and more recently in 2001–2, lasting 87 days. Here the focus is on the 1997 and 2001–2 strikes as these took place over related issues.

A fresh wage agreement had been signed in 1995 providing for a wage increase as well as an increase in productivity target. However, following the settlement, a large number of workers felt that the new productivity target was too harsh. As a result of agitation, management dismissed four workmen and thirteen were suspended. At this time, the All India

Trade Union Congress (AITUC) – associated with the Communist Party of India – was replaced by the Centre of Indian Trade Unions (CITU) – associated with the Communist Party of India (Marxist) – in the Union elections. CITU adopted a more aggressive style of functioning, particularly over the matter of suspensions. A strike was announced and continued for 99 days. The government of Karnataka finally banned the strike and referred the suspensions to the Labour Tribunal. Subsequently, in 1998, the Tribunal ordered that the suspended employees should be reinstated. But management took the matter to the High Court, where the case is still pending while the thirteen employees remain suspended.

Given the impasse over the issue of suspensions, the relationship between the management and the CITU-led union became extremely bitter. In the meantime, a new charter of demands for wage increase had been placed. But management refused to negotiate a wage rise, unless there was a 50 per cent rise in productivity. Workers were not prepared to accept such a productivity increase. As negotiations failed, a strike was declared (July–December 2001). After several hearings, the government banned the strike, and workers returned to work.

With the subsequent return of the AITUC, union–management relations became smoother, and workers agreed to a rise in the production target. In December 2002, a new settlement was reached with 40 per cent rise in productivity. It is important to note the following two points: first, the suspension orders – that had, in fact, been the central issue in the earlier strike – remained unrevoked. Secondly, the dispute was settled to the advantage of the management, and with the mediation of the AITUC which in a way played into the hands of the management by not demanding the reinstatement of the suspended workers, and by agreeing to a substantial increase in the productivity target.

In the perception of many workers, the advent of Komatsu led to a marked change in the company's approach towards labour. There emerged a clearly stated stand on the need to reduce the workforce. In August 2002 a Voluntary Retirement Scheme (VRS) was announced. Between 2002 and 2003, 250 workers took the VRS. However, the implementation of the VRS is itself taking place against the backdrop of a serious contestation between management, workers and the unions. The CITU, although in principle opposed to the VRS, had laid down the condition that the minimum package should be Rs 7 lakhs and that for skilled workers it should be 12 lakhs. The AITUC, on the other hand, decided to go along with the management's proposal of two and a half months' basic pay plus Dearness Allowance for every completed year of service, with a maximum limit of Rs 5.5 lakhs. While the CITU's claims regarding the VRS have been ignored, this was possible because of the split in the workforce between the two unions, although a large number of workers are in fact extremely dissatisfied with the terms and conditions of the VRS that have been offered.

This discontent came to the surface particularly in the discourse of workers who owed their allegiance to the CITU-led union. Many felt that a strategy of subtle coercion had been adopted in order to force employees to opt for the VRS; a large number of workers said that a general environment of intimidation had been created, wherein any kind of union activism was potentially punishable. In this context of intimidation, the VRS was sought to be further implemented by a combination of force and persuasion. Behind the calm that appeared to have been restored in the industrial relations climate in Larsen and Toubro, and the relative ease with which the latest dispute was settled, there was, therefore, a sub-narrative of incipient and undirected labour discontent.

3.2 Kirloskar Electric Company[2]

Kirloskar has manufactured AC motors, AC generators, DC motors, and traction motor transformers for 53 years. There is a total of 1,300 employees, of whom 720 are blue-collar workers. From 1997–8, the company experienced a serious downturn in market share and profits. From 1998–99 to 2000–1, there was a 30 per cent net drop in sales. The company's losses rose from Rs 27 crores ($5.8 million) in 1998–9, to Rs 72 crores ($15.5 million) in 2000–1. In a written memorandum submitted to the government of Karnataka (dated 25 June 2001), the management of Kirloskar sought permission to lay off 460 employees in Shop 2 of their establishment, on grounds of increased competition and declining sales and orders which meant that the company was facing a financial crisis, marked by unsold stocks and inability to buy raw materials and to provide work.[3]

The Kirloskar Employees Association, independent, but with strong links to the CITU, contended before the Labour Commissioner that the management intended to get the same work done by outside subcontractors and had also floated another company for manufacturing motors and generators. The government of Karnataka took a decision to refuse permission for layoff. This decision was taken for the following reasons: the company had failed to provide any evidence of piled-up stocks or of declining orders, although they had made claims about both. The company was using the services of nineteen contractors.

Additionally, the company had set up another company in the name of Dinky Toyo Power Systems and had been shifting both machines and managerial personnel to that company. In view of these considerations the government considered that the layoffs could not be justified.[4]

To all appearances this was a verdict that went in favour of the union. However, this case needs to be seen in the context of the Kirloskar company's broader restructuring efforts in the recent past and its impact upon workers. The blue-collar strength has been brought down from 2,158 in 1998 to 720 at the present time through the VRS, and by a sustained policy of not filling up superannuated positions. The proposed layoffs were in a way a continuation of this policy of systematic downsizing. The company has sold off eight acres to a consumer goods retail store called Metro for Rs 250 crores. The immediate plan is to sell off the present land and premises of the company and to relocate to a location in Bangalore Rural. This will in many ways address the problem of labour cost, as a large number of employees will take the VRS rather than relocate, and labour costs will be much lower in the rural areas than they are in a prime location in the city. The broader implications of Kirloskar's restructuring are discussed in section 4 below.

3.3 WIDIA India Ltd.[5]

WIDIA India Ltd. was established by the TVS group of Madras, with a German collaborator, for the production of machine tools, in 1964. In 2002, the company's Bangalore unit was completely taken over by an American company (Kenne Metal Inc.). The new management, almost immediately after taking over, introduced a VRS scheme and between September 2002 and December 2003, the workforce was reduced from 855 to 600.

The present case study is of a strike called by the WIDIA India Employees Association on 21 January 2004. The dispute between workers and management was over the manner of sharing of improved profits in recent years. According to section 36 of a memorandum of understanding (MOU) signed in January 2003, there would be a performance review for the fiscal year ending June 2003, and improvements made in profitability would be accordingly translated in terms of additional payment to the workers. According to the union, there had been a quantum improvement in profits by Rs 19,300,000 and one-third of this, Rs 6,433,333 should be paid to the Bangalore plant employees. The management, on the other hand, used the percentage of the wage cost of the Bangalore plant employees to the total personnel cost of the company as a basis to determine the share of the Bangalore plant employees. The amount which the management came up with was Rs 2,622,870.

A strike was called on 2 January 2004, generating increasing bitterness in employee–management relations. At the inception of the strike, the management made it clear that at any point in time the workmen in continuous operations should not strike. Ultimately, however, they joined the strike on 18 January 2004. A suspension order was taken on account of physical violence between two union office bearers. The union decided to refer this matter to the Labour Commissioner's office for adjudication.

In the eyes of the management the strike was necessarily an illegal instrument of action. In a letter dated 17 January 2004, the management communicated the matter to the union in the following terms: 'You have threatened that workmen in continuous process would join the strike on 4/1/04 and 10/1/04. You are aware that there exists a settlement under which the workmen have agreed that workmen in continuous operations and in essential services would not strike work even when other workmen strike.' The strike was thus deemed illegal as per the terms of the Certified Standing Orders of the company. 'Management will make permanent and alternate arrangements resulting in equally permanent elimination of these jobs in workmen category.'[6]

The posture of the management highlighted that traditional means of collective bargaining are being rejected by management. This, in itself, is a serious challenge to the democratic rights of workers. In this particular case, not only were the workers compelled to call off the strike, but their major demands of revocation of the suspension order and reviewing the payments on increased profits remained unfulfilled.

3.4 Guest Keen Williams (GKW)[7]

GKW has two divisions located in Bangalore: Sankey Electrical Stampings Division and Head Treated Product Division. The unit had earlier employed 1,300 workmen. Over time, many manufacturers of electrical motors started in-house production units for electrical stampings to meet their requirements. Several small units have also sprung up, cutting GKW's market. The Bangalore unit has downsized, by terminating the services of 245 workmen.

In 1997–8, the company incurred a loss of Rs 30 crores ($6.5 million). This brought accumulated losses to Rs. 100 crores ($21.6 million), and the net worth of the company became negative. The Board for Industrial and Finance Restructuring (BIFR) was approached at this time.

A new wage settlement came up for consideration in October 1997. On the intervention of the Labour Commissioner's office, an interim settlement was signed in March 1999. As per the settlement, the management was required to pay Rs 500 per month as special incentive, subject to a final judgement. However, in the following months, management–union relations deteriorated sharply. The GKW Nowkara Sangha, the only union in the company, perceived this period as one where management, instead of going in for negotiations for a future settlement, increasingly resorted to strategies of worker victimization.

In May 1999, management cut wages and stopped paying the interim relief of Rs 500 per month, on grounds that the workers had violated the terms of the March settlement. The union decided to go on an indefinite strike from July 1999. The management made several attempts to break the strike, but finally filed an application before the government seeking permission for closure of the Bangalore plant under section 25-O of the Industrial Disputes Act 1947. The government rejected the application, and gave an order (dated 17 December 1999) to the effect that wages as well as the interim allowance must be paid. The government prohibited the strike on 13 January 2000. The strike was called off on 17 January 2000.

However, by a strange twist, when the workers reported for work, the management had locked the gate. Workers were exempted from work until further notice. The workers had not been paid since May 1999, contrary to orders passed by the government. Thus the management had violated the orders of the government under section 25-O of the Industrial Disputes Act. The union approached the Labour Commissioner with a request for recovery of wages. The Labour Commissioner ordered payment of arrears to workers. In response, the management filed a Writ Petition before the High Court challenging the Labour Commissioner's order. The High Court granted a stay on this order.

The management stated that its reason for seeking closure was that the strike had led to the loss of the customer base, and as such, the company was unable to provide work any longer as there were no orders. The union maintained, first, that workers were fully within their rights to resort to a strike, and at the same time, it was emphasized that the strike had been called off as soon as the government had prohibited it. As such, the workers, according to the union presentation, were entirely on the right side of the law. Secondly, the union maintained that the management's decision regarding refusal to provide work amounted to an illegal closure. If indeed this cannot be termed closure, then it had to be termed lock-out or layoff. At present, the BIFR report is awaited, and as such there has been no resolution of the workers' dismissal from work and of their pending wage payment.

3.5 Binny Textiles[8]

Binny Textiles has been a part of the general decline that has struck many firms in the textile sector. Incurring losses of several crores, the company has been declared 'sick' by the BIFR. While the production of cotton textiles is no longer financially feasible, the company is attempting to stay afloat by shifting its operations to spinning and other related activities.

The company union, the Binny Karmikara Sangha, stated in its application (of 11 December 1999) to the Labour Commissioner's office that the management of Binny Ltd. had declared an illegal layoff of 35 *badli* workmen from March 1998 on account of scarcity of raw materials. The company employs more than 100 workmen and therefore falls within the framework of the Industrial Disputes Act, making it mandatory for it to seek government permission for layoff. Hence its action is a violation of section 25-M of the Industrial Disputes Act. Accordingly the workers are entitled to all their benefits as if they had not been laid off. They thus claimed their wages for the period from May 1998 to January 1999, as well as layoff compensation for the 35 *badli* workmen.

The management claimed that the failure to provide employment for financial reasons cannot be deemed to be layoff. Moreover, *badli* workers cannot demand work as a matter of right. *Badli* workers are given work as and when it is available, or when permanent workers are unavailable. The management also held that the concerned *badli* workmen had been employed in carding, and cotton weaving. These departments had been closed down in April 1998 on the grounds of non-viability. Therefore, in order to reduce the workforce, a settlement had been reached in August 1998 on reduction of workforce through a VRS. Under this scheme, 619 permanent workers had opted for retirement.

When the matter came up before the Labour Commissioner's office, the Commissioner expressed the opinion that the company management had not produced a balance sheet and other documents to prove the financial crisis. It was also pointed out that a VRS had been introduced for the benefit of regular workers. Thus it appeared that the management was attempting to retrench only *badli* workers without paying them severance compensation. The attempt to get rid of *badli* workers could therefore be termed a layoff. As no permission was given by the government for laying off, this was an infringement of section 25-A of the Industrial Disputes Act.

Secondly, the government further held that the right to demand work by *badli* workers must be seen in the context of the evolution of the *badli* system and of the legal framework surrounding it. Under section 25-C of the Industrial Disputes Act, a *badli* worker who completes 240 days of service on an average in the preceding twelve months would cease to be a *badli*. He or she will acquire the status of a permanent worker, to the extent of being able to claim layoff benefits on par with permanent workers.

The case was heard on 10 and 24 April 2003. The management held that whether or not a worker had completed 240 days of service should be decided by the Labour Court. The Court, however, held that the management had not submitted the muster roll. On 21 April 2003, the government ordered that the claims of the *badli* workers were justified and that the amount should be recovered by the Deputy Commissioner, Bangalore Urban, as land revenue arrears, and paid to the workers. However, the order has not been implemented until now.

4. Industrial conflicts and trade union power

The industrial disputes reviewed above show a certain pattern. First, a remarkable feature in each of the case studies is that the focus issue in a given industrial dispute was perceived as a problem that was specific to the company, and could be resolved within that framework. *What did not take place was the anchoring of a worker-related issue, or an industrial dispute, in the wider context of economic policy.*

For example, in the case of Binny Textiles, management's intention to get rid of *badli* workers without payment of compensation fits into the logic of the present economic framework where there is a clear bias towards casualizing the workforce in order to reduce employers' commitments to workers. A large number of contract workers in Karnataka are similarly affected by the absence of job security and the absence of compensation or other social security provisions.[9] However, union leaders articulated the problem as specific to the firm, limited in space and time, and were unable to forge broader networks with similarly placed workers, affected by similar issues.

In the dispute at Guest Keen Williams, the company had already been running with heavy losses for several years and a strike created a situation that led to the closure of the company, and loss of workers' livelihoods. The question posed by situations such as the one in GKW is not whether the state should take over companies in order to preserve employment; but, rather, that of what should be the state's responsibility towards workers in terms of indirect income (social security, public health, education and so on) in a situation of rapid restructuring. Unfortunately, trade unions, which are struggling for wage increases or similar issues, have not addressed themselves to the broader question of worker welfare in a marketizing economy where some amount of dislocation is inevitable.

In the case of Kirloskar, the attempt of the company to retrench a few hundred workers was thwarted. However, the dispute at Kirloskar must be seen in the context of the larger programme of restructuring that the company was undertaking at the time, and through which substantial downsizing had already occurred. The company's plans for physical relocation from the heart of Bangalore to a semi-rural location[10] raise several issues in this context. The selling of land owned by private companies in order to bail themselves out of financial crises has typically been a contentious issue of industrial relations.[11] In most cases, such companies have been closed, spelling great hardship for workers. On the other hand, the selling of land generated huge profits to owners who were not under any obligation to use this for reinvestment into the company or for worker compensation. In the case of Kirloskar, however, the selling of the property in which the company is currently located is proceeding without any major challenge from the workforce. Secondly, Kirloskar has begun its restructuring effort by selling a portion of its land to a foreign trading company, the Metro. The agitation against Metro has emerged mainly from local traders, couched in an anti-liberalization position against multinationals perceived as threatening the interests of Indian business and trade.

The selling off of Kirloskar land to Metro can in fact be seen as a situation where the admission of the multinational into an urban space embodies a direct threat not only to local traders but also to thousands of workers who had earlier earned their livelihoods within that space. The feeling amongst a large section of the workers is that this is a process of indirect layoff, as most workers would not be willing to move from their nearby homes to a far-off place of work, where the company would relocate. Finally, one of the major factors in relocation appears to be the possibility of paying lower wages in rural or semi-rural locations. All of these point to the consideration that the process of restructuring in Kirloskar is part of certain tendencies in the larger political economy, whether it is the advent of multinationals into the urban land market, or the casualization of labour.

However, the union's representations to the government remained confined to the narrow question of the possible retrenchment of 464 workers. There was virtually no attempt to link this issue substantively to the broader economic policy environment wherein selling off of land to multinationals and casualization of labour are occurring as part of the larger process of restructuring.

The struggle of industrial workers is now mostly framed within the paradigm of firm-based activities. What is absent is both a movement character in the activities of trade unions, and a broad class-based character in workers' struggles. Additionally, there is a disconnect from central trade union organizations and from political parties. The character of the trade union movement, as outlined above, to an extent underlies the absence of class activism in workers' struggles.

A certain amount of opaqueness in industrial workers' perspectives, which are limited to purely economic and firm-based issues (economism), is not entirely puzzling. Nevertheless, in the present context, an obvious question would be, what factors account for the inability of trade unions to place the interests of their constituencies within a broader political/policy paradigm?

A more specific question here of course is that of the ineffectiveness of union activities, which is highlighted in the industrial disputes reviewed in this chapter. The question is, of course, the extent to which this is a new phenomenon. Trade unionism in Karnataka has not been associated with the kind of militancy that has characterized union activities in places like West Bengal and Kerala, where the backbone of union activism was shaped by their close alliance with leftist parties. While the CITU (affiliated to the CPI-M) has had some presence in Karnataka, the defiant edge of working-class politics has been more or less absent here.[12] Janaki Nair's work has documented, for example, that given the predominance of the public sector in Bangalore, the city's workforce has been more middle class than proletarian in nature, physically removed from the city (located in self-contained public sector campus/colony environments), and that its defining culture has been one of enhanced consumption rather than one deriving from working-class movements. Unionism in the private sector has been shaped by this broader character of unionism in the city.

On the other hand, the invisibility of workers could be seen as only part of the story. Indeed there have been moments in the history of workers in the city that depart significantly from the image of the invisible worker. Thus the 1980s saw two remarkable strikes in Bangalore (Subramanian, 1980, 1997). The first was a strike that involved central public sector workers over an issue of wage parity between Bharat Heavy Electricals Ltd. (BHEL) and the other central public sector units (PSUs). Involving some 80,000 workers in five PSUs, and resulting in stoppage of work for over two months, this was the longest public sector strike in Indian history. The objectives of the strike remained unachieved. But the strike went beyond company gates by building area solidarity committees as communication links between workers and leaders, and extended to a general Bangalore *Bandh* with the backing of other trade unions. Thus a broader engagement, in terms of issues, numbers and movement scope, was possible.

During 1979–80, workers at the German-owned MICO factory in Bangalore held an 88-day strike to protest against increasing workload. This strike, too, was unsuccessful, but had many features of a full-blown workers' movement. The agitation within the Bangalore MICO factory led to the formation of the MICO Employees Association (a union of MICO workers across the country) which held a one-day token strike in support of the Bangalore MICO workers. Within Bangalore, the strike generated a Solidarity Meeting of major trade unions in the city. When the government of Karnataka finally banned the strike, this brought forth an avalanche of protest from trade unions across the spectrum. The strike, therefore, reflected as well as contributed to the creation of a certain level of working-class solidarity.

This dimension would be completely lost in the character of industrial disputes in the years to come, some instances of which have been reviewed above. In the late 1990s, and the 2000–4 period which has been examined, industrial disputes appeared to occur in a relative vacuum, led by trade unions that were only tenuously connected, and in some cases not connected to the mainstream trade unions. These were isolated events which evoked little or no response from the larger body of industrial workers. The invisibility of the workforce is much more pronounced in these cases of industrial disputes than in the earlier period in which the PSU strike and the MICO strike occurred.

Would a labour historian, then, view the PSU strike and the MICO strike as exceptions to a general pattern of pacifism in industrial disputes, and the more recent industrial disputes presented in this chapter as representative of a continuing pattern? Alternatively, do the recent cases represent certain trends that set apart the current phase of industrial disputes from the earlier phase?

The grey area here is the question, if indeed broad-based class resistance is absent, of whether it is because of the peculiar nature of politics, or whether politics itself is determined by a deeper structurality.

In other words, can we meaningfully talk about the absence of class struggle if indeed there is no context for talking about it? Is there an absence of class conflict? Or, alternately, is this a situation where there is a class struggle without classes (Edwards, 2000)? In other words, is there an objective situation of conflict, without classes, the working class in particular, being actually aware of, or functioning within the framework of class conflict? Can we talk of an antagonistic relationship even when the opposed classes are themselves not using that language of opposition or antagonism? One response, typically, has been to reiterate that working-class consciousness is not something that is 'there', ready to spring up, but is necessarily contingent on the politics of the given moment (Chandravarkar, 1999). Essentially, the debate thus falls into two sets of questions: first, is there, indeed, a structural basis to class conflict? And second, what is the role of politics in shaping class conflict?

Much of this debate has revolved around locating what might be the objective, or structural, foundations of a class conflict. Contemporary Marxists have sought to refine, for example, the concept of surplus value by talking about rents (Castells, 1978; Edwards, 2000); or locating the power of capital in its control over the labour contract (Giddens, 1984). While the interpretations vary, the problem that has driven these responses appears to have been the search for a theory of exploitation – appropriate to the changing dynamics of contemporary capitalism – that could provide the foundations for a refurbished theory of class conflict. Indeed there can be little doubt that problematizing exploitation and class conflict in the current context would require conceptual and theoretical tools more refined than those given in classical Marxist theory. Today, global finance capital presents to the working class a largely invisible and ill-defined form of power. At the same time, the incorporation of the working classes into mainstream capitalist society and culture occurs through advancing technologies of communication and the spread of consumerism. In that sense, certainly, the objective basis of exploitation and the face of class conflict are more amorphous than they were during earlier phases of industrialization where manufacturing capital met labour face to face on the shopfloor.

Having said this, however, perhaps it should also be pointed out that the changing nature of capitalism represents only shifts in colours, angles and appearances of conflict, not in the fundamental opposition of interests. The manifestation of that opposition is indeed different. The outrage in the United States at the emerging scale of business process outsourcing, which is costing the American public several thousand jobs is of course different from the shopfloor-located capital–labour conflict. But the fundamental opposition is still between a profit-driven, now globalizing capital and domestic job seekers. Similarly, in the cases reviewed above, industrial disputes arise over issues that represent capital–labour conflicts.

As the contrast with strikes in the 1980s, outlined above, would indicate, working-class *politics* is in many ways different from the sharply polarized capital–labour antagonism of previous decades. A working population that is numerically weakened through ongoing policies of workforce reduction marked the industrial disputes reviewed here. There have been wide-ranging efforts by management not only to replace regular employees with a casualized workforce, but also to recast the institutions of industrial relations such that traditional forms of collective bargaining are no longer available or appropriate even to workers within the formal sector. There have occurred, additionally, subtle shifts in the state's position vis-à-vis labour. In an economic climate demanding greater attention to profits than to employee welfare, the state's approach to labour in industrial disputes is no longer one of guaranteed support. As one official in the Labour Department expressed it, 'The government is now, at best, a neutral onlooker; the outcome of an industrial dispute therefore depends on the relative power of management and labour. In most cases, the power of management is determined by the fact that they now have access to contract labour, outsourcing and so on.'[13] Finally, mainstream trade unions continue to speak for a shrinking formal sector workforce, while the informal sector is sought to be represented by a large number of new unions, NGOs and civil society organizations. In remaining focused on the formal sector, mainstream unions have distanced themselves from the issues that affect the workforce as a whole, while the amorphous character of unionization in the informal sector lacks the political anchoring and resources which the long-established trade union movement might have given it.

The question here then may be as much, or perhaps more so, one of an *appropriate politics* as of reframing a new theory of exploitation. It is only through a broader definition of the working class and a more energized politics than is available at the present moment that a more broad-based awareness would be possible of the conflicts of interests that characterize emerging forms of capitalism in the present era. To this extent, then, what needs to be underlined is, first, that the objective conditions of conflict and exploitation between capital and labour remain, although the modalities have changed. And second, labour activism could perhaps be re-energized through a re-reading of the new structures of conflict and what could be a possible politics thereof.

Notes

1. Information on this case study was collected from Mr Hallemane, Assistant General Manager, Personnel, Larsen and Toubro Komatsu Ltd., Mr Sabbaiah and Mr Hanumantha Rao, Union office bearers, Mr K. R. Narayan, General Secretary L&T Komatsu Ltd. Press note dated 7 August 2001.
2. Information on this case study was collected from documents (quoted below) provided by the Kirloskar Employees Association, and the Commissioner of Labour's Office, Karmikara Bhavan, interviews with Mr Naik, General Manager, Human Resource Development, Kirloskar Electric Company, and Mr Subramani, General Secretary Kirloskar Employees Association.
3. Proceedings of the Commissioner of Labour and Authority under section 25-M of the Industrial Disputes Act, 1947 (dated 14 September 2001).
4. E. Venkataiah, Commissioner of Labour, in Proceedings of the Commissioner of Labour and Authority, under section 25-M of the Industrial Disputes Act, 1947.
5. Information on this case study was collected from the office of the Labour Commissioner, Government of Karnataka, as well as from office bearers of WIDIA India Employees Association.
6. This letter was made available by the office of the Assistant Labour Commissioner, Government of Karnataka.
7. Information was collected from the office of the Labour Commissioner, Government of Karnataka.
8. Information on this case study was collected from the office of the Labour Commissioner, Government of Karnataka.
9. See Rajeev and RoyChowdhury (2004).
10. It should be noted that the entire relocation/restructuring plan of Kirloskar is anchored in the selling of acres of land that the company owns in a prime location in the city. In terms of land, the company's assets are 52 acres in Malleswaram (valued at Rs 116 crores); 11 acres in Peenya (Rs 8 crores – both in Bangalore); and 4 in Pune (Rs 2 crores) (CMIE, May 2003).
11. This has been particularly true in the case of closed textile mills.
12. Interview with Mr V. J. K Nair, President, CITU, Karnataka, on 30 September 2004.
13. Interview with Mr Sanjiv Kumar, Commissioner of Labour, Government of Karnataka, on 11 October 2004.

References

Castells, M. (1978) *City, Class and Power*, London: Macmillan Press.
Centre for Monitoring the Indian Economy (CMIE) (2003) *Monthly Review of the Karnataka Economy* (May).
Chandravarkar, R. (1999) 'Questions of Class: the General Strikes in Bombay 1928–29', in J. Parry et al. (eds), *The Worlds of Indian Industrial Labour*, New Delhi: Sage.
Edwards, P. (2000) 'Late Twentieth Century Workplace Relations', in R. Crompton et al. (eds), *Renewing Class Analysis*, Oxford: Basil Blackwell, pp. 141–64.

Gayatri, K. (2002) 'Genuineness of the Capital Investment Subsidy: a Study of Bangalore Division', Institute for Social and Economic Change, Bangalore (mimeo).

Giddens, A. (1984) *The Constitution of Society: Outline of a Theory of Structuration*, Cambridge: Polity Press.

Rajeev, M. and DasGupta, P. (2003) 'Karnataka Public Enterprises Reform Program (2000–2003)', Institute for Social and Economic Change, Bangalore, and World Bank, New Delhi (mimeo).

Rajeev, M. and RoyChowdhury, S. (2004) 'Contract Labour in Karnataka's Manufacturing Industries', Institute for Social and Economic Change and Sir Ratan Tata Trust Project, Bangalore.

RoyChowdhury, S. (2005a) 'Labour and Economic Reforms: Disjointed Critiques', in Jos Mooij (ed.), *The Politics of Economic Reforms in India*, New Delhi: Sage Publications, pp. 264–90.

RoyChowdhury, S. (2005b) 'Labour Activism and Women in the Unorganised Sector: Garment Export Industry in Bangalore', *Economic and Political Weekly*, 40, 22 and 23, 28 May–4 June.

Subramanian, D. (1980) 'The MICO Strike: a Retrospective', *Economic and Political Weekly*, 15, 22 (31 May).

Subramanian, D. (1997) 'Bangalore Public Sector Strike, 1980–81: a Critical Appraisal, Parts I and II', *Economic and Political Weekly*, 32, 15 and 16.

10
Labour and Globalization: Union Responses in India

Rohini Hensman

1. Introduction

The economic liberalization programme begun in July 1991 initiated the globalization of the Indian economy. Faced with a crisis resulting from foreign exchange reserves sufficient for just a fortnight's imports, the Congress government undertook some of the measures recommended by the International Monetary Fund (IMF) and World Bank in the late 1980s, including abolition of licensing procedures for manufacturing investment (which had popularly come to be known as a corruption-ridden 'licence-permit raj'), reduction of the high import tariffs on most goods (but not consumer goods), liberalizing terms of entry for foreign investors, and liberalizing capital markets (Balasubramanyam and Mahambare, 2001). These changes were not simply imposed on India. Many were designed to encourage the expansion of big business after what were perceived as decades of stagnation, for example by removing restrictions on mergers and acquisitions, encouraging businesses to seek finance abroad, and sparking a wave of expansion into new sectors which had barely developed (e.g. telecom), or had been reserved for the public sector (e.g. banking).

When the World Trade Organization (WTO) was established on 1 January 1995, India was a member from the beginning. This involved new pressures, for example to eliminate quantitative restrictions on imports, simplify and reduce tariffs, reduce export constraints, reduce the number of activities reserved for the public sector and small-scale sector, further liberalize the Foreign Direct Investment (FDI) regime, and address the fiscal deficit. The process of integrating India more closely into the world economy has been more or less continuous since 1991, despite changes of government, and the world economy itself has globalized rapidly during this period.

The meltdown of the US subprime mortgage market in August 2007, leading to the global economic crisis that hit the world in September 2008, not only had an impact on labour in India, but called into question the stability of the whole system. The Ministry of Labour and Employment estimated that approximately 500,000 workers lost their jobs in selected industrial sectors during October–December 2008, with total earnings declining by 3.45 per cent. Production for export was hit harder than production for domestic consumption (Ministry of Labour and Employment, 2009).

However, the extent of the damage was less in India than in Europe and the US. Paradoxically, the most effective stimulus package was probably the scheme put in place by the National Rural Employment Guarantee Act (NREGA) *before* the crisis, as the result of a sustained Right to Food campaign by social activists. Promising to provide 100 days of employment (or unemployment benefit) per year to each rural household demanding it, it sustained livelihoods and consumer demand while building assets like irrigation wells and roads. In the words of some of the leading activists working for the scheme, 'the NREGA is having an impact: wages are rising, migration is slowing down, productive assets are being created, and the power equations are changing too' (Drèze and Khera, 2009: 4–6); 'It has given people a right to work, to re-establish the dignity of labour, to ensure people's economic and democratic rights and entitlements, to create labour intensive infrastructure and assets, and to build the human resource base of our country' (Roy and Dey, 2009). By mid-2009, predictions that the global economy would be pulled down by the crisis in the US were beginning to be replaced by hopes that the resilience of the Chinese and Indian economies would help to pull the rest of the world out of recession.

2. Right-wing opposition to globalization

In order to understand the responses of party-affiliated unions to globalization, it is necessary to examine the ideologies of their respective parties. The Bharatiya Mazdoor Sangh (BMS) is the union affiliated to the Rashtriya Swayamsevak Sangh (RSS);[1] the Swadeshi Jagran Manch (SJM) and Bharatiya Janata Party (BJP) are also part of the Sangh Parivar or 'family' of Hindu right-wing organizations. These organizations on various occasions protested against 'handing over the nation's consumer market to foreign companies' (*Business Standard*, 1994), 'globalization and foreign investment' (*Business Standard*, 1995), India's accession to the WTO (*Business Standard*, 1998) and, more generally, liberalization and globalization (*Economic Times*, 1999). Opposition to international capital has been the hallmark of the extreme right since Hitler wrote, 'The development of Germany was much too clear in my eyes for me not to know that the hardest battle would have to be fought not against hostile nations but against international capital' (Hitler, 1943: 213, cited in Henwood, 1993: 303). Hindutva – the ideology of the Sangh Parivar – follows in this tradition.

It has been argued that 'What we might call the *political projects* of Hindutva and neoliberalism share certain socio-political agendas', including '*Reduction of social processes to individual choice*' (Gopalakrishnan, 2008). But this proposition is not supported by Hindutva's hostility to free markets and international capital, nor is it credible that an ideology that discourages inter-caste and inter-community marriages has much to do with individual choice. In India, religious nationalism and neoliberalism do converge in their unqualified opposition to workers' rights and any form of social democracy, but they are distinct agendas, and the reasons that motivate this opposition are quite different. Hindutva's opposition is grounded in a caste and gender system that puts workers (*Shudras*) at the lowest level, with Dalits and Adivasis even below that (in the sense that they are outcaste), and women below men. Any attempt to organize and fight for workers' rights is seen as antithetical to their culture, which is consciously based on hierarchy. This stance provides practical benefits to capitalists (including farmers) whose predominant method of competing is by absolute surplus value production. Their defence of domestic business groups (i.e. their economic nationalism) explains their hostility to international capital. By contrast, neoliberal opposition to trade unions draws its inspiration from the ideology of 'free markets' in everything including labour, and is not only compatible with free trade and the internationalization of capital flows, but actually requires these. However, the observation that hostility to workers' rights is shared by the Hindu right and neoliberalism is a useful one, and helps to explain the trajectory of attacks on labour in India.

3. Left-wing opposition to globalization

Left-wing opposition has relied on construing globalization as imperialism and neoliberalism, and on defending 'national sovereignty' against international institutions and large international firms. Thus, in replying to Amartya Sen's criticisms of the left, a Communist Party of India (Marxist) (CPIM) leader writes, 'Surely Dr Sen recognises our concern about the links between food security and national sovereignty ... Dr Sen ... would accept there are some exceptional imperialist acts such as the war on Iraq, but for the rest, imperialist-driven globalization with its twin instruments of neo-liberal policies and military interventions are not germane to the central issues of social justice that are close to Dr Sen's heart' (Karat, 2009).

The definition of globalization as imperialism draws on Lenin's analysis in 'Imperialism, the Highest Stage of Capitalism', written in 1916 and published in 1917. This was never intended to be definitive, and now, almost a century after it was written, its flaws have become evident. Lenin's analysis pulled together two phenomena coexisting at the time that he was writing – finance capital and colonialism – and assumed there was an intrinsic link between them. Yet going into the separate dynamics of each would reveal that decolonization has been accompanied by the exponential growth of finance capital globally: 'The fundamental point is to see the territorial and the capitalist logics of power as distinct from each other', and in the early twenty-first century 'there appears to be a deep inconsistency if not outright contradiction between the two logics' (Harvey, 2003: 29, 204).

In fact, *imperialism and globalization are characterized by very different relationships between capital and the state.* Under imperialism, capital depends on the state to control territory outside the borders of the nation politically and militarily in order to secure cheap raw materials, labour, markets and profitable investment opportunities. Colonies have to be subjugated and other powers fought off, so military might is an asset for imperialism. But in a globalized world, the most competitive capitals rely not on state backing but global regulation to aid their expansion, and this is best achieved not through militarism but through multilateralism. Indeed, it can be argued (see below) that militarism constitutes an obstacle to capital accumulation in a globalized economy.

The conflation of globalization with neoliberalism is understandable, since there is an area of overlap between the two: namely, the elimination of barriers to the international flow of goods, services and capital. But there are differences. Neoliberal policies, in the sense of the economic stabilization and structural adjustment programmes imposed by the Bretton Woods institutions, go much further than the free trade policies envisaged by the classical economists or the policies demanded by globalization. The short-term stabilization measures include cut-backs in government expenditure, high interest rates and currency devaluation, while the longer-term adjustment measures include deregulating the economy and privatizing public services, none of which are required by globalization.

Another difference is far greater multilateralism in the WTO, illustrated by the fact that the Doha Development round of WTO negotiations was stuck for years due to the stubborn refusal of developing countries to agree to US and EU proposals on agricultural policy (Khor, 2006; Subramaniam, 2003), whereas the IMF and World Bank could effectively compel developing countries to accept the policies they recommended. The emphasis on 'deregulation' that is characteristic of the IMF and World Bank, and which resulted in privatization efforts being marked by corruption and the creation of private and often criminal monopolies (Stiglitz, 2002: 54–6, 71), is not shared by the WTO; on the contrary, the avowed purpose of the WTO is to *regulate* the world economy, and this makes it possible to contest the question of whose interests its regulations should serve. Thus, although there is an area of overlap between neoliberalism and globalization, there is more to each than this area. And while they are compatible with each other in the short run – indeed, the dominant model of globalization thus far has been a neoliberal one – it can be argued (see below) that the global economic crisis is a signal that this model is in serious trouble.

Globalization can be defined as a new stage of capitalism emerging out of imperialism, and distinguished from all previous epochs by (a) the existence of communication and information technologies that allow capital to operate worldwide in a way that has not been possible before; (b) a partial reversal of the distortion of Third World economies imposed by imperialism, and reintegration of key Second and Third World countries into the capitalist world economy on a more equal basis; (c) a dynamic sector of capital which depends not on the support of a nation-state for its expansion, nor on rigid national borders to protect it from imports, but on porous borders and global regulation that will allow it to expand globally; (d) the growing dominance of institutional investors, including pension funds; and (e) new institutions of global governance.

4. Attacks on labour rights

The assault on labour rights in India does not follow the trajectory of globalization. Independence made no difference to the preponderance of informal labour which lacked the most basic rights. The bulk of labour legislation deliberately excludes informal workers – defined as workers either in small-scale unregistered establishments (in India referred to as the 'unorganized sector') or as workers in irregular employment relationships – and this provides employers with a variety of ways to evade these laws: splitting up an establishment into small units which are supposedly independent of each other, creating artificial breaks in employment so that workers never attain permanent status, employing large numbers of contract workers on site who are controlled by labour contractors and therefore do not appear on the payroll of the company, or sub-contracting production to smaller workplaces. In theory informal workers have the right to organize, but it is almost impossible to organize without being dismissed. And once dismissed, they have no access to legal redress, because there is no legal recognition of their employment or even their existence as workers.

In 1977, when the emergency was lifted and the Janata Party came to power, there was a massive strike wave as workers fought for long-repressed demands. There was an opportunity to strengthen union rights, but the new government's policy had the opposite effect. Its Industrial Policy Statement issued in December 1977 declared that 'The emphasis of industrial policy so far has been mainly on large industries ... relegating small industries to a minor role. It is the firm policy of this government to change this approach' (Government of India, 1977). More than 500 items – many more than before – were reserved exclusively for the small-scale sector. Financial and marketing assistance were provided to these units, but there was no mention of extending basic rights to the workers employed in them.

When Indira Gandhi came back to power in 1980, her government scrapped the Janata industrial policy and launched a new Five Year Plan. But instead of abandoning the emphasis on small-scale production, the Industrial Policy Statement of 1980 – and thus the Sixth Five Year Plan that followed – reiterated and expanded it. With the boost for small-scale units in the new industrial policy, they could afford modern technology, and having much lower overheads and labour costs, could compete successfully with the large-scale sector. In addition, the government 'decided to encourage dispersal of industry and setting up of units in industrially backward areas. Special concessions and facilities will be offered for this purpose' (Government of India, 1980).

The consequences were predictable, and, indeed, were predicted: 'If the projected rate of growth for this sector by the planners does materialize, then, by the end of the Sixth Plan period, it should account for about a third of the manufacturing output in the country. Such a large part of the production system will be receiving Government assistance, such as cheap credit, reserved markets, tax concessions, etc. but will not have to accept any regulations as to ... how it should treat its workers, etc. Do we really want to encourage subminimal wage rates, a weakening of the bargaining strength of the industrial workers, or the very high profit margins which go without taxation?' (Banerjee, 1981: 280, 293). That, it seems, was exactly what the government wanted, and it succeeded only too well.

Employers in large-scale industry found it hard to compete with the upgraded small-scale sector; most responded by transferring more jobs to informal workers, using the methods outlined above. Having shifted production, the company could liquidate the existing workforce. It is estimated that the Bombay textile strike of 1982–3 was followed by the loss of roughly 75,000 jobs due to closures and downsizing, with another 25,000 lost soon after (van Wersch, 1992: 234–44). In Ahmedabad, the decline started in 1982, with the loss of almost 100,000 jobs over the next fifteen years, the majority in the 1980s (Patel, 2001: 6). Textile centres like Kanpur and Coimbatore witnessed similar declines (Baud, 1983; Joshi, 2003: 314). In every case, weaving was transferred to the decentralized powerloom sector (Baud, 1983: 31–2; van Wersch, 1992: 40–6). Modern industry was the next target. Where workers posed resistance, there were ways of dealing with them: in 1985–6, workdays lost due to lockouts outstripped workdays lost due to strikes, a trend which began much earlier in Bombay; by 1989–90, the former were double the latter at over 20,000 per annum, and although the number fell steeply in subsequent years, it remained consistently above the level of days lost due to strikes (Nagaraj, 2004: 3389). The generous incentives for setting up units in industrially backward areas encouraged transfer of production from highly unionized workforces in cities like Bombay to non-unionized workers in greenfield sites. In both textiles and modern industry, an attack on secure, well-paid jobs for women preceded the wholesale demolition of jobs (Hensman, 1996).

Another common method of eliminating trade unionism and workers' rights was to exclude sections of workers from them, and here managements were assisted by ambiguities in the Industrial Disputes (ID) Act, which protects only those who are designated as 'workmen' from dismissal for trade union activities. Courts interpreted this to mean that there is a 'non-bargainable category' of employees, who do not have the right to belong to a union or bargain collectively: an interpretation which is a clear violation of ILO Conventions 87 and 98 on Freedom of Association and the Right to Organize and Bargain Collectively, as well as the Constitution of India. Starting from the second half of the 1970s, an important section of employees to be attacked in this way were Medical Representatives of pharmaceutical companies. The Supreme

Court judgement of August 1994 in the Sandoz case, excluding Medical Representatives from protection for trade union activities, opened the floodgates to managements attempting to push more and more sales, technical, clerical and even service staff into the 'non-bargainable' category. The ID Act forbids 'promotions' to the 'non-bargainable' category when job content remains unchanged, but once the category had been created, it was impossible to prevent the expulsion of unionized workers into it.

So the assault on labour rights began long before 1991 and without any change in the labour laws. Chapter V B of the ID Act stipulates that in workplaces with 100 workers or more, the employer has to get permission from the government before laying off workers or closing the unit. For smaller workplaces, this was no impediment to closure, but even in larger ones, everything was left to the government. So long as the prevailing public policy was opposed to making workers redundant, permission was routinely denied. But in an ideological climate that asserted the superiority of small-scale production, it was easy for government to reverse its policies and allow closures of units in the formal sector. If state authorities did not give permission for closure or dismissals, the company was still at liberty to go ahead with its plans in the absence of a response from them within three months.

The assault on workers' rights reached new heights when the BJP-led National Democratic Alliance (NDA) government was in power from 1998 to 2004. Two proposals for 'reform' of labour laws were made: (a) employers wanted deletion of Section 10 of the Contract Labour Act which restricted the use of contract labour (Hakeem, 2000); and (b) they wanted revision of Chapter V B of the ID Act, to allow employers the freedom to dismiss workers and close down units with less than 1,000 workers (Mitra, 2001). There were frequent full-page advertisements in the newspapers alleging that the very existence of permanent workers was responsible for unemployment, and Finance Minister Yashwant Sinha announced, in his budget speech of 2001, that the government would liberalize the use of contract labour and permit employers to dismiss employees and close down units employing up to 1,000 workers with no questions asked. The *Report of the Second National Commission on Labour (SNCL)*, which came out in 2002, made recommendations for the formal sector that followed the guidelines laid down by employers and the government (Ministry of Labour, 2002). The absolute number of formal jobs declined, falling by 420,000 in 2001–2 alone, and the ratio of workers in formal employment fell to less than 7 per cent of the labour force (*Business Standard*, 2003; Soman, 2003).

5. Unions and labour law changes

The labour law changes proposed in 2000–1 brought unions together in Maharashtra. The Trade Union Joint Action Committee (TUJAC) of left-of-centre unions undertook a series of rallies, demonstrations, local meetings and other actions, culminating in the Maharashtra *bandh* (general strike) of 25 April 2001. The complete success of this strike (*Business Standard*, 2001a), and the unprecedented unity which ensured this success, required the TUJAC to approach unions affiliated to the Congress, BJP and Shiv Sena, which at times had been involved in bitter conflicts with its own constituents. It is likely that this unity would never have materialized if not for the feeling of extreme insecurity among members of all unions, and the pressure they exerted on their own leaderships.

On 10 May the Chief Minister of Maharashtra assured trade union leaders that the proposed labour law changes had been 'nullified' (*Business Standard*, 2001b). At the national level, however, the campaign for the same labour law changes continued. On 26 February 2003, over 350,000 workers and activists from left unions throughout India held a rally in Delhi against the anti-union policies of the government (Nicholas Employees' Union, 2003). Members of independent unions affiliated to the Trade Union Solidarity Committee in Bombay and the New Trade Union Initiative (NTUI) nationally not only campaigned against the NDA before the parliamentary elections in 2004, but also approached opposition parties, including the Congress, and pressed them to include protection for labour rights in their party manifestos (NTUI, 2004). Their activities no doubt played a role in the defeat of the NDA and the fact that the new Congress-led United Progressive Alliance (UPA) government did not pursue the labour law changes which had been the hallmark of the previous regime.

Thus the trade union movement was successful in staving off policies that would have precipitated the remaining 7 per cent of workers in formal employment into informal employment at one blow. Paradoxically, one of the main ways in which this was achieved was by voting back to power the very party – Congress – which had initiated globalization in the first place, confirming that it was not globalization which was responsible for the particularly vicious attack on labour that took place in India over the turn of the twenty-first century. However, trade unions were not successful in stemming the more gradual contraction of formal employment.

One effort that might have constituted a major step forward was the struggle by informal workers' organizations for legislation to regulate their employment. Such legislation did exist in particular sectors – for example, the Dock Workers (Regulation of Employment) Act (1948), the Maharashtra Mathadi, Hamal and Other Manual Workers (Regulation of Employment and Welfare) Act (1969), and the Building and Other Construction Workers (Regulation of Employment and Conditions of Service) Act (1996) – but it differed from state to state, and was fragmented by occupation. These Acts required the formation of state-level tripartite boards, consisting of employer, employee and government representatives, to register all employers and workers and regulate employment (Subramanya, 2005: 28), and enabled workers to organize successfully in extremely casualized and apparently unpromising occupations.

The Unorganized Sector Workers' Bill (2004) mentioned registration, but made it clear that it would not be compulsory for employers to register, which would make regulation of employment impossible. Given that the bulk of the proposed legislation pertained to the setting up of Welfare Boards for informal sector workers, labour activists described it as a 'truncated social security scheme' (Menon, 2005: 13). The truncated version was finally passed in December 2008 as the Unorganized Workers' Social Security Bill. This approach to legislative reform lumps together workers who are employees with those who are self-employed, whereas their needs are very different. It also accepts the differential treatment of formal and informal employees, instead of attempting to ensure that all employees are covered by the same labour laws. Consequently, it has less chance of success, since the more powerful formal sector workers do not perceive it to be in their interest, and even if successful, it still leaves one section of workers with weaker rights than the other. Unions in India have failed to make any dent in this system of industrial apartheid for over sixty years.

6. Nationalism versus internationalism

Globalization could potentially act as a positive force, helping to push the level of labour rights in India upwards. By breaking down barriers to the mobility of commodities and capital across national borders, globalization created problems for workers in countries with higher labour standards, many of whom have seen their jobs moving to countries with lower standards. The most important proposal by unions globally aimed at protecting workers from this effect has been a 'social clause' in WTO agreements, affirming respect by all members for the fundamental workers' rights embodied in the Core ILO Conventions as well as environmental protection. This would not equalize labour standards immediately, but would at least prevent production being shifted to certain countries simply because they allowed core workers' rights to be violated.

A few independent unions, organizations of informal workers, and groups working with child labour in India supported this proposal, but the overwhelming majority of responses to it were negative. All the central unions, across the political spectrum, rejected the idea (Central Trade Union Organizations of India, 1995). At the forefront of this rejection was the notion that it was a protectionist measure, and therefore against the national interest (Ganguli, 1996; Mahendra, 1996). This was not just a criticism of the particular proposal that the International Confederation of Free Trade Unions (ICFTU) and some First World unions had made, but a rejection of the very idea of a workers' rights clause in WTO agreements.

Arthur Dunkel (cited by Ferguson, 1994: 4) and the World Bank (1995: 6) also rejected the social clause as a protectionist measure, recognizing the advantages of international trade liberalization for developing countries, but opposing any corresponding international regulation of labour. One of the main proponents of this position, Jagdish Bhagwati, argued strongly that labour was not a trade-related issue, and the WTO should concentrate on trade issues while the ILO concentrated on labour (Bhagwati, 2002: 79–80). Yet it is obvious that ILO Conventions protecting labour are widely flouted, whereas WTO rules are much more enforceable. What was being advocated by Bhagwati and, paradoxically, echoed by the central trade unions of India, therefore, was enforceable protection for capital without enforceable protection for labour.

Another reason why left-wing unionists rejected the social clause was their analysis of globalization: for them, the social clause was simply a cover for the agenda of imperialism and neoliberalism. Yet a mistaken analysis of globalization alone cannot account for the way in which the anti-union policies of domestic employers and the government were blamed on globalization: an element of nationalism was also involved. An obvious problem with this approach is that it fails to tackle key domestic sources of attacks on workers' rights. Less obviously, but perhaps even more dangerously, the prejudice against international as opposed to national capital strengthens the xenophobic agenda of the extreme right, and constitutes an obstacle to solidarity with workers of other countries (see Hensman, 2001 for a more extended discussion of the union debate on the social clause).

Ironically, then, an important task for those who wish to confront the challenges of globalization in India is to make a much more thorough study of social practices and government policies which deprive workers of their fundamental rights, and oppose them in a way that has never been done by the Indian trade union movement. In fact, this is not as paradoxical as it may seem. With globalization, the local and national become essential parts of the global; the distinction no longer makes sense. The abysmal record of labour rights in India has helped to pull down standards elsewhere, both by encouraging a shift of employment to informal labour in India, leading to job losses for workers with better rights, and by providing models for employers elsewhere to emulate, for example by carrying out a similar informalization of employment in their own countries.

The second requirement is a better understanding of globalization as neither imperialism nor neoliberalism but a new stage of capitalist development which began to emerge in the middle of the twentieth century with the struggles for independence and national liberation in the Third World, and progressed further as some of the largest of these countries industrialized. As early Marxists recognized (for example in the *Communist Manifesto*), capitalism is inherently global, and therefore solidarity between workers of different countries is crucial in the struggle against it. In the modern globalized world economy, this becomes even more indispensable. The anti-globalization agenda, by itself, is both unrealistic and reactionary, because it seeks to reverse the decline of a nation-state system which has been used against workers in so many ways, ranging from the divide-and-rule policies of international capitalism to the use of workers in uniform to kill each other in the interests of their ruling classes. Opposition to globalization retards the transition from imperialism to a world order marked by more egalitarian and peaceful relationships between peoples; furthermore, it distracts attention from the task of shaping the new global order, leaving the field open for advocates of traditional authoritarian labour relations and modern neoliberal policies to impose their own agendas on it.

If unions worldwide were to put pressure on their governments to incorporate a workers' rights clause in WTO agreements requiring the ILO to assist governments genuinely striving to improve labour rights, and penalizing countries and companies which persisted in the denial of basic workers' rights, some of the gross violations prevalent in India would surely decline. The ILO is already providing assistance to eliminate child labour, but this could be stepped up, and it could also help to set up machinery to register informal employees and employers, redress discrimination complaints, and so on. The global coverage of the clause would ensure that companies would not be able to threaten to shift production to other countries, because they would face the same regime wherever they went.

However, it would be impossible to formulate such a clause, much less work for it, without an enormous amount of discussion and debate between workers in all their diversity, including differences of nationality. A weakness of the original social clause proposal was the lack of input from Third World union activists. As Bennet D'Costa of the Hindustan Lever Employees' Union put it in 1998, 'Third World workers must have a say in defining the social clause and putting what we want into it; we can't just accept what trade unions in the imperialist countries suggest' (cited by Hensman, 1998: 83).

Opening up communication channels between workers across the world so that this discussion and debate can take place is therefore a priority. For this to happen, several conditions need to be met. If the channels of communication are hierarchical ones set up by national union bureaucracies, it is not likely that much progress will be made; a more democratic model would need to be utilized. Fortunately, globalization has provided the wherewithal for such a process through the internet and email. But not all workers have access to the internet, nor do they all speak the same language: translations and other forms of dissemination would also be necessary. A research, education and consultation project aimed at defending the rights of women workers in supply chains in the garment industry organized by Women Working Worldwide demonstrated the possibilities of stimulating communication and solidarity using all these resources (Hale and Wills, 2005).

These are practical requirements. In addition, a minimal degree of mutual respect and trust would be crucial. This was lacking in the earlier debate on the social clause. Many Third World unionists suspected their First World counterparts of being more interested in protecting their own jobs than in helping workers in developing countries, and in some cases this was true. Conversely, many First World unionists thought their Third World counterparts were willing to tolerate child labour and other abuses so long as their countries attracted more investment and employment, and this, too, was in some cases true. But in other cases, unionists from developed countries genuinely wanted to help workers in developing countries to defend their rights, and unionists from developing countries had valid criticisms of the original social clause proposal, yet a consensus was precluded by mutual recriminations. A genuine dialogue would require all sides to be free of such prejudices, or at least to be willing to subject their own prejudices to critical scrutiny.

The most difficult task in India is likely to be convincing trade unionists that nationalism is not a positive value. Nationalism is so closely
associated in the minds of most Indians with the struggle for freedom
from British colonialism that denouncing it is almost taboo, and only
an exceptional visionary like Rabindranath Tagore could see that it has
nothing to do with either freedom or love of country (Tagore, 1976).
These distinctions are as important for trade unionists as the distinctions between imperialism, neoliberalism and globalization: unless they
feel they can oppose imperialism and love their country without being
nationalists, or oppose neoliberalism and value freedom while working for their own vision of globalization, it will be difficult for them to
participate creatively in developing a new global agenda for labour. By
pitting workers in different countries against one another, nationalism
deprives the working class of its most powerful weapon in the struggle
to protect workers' rights in the new global order: global solidarity. By
contrast, fighting for an alternative model of globalization that is superior to the neoliberal model would be both realistic and progressive.

7. An alternative model of globalization

What would this model look like? Suggesting the outlines of it has
become fairly urgent, given the danger that the recovery from recession in
mid-2009 might not be sustained once the stimulus packages come to an
end, and the world could once more be plunged into economic crisis.

The first task would be to clear away the debris from the epoch of
imperialism and nationalism, namely ruinous military spending. In
the epoch of globalization, militarism plays no useful role for capitalism; indeed, large-scale military spending actually becomes a liability
in a globalized economy. The fact that it constitutes a deduction from
social spending on the labour force is obvious. But it is also a deduction
from state investment in civilian research and infrastructure that could
increase efficiency and productivity in capitalist production as a whole.
Excessive military spending by the US in the 1990s resulted in productivity lagging far behind that of Japan and Germany; the failure to mod-
ernize resulted in its manufacturing base being decimated by the turn of
the twenty-first century, and contributed greatly to the economic crisis
in 2008 (Johnson, 2008; Melman, 2001: 110–14, 124–6).

Military spending by the US is greater than that of the rest of the world
put together (GlobalSecurity.org, 2007), and constitutes a huge drain on
the world economy. Ending the occupations of Iraq and Afghanistan
and the bankrolling of Israel's occupation of Palestine, winding up

foreign bases and downsizing the military-industrial complex would go a long way towards shrinking the outsize US fiscal deficit (*Business Standard*, 2009), reviving the US economy, and thereby contributing to global economic recovery. But India's military spending too is massive, with $3 billion spent on building a nuclear submarine, plans to build four more, buy seven from France and two from Russia, and buy $2 billion worth of missiles from Russia, all in a country where 47 per cent of children are malnourished and around 2 million die each year of malnutrition and preventable diseases (Janson, 2009): surely the 'national sovereignty' defended by this expenditure not only does *not* promote food security, but is actually inimical to it! Rapid steps towards global nuclear disarmament, eliminating other weapons of mass destruction and slashing military budgets would be important features of an alternative model of globalization.

The economic downturn has also made it clear that the neoliberal model of globalization is fatally flawed. By impoverishing the vast majority of the world's working people, it restricts market expansion drastically and thus becomes a fetter on capitalist accumulation. One powerful and obvious way in which this can be remedied is by extending to the workers of the world the basic human rights stipulated in the ILO's Core Conventions. This would help to curtail debt, while strong regulation would help to direct finance capital into socially useful production. Another requirement is employment creation programmes like the NREGA scheme in which workers are registered and guaranteed basic rights, as well as state support for workers' cooperatives. Finally, if the bulk of state expenditures on militarism were redirected towards health care, education, social security, welfare, infrastructure and civilian research, this would create socially useful employment, upgrade productive resources and create the conditions for far stronger protection of the environment.

In other words, globalization minus militarism and neoliberalism is a realistic goal for which workers around the world can launch a coordinated struggle.

Note

1. Nathuram Godse, the Hindu fanatic who murdered Mahatma Gandhi, was associated with the RSS.

References

Balasubramanyam, V. N. and Mahambare, V. (2001) India's Economic Reforms and the Manufacturing Sector', Lancaster University Management School Working Paper 2001/010, Lancaster University Management School, Lancaster.

Banerjee, N. (1981) 'Is Small Beautiful?' in A. Bagchi and N. Banerjee (eds), *Change and Choice in Indian Industry*, Calcutta: Centre for Studies in Social Sciences, pp. 177–295.

Baud, I. (1983) *Women's Labour in the Indian Textile Industry*, Research Project IRIS report no. 23, Tilburg: Tilburg Institute of Development Research.

Bhagwati, J. (2002) *Free Trade Today*, Princeton: Princeton University Press.

Business Standard (1994) 'RSS Asks Left to Join Swadeshi Stir', 21 November.

Business Standard (1995) 'RSS to Continue Attack on Globalization, MNCs', 28 March.

Business Standard (1998) 'RSS Plans Stir Against Govt Today', 30 November.

Business Standard (2001a) 'Bandh Brings Maharashtra to a Halt', 26 April.

Business Standard (2001b) 'Labour Law Changes Nullified, Assures CM', 11 May.

Business Standard (2003) 'Employment Levels Fall 1.5% in Organized Sector', 16 May.

Business Standard (2009) 'US Fiscal Deficit to Touch $9.05 Trillion in 10 Years', 29 August.

Central Trade Union Organizations of India (1995) 'Appeal from the Central Trade Union Organizations of India to the Fifth Conference of Labour Ministers of Nonaligned and Other Developing Countries', New Delhi (mimeo).

Drèze, J. and Khera, R. (2009) 'The Battle for Employment Guarantee', *Frontline*, 26, 1 (16 January): 4–25.

Economic Times (1999) 'BMS Joins Left in Slamming Govt's Economic Policies', 14 January.

Ferguson, M. (1994) 'International Trade and Workers Rights', *International Union Rights*, 1, 7: 3–5.

Ganguly, P. K. (1996) 'Labour Rights and National Interests', in J. John and A. M. Chenoy (eds), *Labour, Environment and Globalization – Social Clause in Multilateral Trade Agreements: A Southern Response*, New Delhi: CEC, pp. 43–6.

GlobalSecurity.org (2007) 'World Wide Military Expenditures', http://www.globalsecurity.org/military/world/spending.htm, accessed 28 August 2009.

Gopalakrishnan, S. (2008) 'Neoliberalism and Hindutva: Fascism, Free Markets and the Restructuring of Indian Capitalism', *Radical Notes*, http://radicalnotes.com/content/view/77/39/, accessed 26 August 2009.

Government of India (1977) 'Industrial Policy Statement', in *India's Industrial Policies from 1948 to 1991*, www.laghu-udyog.com/policies/iip.htm, accessed 26 August 2009.

Government of India (1980) 'Industrial Policy Statement', in *India's Industrial Policies from 1948 to 1991*, www.laghu-udyog.com/policies/iip.htm, accessed 26 August 2009.

Hakeem, M. A. (2000) 'Labour Flexibility for Competitive Edge', *Economic Times*, 30 November.

Hale, A. and Wills, J. (eds) (2005) *Threads of Labour: Garment Industry Supply Chains from the Workers' Perspective*, Oxford: Blackwell Publishing.

Harvey, D. (2003) *The New Imperialism*, Oxford: Oxford University Press.

Hensman, R. (1996) 'The Impact of Industrial Restructuring on Women, Men and Trade Unions', in T. V. Sathyamurthy (ed.), *Class Formation and Political Transformation in Post-Colonial India*, Delhi: Oxford University Press, pp. 80–104.

Hensman, R. (1998) 'How to Support the Rights of Women Workers in the Context of Trade Liberalization in India', in A. Hale (ed.), *Trade Myths and Gender Reality: Trade Liberalization and Women's Lives*, Sweden: Global Publications Foundation and International Coalition for Development Action, pp. 71–88.

Hensman, R. (2001) 'World Trade and Workers' Rights: In Search of an Internationalist Position', in P. Waterman and J. Wills (eds), *Place, Space and the New Labour Internationalisms*, Oxford: Blackwell, pp. 123–46.

Henwood, D. (1993) *Wall Street*, London: Verso.

Hitler, A. (1943) *Mein Kampf*, trans. Ralph Manheim, Boston: Houghton Mifflin Co.

Janson, J. (2009) 'Should Indian Leaders Who Spend Billions on Submarines While Others Starve Go Unpunished?' *Countercurrents.org*, 12 August, http://www.countercurrents.org/janson120809.htm, accessed 29 August 2009.

Johnson, C. (2008) 'Going Bankrupt: the US's Greatest Threat', *Asia Times Online*, 24 January, http://www.atimes.com/atimes/Middle_East/JA24Ak04.html, accessed 29 August 2009.

Joshi, C. (2003) *Lost Worlds: Indian Labour and its Forgotten Histories*, Delhi: Permanent Black.

Karat, P. (2009) 'A Fraternal Argument with Dr Sen', *People's Democracy*, 33, 33 (16 August), http://pd.cpim.org/2009/0816_pd/08162009_2.html, accessed 27 August 2009.

Khor, M. (2006) 'Failure of WTO Geneva Mini-Ministerial', *Economic and Political Weekly*, 41, 29 (22 July): 3143–6.

Lenin, V. I. (1964) 'Imperialism, the Highest Stage of Capitalism: a Popular Outline', in *Collected Works*, Volume 22, Moscow: Progress Publishers, pp. 185–304.

Mahendra, K. L. (1996) 'A Protectionist Measure', in J. John and A. M. Chenoy (eds), *Labour, Environment and Globalization – Social Clause in Multilateral Trade Agreements: A Southern Response*, New Delhi: CEC, pp. 47–50.

Melman, S. (2001) *After Capitalism: From Managerialism to Workplace Democracy*, New York: Alfred A Knopf.

Menon, S. (2005) 'Endorsing an Unorganised Bill: a Game of Hide and Seek', *Labour File*, 3, 2 (March–April): 7–20.

Ministry of Labour (2002) *Report of the National Commission on Labour*, New Delhi: Government of India.

Ministry of Labour and Employment (2009) 'Report on Effect of Economic Slowdown on Employment in India (October–December 2008)', Government of India, http://labourbureau.nic.in/Report_on_EOFEMP_Jan09.pdf, accessed 27 August 2009.

Mitra, S. K. (2001) 'Capitalise on Labour Flexibility', *Economic Times*, 8 March.

Nagaraj, R. (2004) 'Fall in Organised Manufacturing Employment: a Brief Note', *Economic and Political Weekly*, 39, 30 (24 July): 3387–90.

National Trade Union Initiative (NTUI) (2004) Minutes of meeting on 14–15 February at Shramik Union office, Bombay.

Nicholas Employees' Union (2003) 'Trade Union Rally Jams Capital', *Samvaad* (March): 1.

Patel, B. B. (2001) 'Socio Economic Marginalisation of Displaced Textile Mill Workers in Ahmedabad, Gujarat, India', paper presented to IDPAD workshop on Collective Care Arrangements Among Workers and Non-workers in the Informal Sector, Centre for Economic and Social Studies, Hyderabad, 1–2 March.

Roy, A. and Dey, N. (2009) 'NREGA: Breaking New Ground', *The Hindu Magazine*, 21 June: 1–4.

Soman, M. (2003) 'India Inc Cuts More Jobs in '01–02 Than in Past Three Years', *Economic Times*, 6 May.

Stiglitz, J. (2002) *Globalization and its Discontents*, London: Penguin Books.

Subramaniam, G. G. (2003) 'Dark Secret: Who Killed the Cancun Conference?' *Economic Times*, 20 September.

Subramanya, R. K. A. (2005) 'The Importance of Employment Regulation and Unorganized Sector Workers' Bill', *Labour File*, 3, 2 (March–April): 26–30.

Tagore, R. (1976) *Nationalism*, New Delhi: Macmillan India.

van Wersch, H. (1992) *The Bombay Textile Strike 1982–83*, Delhi: Oxford University Press.

World Bank (1995) *World Development Report: Workers in an Integrating World*, Washington, DC: World Bank/IBRD.

Part IV

International Dimensions and Responses

11
Using Domestic Legal Tools to Further Western Labour Internationalism

Greg Flynn and Robert O'Brien

1. Introduction

The labour movement faces a number of profound challenges in the twenty-first century. Chief among those difficulties is coping with the labour market consequences of the industrialization, modernization and globalization of the Chinese and Indian economies. The surge of a numerically large, relatively low paid and politically weak labour force into the global economy threatens to undermine existing economic protection and achievements by Western labour movements and has the potential to lead to destructive conflict between nations and states. The globalization of the US financial crisis in 2008–9 and the ensuing global recession provide further challenges because of reduced employment levels in most states. As a result, governments have been tempted to spark economic growth through measures that undermine or threaten the welfare of other countries, such as the 'Buy America' provisions in the US. The potential for the further use of the beggar-thy-neighbour policies of the 1930s could reappear and further exacerbate the economic crisis.

The traditional options available to workers have often been presented as falling into one of two camps. Workers can cooperate with 'their' companies or their states to ensure local and national competitiveness or they can attempt to cooperate internationally to limit the exploitation of corporations and states. The choice often appears to be between nationalist or internationalist strategies, either of which is problematic. The real challenge is not to choose between nationalist and internationalist strategies, but rather to integrate them. This requires the combination of a recognition that state power is required to improve labour conditions with a sensibility that such power only be deployed in a way that does not threaten workers in other countries.

In this regard, one fruitful way forward for Western labour movements is to put increased energy into changing domestic legal environments so that Western based transnational corporations (TNCs) can be held accountable in their home countries for labour violations of their foreign subsidiaries and sub-contractors. This is a difficult and complicated task, but putting more emphasis on such a strategy is likely to further labour internationalism by integrating nationalist and internationalist strategies. The challenges of altering domestic legal regimes are immense. The importance and possibilities of such an approach can be highlighted through a consideration of the past experiences of internationalism, developments in labour standards debates and practices and changes that have occurred in both international and domestic legal arenas arising from increased global integration and the consequences arising therefrom.

2. Labour internationalism

Over the past two centuries internationalism has taken a number of different forms, ranging from the dogma of free trade liberals and the advocates of humanitarian intervention to the alleged civilizing mission of imperialists and missionaries to the revolutionary slogans of workers, republicans and Islamists (Halliday, 1988). Labour internationalism is one variant of the Internationalist movement and the nineteenth and twentieth centuries have featured extensive international projects by workers' organizations and socialist parties. Most visible were the First (1864–76), Second (1889–1917) and Third Internationals (1919–43) that were influenced by a variety of anarchist, Marxist, social democratic and communist groups (Forman, 1998). They varied in their structure and reach, with the First and Second Internationals being federal structures that were confined mostly to Europe, while the Third was world spanning, but tightly controlled by the Soviet state.

Despite differences, these labour internationalist groups shared two key features (Colas, 1994). First, they were reactions to concrete problems facing workers, including the need to deal with strike-breaking by foreign workers, the creation of labour legislation and the defence of socialist revolutions. Second, the Internationals struggled to reconcile the solidarity of workers with the demands of nationalism. Groups interested in improving labour conditions in the modern world, whether they are trade unions, labour-oriented NGOs or concerned consumers, face the same basic problem of internationalism. How can one reconcile the need and desire to show solidarity across borders with the forces of nationalist politics and inclinations? The history of the Internationals flag three key dangers. The first is the problem of Western ethnocentrism. The First and Second Internationals were European organizations that did not greatly engage with the outside world and were largely ignorant of other regions. The second danger is the risk posed by the threat of and mobilization for war. The Second International collapsed because its members were swayed more by the call to arms than the call to peace as Europeans rushed to war in 1914. This was partially due to the fact that the socialist project was so closely associated with nation-building that engaging in war to protect the state seemed logical. The third problem is the linkage of internationalism to state-driven foreign policy concerns. The Third International showed the danger of linking an internationalist project to the needs of a particular state's foreign policies as it evolved into a foreign policy tool of the Soviet Union. Workers' interests around the world were sacrificed to the power and political strategies of the Soviet Union. Similar problems plagued the international role of the US labour movement during the Cold War (Sims, 1992).

The twenty-first century is unlikely to see a reincarnation of the formal labour and socialist Internationals of the nineteenth and twentieth centuries. And while modern internationalism takes a much different organizational form in that it is decentralized, networked and heavily reliant on information technology communications (Waterman, 1998), it could still benefit from consideration of past experiences. In other words, an effort should be made to construct an internationalist approach that is sensitive to the views of workers in other parts of the world, avoids actions that increase political tensions between states and resists being an accomplice of the unsavoury aspects of their own state's foreign policy. The question is how to do so in a modernized and globalized world with an increased prominence of labour standards issues.

3. International labour standards and the North–South divide

International labour standards emerged as a key debate between and amongst states and civil societies in the North and South in the early 1990s. The debate centred around the creation of mechanisms which would lead to the enforcement of 'enabling rights' or core labour standards, including: freedom of association, collective bargaining, freedom from forced labour, abolition of child labour and freedom from discrimination. These enabling rights constitute the basic minimums that allow workers to organize their affairs and participate as partners in economic negotiation and regulation. Enabling rights do not confer all of the other labour protections advocated by the International Labour Organization (ILO), but they do allow workers to pursue those rights from a position of stability and independence.

International labour standards have became a significant issue because state and corporate economic strategies in the North and the South increasingly relied upon cheap and passive labour as a source of development and profit. Since the debt crisis of 1982 and the collapse of communism in Eastern Europe in 1989, most developing countries have abandoned the notion of autonomous development in favour of a strategy of comparative advantage in the global economy, often through export-oriented industrialization. In this context, the key to development lies in attracting foreign direct investment (FDI) to build factories to export goods, resources and occasionally services to the North. In turn, Northern countries have increasingly relied upon imports from several key Southern countries to provide low-cost, mass-produced consumer goods which provide for steady levels of consumption in the face of stagnant real wages and reduced risk of inflation. Transnational corporations are the key vehicles for these economic strategies as they possess the ability to channel the movement of investment into productive enterprises in numerous locations and manage the distribution of the end product. In this evolving global economic environment, international labour standards have been brought to the fore.

In Northern states, three factors have increased the prominence of enforceable labour standards. First, the decline of the standard employment relationship with the advent of increasingly insecure, low-waged employment has corresponded with a flood of manufactured goods into Northern states from the South. The second factor has been the rise of social movements concerned with ethical consumption. The proliferation of information technologies, which facilitate global production, have also allowed workers and consumers to communicate about the conditions under which products are created. A growing number of consumers have accepted responsibility for the impact of their spending decisions on workers and the environment in other parts of the world. The third factor has been a more general debate over global regulation and the public interest. In particular, the lack of protection for basic worker and social rights is contrasted with the elaborate new intellectual property protections afforded to Western corporations.

While enforceable labour standards have become an important issue in Northern states, they remain extremely sensitive for Southern countries for three main reasons. First, because many developing states have based their development on low-cost export strategies, changes in the labour standards regime threaten to undermine one of the cornerstones of their competitive advantage. Second, many developing countries have historically experienced Northern protectionism in the international trade regime. They suspect that the labour standards issue will only be the latest incarnation of Northern protectionism. A third reason is that many developing countries have export models based upon an authoritarian political culture, which systematically excludes labour from decision-making. This was certainly the case with the successful East Asian development state (Deyo, 1993). Respecting 'enabling rights' risks empowering groups that may become political opponents of existing regimes. Authoritarian states have some reason to fear independent labour unions as demonstrated by the democracy struggles in countries as diverse as Poland, South Korea, South Africa and Brazil.

Despite the prominence to which these issues have arisen, labour groups have largely failed to link social and economic rights on the international stage (O'Brien, 2008), and efforts to do so have highlighted political divisions. The politics around the labour standards debate are complex and cut across state, corporate and class lines. The view that Northern states advocate for labour standards and Southern states resist is a mistaken over-simplification. A better understanding of the motivations of the various actors could potentially assist in developing a more collaborative approach to the issue in the future. In this regard, advocates and opponents of enforceable labour standards can be divided into three different groups: proponents, those who will accept and implement labour standards under pressure or rewards and those strongly opposed.

3.1 Proponents

The group strongly in favour of enforceable global labour standards believes that the state must play a role in ensuring fair working conditions in a global marketplace and includes virtually all trade unions in Northern states and many trade unions in Southern states, social democrats in various states and the leadership of traditionally social democratic states, such as the Nordic countries. The primary approach of this collection of interests is to attempt to ensure that international economic agreements and institutions contain provisions that mandate adherence to core labour standards.

In terms of motivation, it is not surprising that social democratic states would seek labour standards at the international level. Ideologically, they are predisposed to creating a social democratic partnership between states, capital and labour on an international basis that mirrors their domestic consensus. Social democratic states also possess some material interest in the issue, since the spread of labour rights should raise labour costs in other countries and marginally reduce the competitive pressure on wages in Northern states. Northern trade unions are committed, on principle, to the spread of an industrial relations model that grants similar rights to all workers, while also providing some material protection from the competition of weak or non-existent labour regimes. In Southern countries there is also a constituency for international labour rights, particularly in countries with highly organized independent militant labour unions such as COSATU in South Africa and CUT in Brazil. These unions are accustomed to collective bargaining, making deals and working within regulatory frameworks and are also motivated by the need for protection from unregulated capitalism and see labour standards as one element to advance their goals.

3.2 Conflicted

A second group contains actors that are either amenable to or have an ambiguous position towards global labour standards, and includes countries like the United States that have both advocated the adoption of core labour rights and taken steps that cast doubt on their commitment to them. There are also a number of corporations that can also live with or, in some cases, even thrive in a world of regulated labour standards, such as those that compete on the basis of quality or brand name. For some of these corporations, labour is a relatively small percentage of their overall costs and they can afford increased labour costs. Other corporations use respect for labour or environmental standards to bolster their brand image and thereby charge a premium for ethical behaviour and use it as a competitive advantage over firms that fail to comply with such standards.

A large question mark hangs over the political position of citizens in Northern countries. On the one hand, the lack of labour standards in many Southern countries may threaten employment prospects, bargaining power and sensibilities of Northern workers and consumers. On the other hand, cheap products produced by such labour allow consumers to enjoy a higher standard of living and greater choice than would otherwise be possible. There are also a number of labour groups in the South that are in a similarly ambiguous position. They agree that labour standards need to be improved and regulated, but disagree that this should be done through a system that imposes penalties on

Southern governments for labour standard abuses in their territories. For example, while many Indian trade unions wish to see basic labour rights extended, they resist linking labour standards to the World Trade Organization (WTO) or other trade agreements because of their anti-imperial stance. At the same time, however, they are unable to suggest feasible alternative enforcement mechanisms.

3.3 Opponents

The group of opponents to international action on labour standards is composed of international business associations, corporations that compete on the basis of price alone, neoliberal states in the North, many neoclassical economists, authoritarian and/or anti-imperialist states in the South, labour organizations in the South that are either tied closely to their state or corporations, and the more radical anti-globalization forces that reject international enforcement of any kind.

International business associations, such as the International Chambers of Commerce, or national associations take a general position against international enforcement of labour standards. Self-regulation suits many businesses in the South and North because it allows them to utilize differences in labour conditions to generate increased profits. Labour is viewed as an exploitable resource, while other factors of production, such as intellectual property rights, are more evidently protected.

A larger obstacle to the implementation of international labour standards are business and consumption models based on the continuous provision of cheaper products. The commitment to constantly reducing prices results in giant retailers demanding suppliers continually reduce costs. When technological advances have been exhausted or ignored, this means squeezing productivity from workers through reduction in wages or changes in working conditions. This has usually meant that Southern workers pay the real price for cheaper mass consumption goods in the North.

Many Southern states, such as India and China, strongly oppose any measures that would link trade access with labour standards. Their general view is that this is another example of Northern states pushing parochial concerns to block imports from developing countries. Given the lack of Northern concessions on issues such as agriculture, there is no desire to address the labour standards issue. Whereas some developing countries can see advantage in some Western proposals on services opening (e.g. India), there are few that see clear benefits to labour agreements, unless they provide access to Northern labour markets.

The path to enforceable global labour standards must learn from the lessons of the past and seek to reconcile as many of those in opposition as possible. While much of the resistance has been generated by business associations, corporations and/or authoritarian states, opposed to enforceable labour standards in any context, other actors could be incorporated into a coalition based on increased economic justice between the North and South. A Western labour internationalism informed by the recent labour standards debates would recognize that while India and China are plagued by poor working conditions and labour rights issues, and these conditions impact the lives of Western workers, the causes and solutions to *some* of these problems lie in Western countries themselves. Acceptance that some responsibility lies with Western corporations and consumers has resulted in states and consumers attempting two different strategies. The first strategy has been to try to increase the consumption of ethically traded goods through a process of persuasion, both in terms of production and consumption. However, what is increasingly clear is that the ethical trade initiative remains in niche markets and the corporate codes of conduct are having a limited impact on the factory floor (Christian Aid, 2004). This lack of success means that the second strategy, an increased focus on attempts to implement more formal legal sanctions against Western TNCs as a means of ensuring the observance of labour standards, must be pursued.

4. Using extraterritorial law to discipline Western multinationals

The concept of 'extraterritoriality' refers to the extension of a state's domestic law and/or judicial jurisdiction to persons located outside of the state or to events that occur beyond the state's territorial borders. The extraterritorial application of state laws has usually been fairly limited because of a general presumption against the application of a country's legal sovereignty to events and persons beyond its territorial integrity. Despite this general presumption, there has been an increase in the use of extraterritorial laws in recent years to create new criminal and civil liability consequences for domestic and non-domestic actors. These developments could be harnessed to protect labour rights.

4.1 Extension of criminal law to domestic citizens outside states

The primary rule in international law governing state jurisdiction in relation to the prosecution of crime has been the 'territoriality' principle. It proscribes that the territorial location in which the commission of the offence occurs provides a state with the jurisdiction to prosecute, regardless of the nationality of the offender (Shachor-Landau, 1980: 282). On this basis, there would be limited recourse in domestic legal arenas to pursue TNCs for labour violations that occurred in other countries. However, one key exception to the territoriality principle is the 'universality' principle. It is the basic principle underlying prosecution of offences in the international criminal law regime. This exception provides *all* nations with the jurisdiction to prosecute offenders for international crimes, such as genocide, piracy, terrorism or hijacking. This exception provides that a country may prosecute an individual suspected of one of these crimes within its own jurisdiction, extradite the accused to the International Criminal Court (ICC) where it has jurisdiction to deal with the offence or offender, or to another country that is willing to prosecute the offence and has sought extradition of the accused. Recent developments in this area also provide some potential, particularly in relation to sex crimes against women and children and in relation to terrorist-related activities of national citizens.

In relation to the sex trade, many civil law-based systems had already extended jurisdiction on the basis of the nationality principle. This development has now also been advanced in the traditionally territoriality based common law systems. The US enacted the Protect Act in 2003 that eased efforts to prosecute US citizens committing crimes against children outside of the United States (Lichtblau and James, 2004). The UK, Canada and Australia have also similarly extended the reach of their criminal law regimes beyond their territorial borders on the basis of the nationality principle. At the same time, civil law jurisdictions have made prosecution less difficult through the elimination of formal requirements, such as the filing of a criminal complaint by the victim, consent of the government of the state in which the offence occurred and/or the requirement of double criminality. The events of 11 September 2001 and the subsequent 'War on Terror' provide a second situation where states have been more willing to prosecute their domestic citizens in relation to events that occur beyond the borders of the state. For example, in 2007, the United States prosecuted Chiquita Brands International Inc., a US incorporated company, for engaging in transactions with a specially designated global terrorist group in Columbia.[1]

While both of these examples provide for the potential application and extension of domestic criminal law to events beyond state borders, it remains unlikely that such an approach will be advanced on a unilateral basis in relation to labour violations. For example, the jurisdiction of the ICC *does not* include corporations (Shamir, 2004: 661). In addition, states have tended to work more cooperatively in their approach to the regulation and elimination of criminal conduct at the corporate economic level. Whether through harmonization of laws, the extension of authority to supranational organizations or through other coordinated efforts, states have sought to control unwanted economic behaviour on a multilateral basis. For example, attempts to control economic criminal conduct such as money-laundering or corrupt business practices have been addressed in the international arena through the establishment of international conventions, the creation of enforcement and advisory bodies and a harmonization of domestic criminal laws (Stessens, 2003: ch. 11). While one notable exception has been the application of US anti-trust legislation and enforcement (Davidow, 2002), it is unlikely that any one state would eschew the cooperative-based approach to unwanted economic behaviour on the part of corporate citizens.

4.2 Extension of civil jurisdiction to non-domestic actors

Generally speaking, most states will only provide civil liability jurisdiction where one of the parties involved is a national citizen or the events giving rise to the claim for liability occurred within the state. A significant exception to this proposition is the Alien Claims Torts Act (ACTA) which provides US courts with jurisdiction over civil actions commenced by non-citizens, in relation to violations of the law of nations or a Treaty of the United States, even where the wrongful conduct occurred outside of the United States and did not involve a US actor. The scope of ACTA was confirmed in the 1980 *Filartiga* case in which the US Second Circuit Court of Appeal permitted a claim advanced by a Paraguayan family, based on the torture and death of their son at the hands of a Paraguayan state official.[2] Following the *Filartiga* decision a number of claims were filed in the US courts by non-citizens claiming civil damages for alleged violations of the law of nations by state actors in their home countries.

In the 1995 *Kadic v. Karadzic* case the courts extended the application of ACTA to claims brought against private non-state actors, such as multinational corporations, for *jus cogens* (higher law which may not be violated by any state) violations and to those situations where the actions of the private defendant were sufficiently tied to state action.[3] This decision was remarkable for the fact that it extended potential liability for a violation of the law of nations, something previously considered under international law to be only possible by a state actor, to private individuals including multinational corporations. The California District

Court and the Ninth Circuit Court of Appeal in the *Doe v. Unocal* series of decisions extended the range of ACTA to include the provision of 'knowing practical assistance or encouragement which has a substantial effect on the perpetration of the crime' by state actors.[4] Unfortunately, given the current state of international law, it is unlikely that traditional labour-related concerns, such as sweatshop conditions, low wages and long hours, would rise to the levels necessary to constitute violations of the law of nations as defined by the Supreme Court (Chanin, 2005).

In addition to ACTA, the US has also extended its domestic legal regime in relation to claims by US citizens for events outside of US territory. In particular, the Helms-Burton Act, the D'Amato Act and the Torture Victim Protection Act all provide US citizens with causes of action in US courts against foreign citizens in relation to extraterritorial events.

In practice, the use of this possible remedy has been relatively limited (Flynn and O'Brien, 2010). However, the enactment of extraterritorial domestic laws appears to provide a potential avenue to impact on the conduct of transnational corporations and enforce global labour standards. In particular, there have been at least three developments that provide some opportunity to hold corporations accountable for their actions in other states. First, the application of the nationality principle reveals that states can hold national private actors accountable for the commission of certain types of crimes in foreign states as is most clearly illustrated in the evolution of sex crime laws. There is no reason to suggest that this principle could not be extended to other types of offences as well. Second, some national security and anti-terrorism provisions can be used to hold corporations responsible for assisting groups engaged in terrorizing foreign populations. Third, in some narrow cases foreign residents and US citizens can both use the US civil law system to hold corporations accountable for acts committed outside the United States.

5. Obstacles and problems in using extraterritorial laws

Despite the promise of extraterritorial laws, immense hurdles remain in actually using this approach to successfully pursue enforceable labour standards on a global basis. Firstly, the primary criticism against any form of extraterritoriality is that it is an infringement upon the sovereignty of other countries. This can result in strained diplomatic and trading relations between states and the use of retaliatory measures by affected states to alleviate the impact of the extraterritorial laws and thereby undermine the effectiveness of this approach.

A second criticism is that it leads to a lack of predictability and consistency for private actors in the international arena. Global corporations are expected to be aware of the laws that emanate from their own domestic jurisdiction, but must also be cognizant of the laws applied by other countries to international transactions. Given the divergent strategies employed by states around the world to address various policy problems, this difficulty raises more than just a concern over the cost of doing business, but also interferes with the ability of these organizations to plan their affairs and generates the potential for a lack of fairness by the enforcement of legislation that was not foreseen. The extension of competing domestic law regimes into the international market creates the real possibility of the enforcement of laws that directly conflict and contradict one another, thereby creating unfairness for international actors and undermining the policies that underlie those measures.

A third obstacle is the ability of corporations to sabotage their application. In particular, corporations will structure their transactions and affairs in such a manner as to avoid a jurisdiction altogether, with a concomitant effect of lessening investment and commercial activity in that jurisdiction and consequent economic repercussions that flow from that event. A fourth difficulty with extraterritorial approaches is the inherent legal nature of the enforcement measures, and in particular the necessity of collecting evidence. In some states, and in some circumstances, the gathering of sufficient evidence to meet the requisite standard of proof will be particularly difficult, depending on the relationship between the nations in question, the transient nature of the parties involved in the events or transactions, the types of offences that are alleged, and the willingness of victims and other witnesses to participate in the process (Collingsworth, 2003).

The last and perhaps most important difficulty that arises is the nature of the purported defendants to the criminal and civil actions. In particular, most of the private actors in the international arena are TNCs and the law, in most states, deems these 'legal persons' and each of their subsidiaries as separate legal entities (Wilson, 2006: 53). As such, in the absence of direct participation in the alleged events by the parent company, criminal or civil liability that is incurred by a subsidiary is usually not attributable to the rest of the multinational corporation (Blumberg, 2001: 301–7). This has two significant ramifications. First, personal jurisdiction for civil claims and jurisdiction in general for criminal prosecutions may be difficult, if not impossible, to assert over foreign subsidiaries that have no direct relationship with the state claiming jurisdiction. Second, even if a court were able to acquire jurisdiction over a subsidiary, the judgement would only apply to the subsidiary and not the parent company. As such, criminal prosecutions may have limited publicity effect and minimal real impact on the larger corporation. Similarly, civil judgements may be difficult to enforce given a lack of resources contained at the subsidiary level and with no recourse against the parent corporation.

While these obstacles are potentially problematic, a novel approach to the enforcement of global labour standards may make it possible to overcome these difficulties. Firstly, the problems of international comity and consistency of laws have already been addressed through the current pursuit of core labour standards. In particular, international standards have already been accepted by all nations through their participation in the ILO. The innovation of an extraterritorial approach is that these universally agreed upon rules would be enforced domestically in Northern states for violations anywhere in the world. In addition, Northern states' legal action would bolster the enforcement capability of Southern states which, in the absence of a global response, may be reluctant to prosecute for fear of driving away investment.

The third obstacle, the threat of divestment, would be lessened if extraterritorial action was taken on in a concerted effort or if it was adopted by the major economic powers. If the United States and the EU were to take action to enforce global labour standards for violations abroad, it is much less likely to be a problem. TNCs continue to have a home nationality and rely upon regional markets and political assistance of Western states. For most corporations there are many advantages to being a US or EU company that would not be outweighed by having to live up to basic labour rights.

The fourth problem, the inability to gather sufficient evidence, may greatly hamper the effectiveness of the extension of domestic laws and jurisdiction beyond the borders of the state, particularly where the violations occur in non-cooperative states. However, while this need to gather evidence would place a burden upon labour movements, it is not an insurmountable problem. A mechanism already exists for nationals outside OECD countries to advance claims for the violation of labour, environmental and social rights against OECD TNCs within OECD states themselves. The OECD Guidelines for Multinationals were revised in 1998 and 2000 and further empowered a set of institutions and rights for citizens outside the OECD (OECD, 2000). As a result, National Contact Points (NCP) have been established in all OECD states to provide a space for people, including persons from non-OECD states, to make claims against the multinationals of OECD states and to publish their activities on an annual basis. Thus, women workers in a Sri Lankan export processing zone can take their case against a Korean TNC to the NCP in Seoul and Ecuadorian mine workers can advance a claim against Canadian TNCs to the NCP in Ottawa. The results of such proceedings will be published yearly.

The problem with NCPs and the Guidelines process has not been an inability on the part of claimants to uncover sufficient evidence to support their claims, but rather the voluntary nature of the process, the role of the NCP as a facilitator in attempting to resolve the conflict through mediation and the advisory nature of the Guidelines. For example, the NCP statement concerning the filing of a complaint against Ivanhoe Mines Ltd. by the Canadian Labour Congress confirms these difficulties – no agreement could be reached between the parties to participate in the process, the NCP's involvement was limited to trying to facilitate a dialogue between the parties and the Canadian government only expected and encouraged Canadian companies to observe the Guidelines (OECD, 2002). Accordingly, it is not the evidentiary requirement that has prevented claims concerning the actions of TNCs from being resolved through this process, but rather that the forum itself cannot be applied to actors that are not interested in resolving potential conflicts. As such, a more robust enforcement vehicle is required in these situations. Evidentiary requirements, like other obstacles to the use of a legal approach including the burden of proof, the need for service of proceedings on the TNCs in the jurisdiction of the courts and possible defences that could be raised in both criminal and civil claims, can be overcome if the appropriate forum for advancing these causes of action were available.

The fifth and final obstacle facing an extension of domestic law is the legal character of the various actors involved. This obstacle cannot be overcome solely through the diligence and efforts of the labour movement or any other global or local movement or organization. In the absence of reform of the manner in which all domestic legal systems treat corporate entities or a stronger legal doctrine that permits the 'piercing of the corporate veil', attempts to pursue legal remedies against multinational corporations will remain relatively limited and ineffectual in most circumstances.

6. Moving forward

Drawing upon the history of previous internationalist practice and the experience of the core labour standards experience, labour groups in the West should consider how they can advance a strategy which takes account of workers' concerns in other states, reduces inter-state tension and keeps an independent stance towards their own state's foreign policy. This should entail some consideration of what Western labour movements can do inside their own territory to control Western TNCs. In comparative terms, labour movements in China and India face much larger challenges than their Western counterparts. Thus, while Western labour has been under constant attack for the past thirty years, it still has greater financial resources and ability to influence the global agenda. In this regard, one possible way forward is for Western labour groups to press for TNCs to be held accountable for their actions in their home states. The outlines for such a development are present, but key changes are needed. The principle that Western citizens should be held responsible for the commission of particular crimes in foreign jurisdictions has already been established and has been applied to at least one major multinational corporation in Chiquita Brands International Inc. This principle needs to be further extended to include corporations in relation to all criminal offences and broadened to include the violation of labour standards.

Of course, there are immense challenges. Legal reforms will need to be introduced which hold corporations responsible for the actions of their subsidiaries and sub-contractors, both in domestic and international settings. This generates a series of technical issues in holding sub-contractors responsible in extended production chains. Courts will also need to recognize that even though formal mechanisms might exist to deal with these issues in developing countries, the difficulty of prosecuting transnational corporations shifts the enforcement burden to Western states.

Such a change to the legal architecture will be vigorously opposed by the most powerful economic actors on the planet. This will require a sophisticated political strategy involving splitting off 'good' corporations from 'bad' ones, demonstrating the financial reward of good labour practices through consumer action, threatening corporate interests in trade or investment agreements and offering corporations the certainty of a robust legal environment which punishes wrongdoing. An internationalist response that builds solidarity between workers and opens up the possibilities for greater cooperation in the future should target the offenders of labour rights – the TNCs and their suppliers. India and China are large states which might resent the application of extraterritorial law on Western corporations operating in their jurisdictions. Yet, by focusing Western labour activity on Western-based TNCs, the conflict generated by a direct attack on the policies of other states should be mitigated. It is in the interest of internationalist minded Western labour groups to push for increased national regulation of Western TNCs. Even if Western labour movements are less than successful in changing the legal structure to hold Western TNCs accountable, the struggle to do so can bear fruit. It would simultaneously build solidarity in the labour movement by demonstrating the goodwill and good sense of Western workers and put pressure on the nationalistic approaches of their own states. This would go some way to meeting the interests of workers in the North, South, East and West.

Notes

1. *US v. Chiquita Brands International Inc.*, Criminal No. 07-055 (US District Court, District of Columbia, 14 March 2007).
2. *Filartiga v. Pena-Irala*, 630 F2d 876.
3. *Kadic v. Karadzic*, 70 3d 232.
4. *Doe V v. Unocal Corp.*, 110 F.Supp. 2d 1294 (C.D. Cal. 2000), *Doe VI v. Unocal*, No. 00-56603, 2002 WL 31063976 (9th Cir. 18 September 2002).

References

Blumberg, P. I. (2001) 'Accountability of Multinational Corporations: the Barriers Presented by Concepts of the Corporate Juridical Entity', in *Hastings International and Comparative Law Review*, 24, 3 (Spring): 297–320.

Chanin, J. M. (2005) 'The Regulatory Grass is Greener: a Comparative Analysis of the Alien Tort Claims Act and the European Union's Green Paper on Corporate and Social Responsibility', *Indiana Journal of Global Legal Studies*, 12: 745–78.

Christian Aid (2004) *Behind the Mask: the Real Face of Corporate Social Responsibility*, London: Christian Aid.

Colas, A. (1994) 'Putting Cosmopolitanism into Practice: the Case of Socialist Internationalism', *Millennium*, 23, 3: 513–34.

Collingsworth, T. (2003) 'Using the Alien Tort Claims Act to Introduce the Rule of Law to the Global Economy', International Labour Rights Fund, available at http://www.iradvocates.org/collingsworth220605.pdf.

Davidow, J. (2002) 'International Implications of US Antitrust in the George W. Bush Era', *World Competition*, 25, 4: 493–507.

Deyo, F. C. (1993) *Beneath the Miracle: Labor Subordination in the New Asian Industrialism*, Berkeley: University of California Press.

Forman, M. (1998) *Nationalism and the International Labor Movement: the Idea of the Nation in Socialist and Anarchist Theory*, University Park, PA: Pennsylvania State University Press.

Flynn, G. and O'Brien, R. (2010) 'An Internationalist Labour Response to the Globalization of India and China', *Global Labour Journal*, 1, 1: 178–202.

Halliday, F. (1988) 'Three Concepts of Internationalism', *International Affairs*, 64, 2: 187–98.

Lichtblau, E. and Dao, J. (2004) 'US is Now Pursuing Americans Who Commit Sex Crimes Overseas', *New York Times*, 8 June.

O'Brien, R. (2008) 'No Safe Havens: Labour, Regional Integration and Globalisation', in A. F. Cooper, C. W. Hughes and P. de Lombaerde (eds), *Regionalisation and Global Governance: the Taming of Globalisation?* New York: Routledge, pp. 142–56.

OECD (2000) *The OECD Guidelines for Multinational Enterprises*, Paris: OECD, available at www.oecd.org.

OECD (2002) Statement of National Contact Point for Canada, Ivanhoe Mines Ltd. and the Canadian Labour Congress, available at http://www.oecd.org/dataoecd/20/ 24/37205653.pdf.

Shachor-Landau, C. (1980) 'Extra-Territorial Penal Jurisdiction and Extradition', *International and Comparative Law Quarterly*, 29, 2/3 (April–July): 274–95.

Shamir, R. (2004) 'Between Self-Regulation and the Alien Tort Claims Act: On the Contested Concept of Corporate Social Responsibility', *Law and Society Review*, 38, 4 (December): 635–64.

Sims, B. (1992) *Workers of the World Undermined: American Labor's Role in US Foreign Policy*, Boston: South End Press.

Stessens, G. (2000) *Money Laundering: a New International Law Enforcement Model*, Cambridge: Cambridge University Press.

Waterman, P. (1998) *Globalization, Social Movements and the New Internationalisms*, London: Mansell.

Wilson, A. (2006) 'Beyond Unocal: Conceptual Problems in Using International Norms to Hold Transnational Corporations Liable under the Alien Tort Claims Act', in O. de Schutter (ed.), *Transnational Corporations and Human Rights*, Portland: Hart Publishing.

12
Assessing China's Future Possibilities in an Unstable Neoliberal World

Manfred Bienefeld

1. Introduction and summary

This volume brings together chapters focusing on the internal evolution of China's and India's labour markets and, taken together, they bear eloquent witness to the power and the ambiguity of the historic transformations occurring in these two societies. We may now draw upon the evidence presented in the book to try to reach defensible on-balance conclusions as to whether these societies are currently on their way to becoming fully employed, high-wage societies in which strong and relatively secure middle classes can anchor stable democratic polities; or whether their current trajectories are more likely to see them fall prey to the tensions and contradictions historically associated with rising inequality, endemic economic instability and increasing social and political conflict.

This chapter takes as its point of departure the two[1] competing accounts of globalization set out so effectively by Bowles: the neoclassical account, which focuses on global welfare gains thought to be associated with the continued liberalization and depoliticization of markets in an increasingly integrated global economy; and an 'anti-neoliberal' account, increasingly concerned about the possibility that globalization may be dangerously undermining the capacity of nation-states to harness the centrifugal tendencies of competitive market forces in the 'public interest'. In this chapter the 'multi-centred state' approach, which Bowles also defines, is treated as a sub-set of the anti-neoliberal approach because analytically, it shares the latter's concern with the dangers posed by the erosion of sovereignty.

Ultimately this chapter asks how each of these two broad perspectives imagines China's eventual emergence as a stable, prosperous high wage society whose citizens are increasingly free to develop their human potential and to resolve their remaining differences through genuinely democratic processes; and how such an outcome could be reconciled with the simultaneous evolution of a stable and rational international economic system in which financial and political stability could be combined with socially desirable and environmentally sustainable growth.

The neoliberal revolution was never about demanding any specific set of *laissez-faire* policies; it was about insisting on, facilitating, promoting and enforcing a direction of change. It was at once pragmatic and ideological, and all the more powerful for that. The ultimate aim has been to protect capital from 'political meddling' by 'special interests'[2] by creating a global level playing field (for investors); by expanding the ambit of markets by privatizing public assets, by subjecting public activities to commercial logic and by creating ever new marketable property rights (the right to pollute, the right to own large segments of the public record, the right to own seeds and natural life forms); by elevating private, individual rights over social rights; by creating an asymmetrical world in which market actors are assumed to be primarily held accountable by market forces, while public officials are increasingly enmeshed in impenetrable and unpredictable webs of bureaucratic accountability; and by changing the language and the concepts that structure our thoughts and our communication, turning working people into human capital. Those who are concerned about the human, social, political and environmental consequences of this version of globalization must understand that it is this direction of change that needs to be altered or reversed and to that end they must focus on the forces and the circumstances that are driving – and contesting – these processes. Similarly, those who wish to understand the future implications of the issues and trends chronicled and analysed in this book, can ultimately do so by understanding how those forces are likely to evolve in future.

In this context, the main argument of this chapter is rooted in the 'multi-centred state' segment of the 'anti-neoliberal' perspective. In essence, it argues that a primary determinant of whether China (and India) will succeed in building stable, prosperous and genuinely democratic societies on the foundations that they have laid to date, will be whether they are able to contain – and attenuate – the relentless neoliberal pressure for market empowerment, both at the domestic, and the international, levels.

The structure of the chapter is as follows. The next section will explain the point of departure, which is that the neoliberal revolution has gone too far and that, despite enormous obstacles, some way will have to be found to restore a more equitable, desirable and sustainable balance between political, social and environmental dimensions of reality on the one hand, and economic realities on the other. The section that follows will discuss how such a perspective shapes the way one projects the current transformations of China into the future, in essence asking whether that challenge is likely to be met. The final section will conclude with a brief discussion of the question of agency, examining the political forces in China that might conceivably play a role in redirecting current national, and ultimately even global, trajectories.

2. Societies, market embeddedness and neoliberal globalization

Ultimately the reason why the world economy needs to be conceived and constructed as a world of sovereign societies is that markets cannot be managed to promote human and social welfare unless they are embedded in societies that can define the parameters within which they operate. While efficiency in the narrow sense of cost minimization is an important objective for any society, the drive under competitive markets for this kind of efficiency must occur within socially and politically defined limits that take due account of other, often conflicting, social objectives. If production costs could be lowered by chaining children to machines and injecting them with drugs to keep them alert, a civilized society would surely define and enforce legal restrictions on the use of child labour. And the same is true of countless other issues. Ultimately choices in the economic sphere must be constrained by rules that recognize – and protect – the primary objective of public policy, namely the creation of peaceful and humane societies in which people can live fulfilling, productive and appreciated lives as members of caring, supportive and sustainable communities; rules that allow societies to determine the relative weight given to workplace demands driven by the need for competitiveness, and other demands linked to people's family and community responsibilities or their need for social and economic security; or rules that determine the relative priority given to short-run profitability, as against long-run objectives linked to environmental protection, social and political stability or national security. None of these trade-offs can legitimately be left to be determined by the competitive process and yet that is precisely what has been happening as international competitiveness has increasingly come to dominate policy choices.

But the creation and enforcement of a framework that can manage market forces in the public interest is no minor task. Indeed many Marxists dismiss the idea as a social democratic illusion based on a failure to understand how easily economic power can be converted into political power in market societies. Such fears are well founded, as the continuing rollback of the post-Second World War welfare state would suggest. On the other hand, it is also true that the emergence – and persistence – of welfare states between 1949 and 1974 demonstrates that markets can be made to function in the public interest for an extended period of time as Figure 12.1 shows so decisively. In fact, the 'social markets' of that early post-Second World War era produced fundamentally different outcomes from the neoliberal markets that came to dominate over the next thirty-five years. Not only was growth more rapid and sustained in that earlier era, but benefits were far more widely distributed. The contrast between these two 'capitalisms' was even greater than these remarkable graphs would suggest, because they take no account of the fact that the social market era saw major improvements in working hours, working conditions, social protection, employment security and economic stability, many of which have been systematically undermined in the neoliberal era as escalating financial crises have become endemic and increasingly destructive. Indeed, as regards financial stability, the contrast between these two eras could not be more stark with a World Bank study reporting *no* 'serious banking crises' between 1947 and 1974, compared to sixty-nine between 1974 and 1992 (Stiglitz, 2001). Since then financial instability has continued to grow as the Asian and Russian crises of 1997/98 were followed by the dot.com collapse of 2001 and then by the global financial meltdown of 2008, which continues to hold the global economy hostage.

Moreover, although Figure 12.1 relates specifically to the United States, the fact that the social market era was associated with similarly superior outcomes in all of the industrial countries, despite significant differences in their domestic political and institutional circumstances, supports the basic argument of this chapter which is that these outcomes were closely linked to the fact that during this era the rules of the international economy emphasized national policy autonomy, in part by providing for national capital controls to manage short-term capital flows. Such policy autonomy allows markets to be embedded and the interests of capital to be more effectively balanced against other interests. Or, in Keynes's words, it allows societies to 'engage in their favourite social experiments' (Keynes, 1933 as cited in Crotty, 1983: 61).

Rising together: change in family income, 1947–1979
by quintile and top 5%

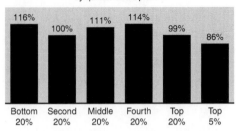

Bottom 20%	Second 20%	Middle 20%	Fourth 20%	Top 20%	Top 5%
116%	100%	111%	114%	99%	86%

Drifting apart: change in family income, 1979–2001
by quintile and top 5%

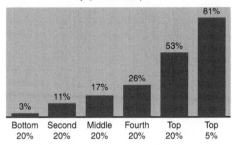

Bottom 20%	Second 20%	Middle 20%	Fourth 20%	Top 20%	Top 5%
3%	11%	17%	26%	53%	81%

Change in after-tax family income, 1979–2000

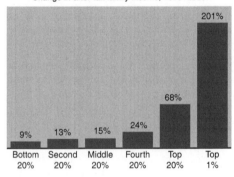

Bottom 20%	Second 20%	Middle 20%	Fourth 20%	Top 20%	Top 1%
9%	13%	15%	24%	68%	201%

Figure 12.1 US: changes in family income 1947–1979 and 1979–2001

Source: US Census Bureau and Congressional Budget Office Data,[3] http://www.faireconomy.
org/research/income_charts.html, accessed 20 September 2004.

Of course capital controls are only a necessary, not a sufficient, condition for embeddedness since they do not guarantee that the resulting
policy autonomy will be used to promote more balanced, sustainable
and socially desirable outcomes. For that one needs societies with the

political will, the sense of social solidarity, and the administrative capacity to establish and enforce fair, transparent and predictable limits to market forces; limits that do not unduly stifle their creativity, or their dynamism, but that do allow other social interests and objectives to be adequately protected. And in the early post-war world those conditions were generally met, partly because depression and war and the widespread fear of communism had strengthened the political will to 'do better', partly because in many countries the war had strengthened social solidarity, and partly because national economies were still far more integrated at the time. In a very real sense, the world had learned a lesson of history, as politicians and policy-makers shared an almost universal commitment to prevent a recurrence of the disasters of the 1920s and 1930s.

But it is not only the positive evidence from the social market era that lends support to the embedded market thesis. Negative evidence from the neoliberal era lends equally strong support to the idea that the disasters of the 1920s and 1930s were ultimately rooted in the destabilizing effects of volatile international capital flows. With escalating financial crises fuelling massive and unsustainable global imbalances, with persistent and chronic levels of unemployment in most leading economies, with growth hobbled by escalating mountains of debt, with inequality at levels not seen for almost a hundred years, with wages stalled and workers' rights in broad retreat around the world it is no exaggeration to say that the worst fears of those who had learned those earlier lessons of history are now coming to pass, as the world once again learns that disembedded neoliberal markets are unstable, divisive, inefficient and ultimately unsustainable, and that endemic instability and economic extremes destroy the legitimacy of markets, breed political extremism, fuel social conflict and undermine the conditions for productive investment.

Just as the regulated Bretton Woods system witnessed the emergence of embedded markets in all industrial countries, so neoliberal globalization is accelerating the disembedding of markets around the world, albeit at differential rates depending on historically determined political and institutional circumstances in particular societies. But it would be wrong to think that the social market era was brought to an end simply because global market forces undermined inherently stable, embedded market economies. In fact, although the social market era demonstrated that market forces could be harnessed in the public interest, it did not set aside the dialectic of history and so it was constantly generating its own contradictions, between more (Germany, Japan) and less (US, UK) successful economies, between capital and labour, and between core and peripheral economies, and these imbalances ultimately provided financial interests with the leverage and the opportunity to roll back the vital safeguards that had been built into the early Bretton Woods agreement – and into many national financial regulatory regimes despite their fierce opposition.[4]

And so, in the 1970s, with the global economy hobbled by massive dislocations linked to huge trade imbalances, the oil crisis and falling profitability, the resumption of international financial flows, fuelled by recycled petrodollars and the rapidly growing Eurodollar markets was greeted with widespread enthusiasm since, in the short run, it allowed conflicts to be defused, investment to be sustained and growing imbalances to be financed. In these circumstances voices of caution were easily ignored, especially since the previous twenty-five years of broad-based prosperity had fuelled the naïve belief that benign socioeconomic outcomes were simply the natural, almost inevitable, outcome of the operation of market forces. Financial interests, led by those of the US and the UK, were able to persuade voters and governments, even in countries with deeply embedded markets, to accept or tolerate developments that would ultimately restore a neoliberal international policy framework. While most were reluctant at first, the process fed on itself because, as economic imbalances grew, as real interest rates rose, as economic instability increased, as competitive pressures intensified, as global wage differentials came to be ever more effectively *arbitraged* by floods of international finance and as production structures were progressively internationalized, markets were progressively disembedded and this, in turn, constrained the choices available to voters by increasingly undermining the capacity of governments to maintain politically, socially or economically sustainable balances between the interests of capital, labour and society.

Finally, the importance of embedded markets as a critically important determinant of a society's capacity to manage market forces in the public interest is also supported by the experience of those few Asian countries that successfully made the transition to modern, prosperous, high-wage societies over the past fifty years. As the literature of the developmental state has clearly shown,[5] these countries – most especially Japan, South Korea and Taiwan – based their success on embedded markets that were significantly insulated from the policy distortions associated with relatively free short-term capital flows, or with direct foreign investment flows that eventually allow powerful international corporate and financial actors to undermine a society's capacity to make policy choices in its long-term national interest.

From this perspective the first, and most pressing, question is whether China (or India) is likely to develop into a social market economy based on the findings presented in the other chapters in this volume, and whether the emergence of a social market in one, or both, of these major economies might play a role in reshaping global trajectories, which is the focus of the final section of this chapter.

As defined here, a social market is one in which decisions about economic efficiency as a social objective are effectively and legitimately balanced against other social objectives. A neoliberal market, by contrast, is one in which the efficiency objective, narrowly defined as international competitiveness, has become dominant because of global competitive pressures and the disproportionate influence of international actors and institutions on domestic policy processes. The contrast was well described in a 1994 paper co-authored for the World Bank by Ramgopal Agarwala, reflecting on his experience as the erstwhile head of a 1986 World Bank Mission[6] to assess the impact of the Bank's structural adjustment policies in Africa. Having described how the participatory approach to that Mission had led him and his team to be persuaded by an 'overwhelming weight of opinion and evidence' that the Bank's market empowering policies were themselves a central part of the continent's deepening problems, he was led to express the hope that:

> The crises in Africa and Latin America, and more recently in the former Soviet Union and Eastern Europe, may in time lead to the emergence of a new paradigm or a synthesis between the Keynesian and neoclassical paradigms. Some elements of such a synthesis exist in the workings of the social-market economy in Germany, the Nordic countries, the Netherlands, and in the experiences of Japan and [South] Korea. Some more time will probably have to elapse before the crisis deepens, anomalies [undermining the neoclassical paradigm] accumulate, and a new paradigm is advocated by a persuasive and powerful proponent.

> The socioeconomic achievements of these [social market] countries are impressive historically and they were attained without following a doctrinaire free-market [or 'neoliberal'] approach. The combination of relatively free-market economic policies and public social policies in these countries could be a recipe for Africa. But a prior condition was an enabling environment, that would (1) provide incentives for prices, markets and the private sector to work, and (2) create an infrastructure (capacity building) so that economic agents can take

advantage of the incentives of free markets and prices. This infrastructure is defined broadly to include the social (universal access to food and nutrition, primary education and health, and family planning), physical, legal, and technological infrastructure. To provide the essential infrastructure and ensure the smooth functioning of markets, the government would need to be activist. Improving governance is essential for development.[7]

But to understand the conditions needed for such 'improved governance' to become possible we do not need 'a synthesis of Keynesian and neoclassical paradigms', we only need to rescue Keynes from his neoclassical interpreters. In fact, the oft-repeated claim that the 'mounting problems caused by the oil crisis and stagflation during the 1970s' destroyed Keynes's credibility completely ignores his insistence on the need for capital controls as a precondition for the effective management of national economies. Once this is acknowledged, the events of the 1970s powerfully validate the Keynesian paradigm in that Keynes would have been the first to argue that 'Keynesian economic management' would be impossible in a world in which volatile international capital flows had come to play such a dominant role.

The two other neglected – or suppressed – elements of Keynes's thought that further reinforce the above conclusion concern his clear and persistent awareness that international capital flows, like domestic investments, are always necessarily political to a degree. Properly understood, this implies that long-term international capital flows need to be managed so as to ensure a balance of political forces – and of underlying material interests – that will allow policy choices to continue to be made 'in the national interest', just as domestic investments need to include provision for politically guided strategic investments.

Indeed, as regards public sector involvement in domestic investment and the implementation of international capital controls, it is hard not to agree with Paul Krugman's (1999: 74) conclusion, soon after the Asian financial crisis, that 'sooner or later we will have to turn the clock at least part of the way back'. While he was only referring to a need to restore capital controls in certain countries, Keynesian logic would extend that conclusion to all countries and to both strategic investment and international capital flows.

Unfortunately, turning the clock back has become even more difficult in the wake of the current financial crisis. Although it has triggered much talk of the need for financial re-regulation, little of substance has been achieved, in part because the issue of national capital controls has been left largely untouched as attention has been squarely focused on the need for better global policy coordination. While national governments and central banks have re-emerged as central actors on the global stage, their interventions have generally been tolerated as unwelcome temporary necessities to be reversed at the earliest opportunity, while those charged with the task of rethinking the structure of the global financial system have chosen – or been required as a condition of remaining 'credible' – to assume that finance is global and must therefore be regulated globally, even though this obscures the most critical task which is to reconnect finance to productive activities and to the meaningful national political processes that must legitimate the regulatory frameworks within which finance must be required to function if it is to serve the public interest. Viewed through this lens, both the domestic and the international impact of China's (and India's) further integration into the global economy will depend critically on whether they can embed their burgeoning markets within viable and representative political structures, while at the same lending support to the recreation of an international policy framework that encourages such developments in all member countries. While this is obviously a long shot, activists and policy-makers around the world must understand that this is the world's best – and possibly only – chance to avert a future in which the recent financial upheavals will be remembered only as the mild, early stages of a process that ultimately led the world into a long dark age of hyper-inflation, depression and war.

3. Interpreting – and projecting – China's global integration

Fortunately for China (and India), both have retained a significant degree of control over international financial flows[8] and this, combined with their substantial holdings of foreign exchange reserves, has provided them with a significant degree of policy autonomy in the short run. Indeed, given current global imbalances and the precarious position of the US dollar, their leverage in global negotiations has increased significantly as a result, even though they also remain significantly dependent on US markets and on the US dollar since their reserves are still largely held in that form.

Important though these points are in the short run, China's medium-term room for manoeuvre will depend on its ability to redirect its production capacities to a rapidly growing domestic market fuelled by rising real wages and other forms of non-debt based domestic consumption and investment, including investment in infrastructure and technology. In fact, given the availability of labour and of foreign exchange to cover the immediate costs of such a transition, there are two primary obstacles to such a strategic shift. The first, which is the willingness – and/or the ability – to sustain investment at lower rates of profit, is critically dependent on the second, which is the speed with which world-class technology can be absorbed and developed by China's national firms in a form that allows the associated technology rents to underwrite the costs of such a high-wage policy in the longer run.[9] Obviously the ability to overcome these obstacles is mainly a political matter, ultimately depending on the government's relative independence from capital domestically, and its ability to develop a capacity to secure national technology rents, first by investing in the development of such capabilities through some form of industrial policy, and second by empowering more independent labour unions that could provide political support for macroeconomic policies to keep labour markets relatively tight and thereby lay the economic foundations for a 'harmonious society' that can provide its citizens with prosperity and security in a sustainable, peaceful, democratic and mutually supportive setting.

As the other chapters in this book show, and as China's leadership has clearly recognized, the dramatic economic growth that has been achieved in recent decades has not been creating such a society. Indeed, these gains have been achieved at considerable cost, including sharply rising levels of inequality, an erosion of social protection and the explosive growth of ever harsher and more competitive informal sectors absorbing armies of marginalized migrants. Moreover, efforts to reverse these trends are running into strong opposition from those riding high on the wave of prosperity so that even though the current leadership has defined the 'harmonious society' as its long-term goal, China's future is shrouded in uncertainty.

While the shifting alignment of political forces that will determine China's future will be discussed in the final section of the chapter, this one will be concluded by considering how the main international actors are likely to react if China were to adopt a strategy explicitly aimed at the creation of a high-wage social market based on strong national technological capabilities generating technology rents that are primarily appropriated by national factors of production – both capital and labour – and by the public authorities responsible for leading and financing such a strategy.

In fact the forces promoting neoliberal globalization would be – and are, as we will see – implacably opposed to any such development since this would violate their primary objective of ensuring that all significant arenas of production and finance are integrated into the global financial system. Indeed it is impossible to overstate the centrality of this objective which, in Keynesian language, ensures that the rate of interest, and hence the return on capital, will be internationally determined and that policy autonomy and the scope for embedded markets will be sharply limited. In fact, once this objective is achieved international capital becomes relatively indifferent to the location of new competitive production capacities. Conversely, it will always be fiercely opposed to the emergence of relatively independent centres of production and accumulation from which international investors are 'unfairly' excluded. And since that is what had happened in the East Asian NICs (Newly Industrializing Countries) it is instructive to remind ourselves of the process by which South Korea was brought to heel in the 1990s.

In fact, between 1965 and 1990 South Korea (like Taiwan) had emerged as a distinct national centre of accumulation based on high levels of domestic savings. These provided 'cheap' capital[10] to build strong, competitive and relatively independent national industrial capabilities that were able to generate and appropriate the technology rents that, in turn, provided the foundation for a full employment economy with steadily, and rapidly, rising real wages, together with massive and sustained investments in economic infrastructure, education and further industrial and technological development. But, because this development model excluded international investors and encroached on their activities, and because it contravened the golden rule that investment must be driven by shareholder interests and not by national, or citizen, interests,[11] South Korea came under increasingly intense pressure to liberalize its financial links to the outside world. For some time these pressures were successfully resisted, partly because the existing system was working so well but also because by the early 1990s, just as the World Trade Organization (WTO) negotiations were drawing to a close, the Korean government agreed to relax some of its controls on international capital movements, despite strong opposition from many quarters, including its own Ministry of Finance. And, just as those critics had feared and predicted, the resulting vulnerabilities played a key role in sucking the country deeply into the Asian financial crisis of 1997/98, despite its rock-solid macroeconomic fundamentals. But, as so often happens, rather than leading to a sober re-evaluation of the earlier decision to liberalize its external financial links, the crisis forced the government to accept International Monetary Fund (IMF) conditions attached to emergency loans demanding radical reforms to increase international capital's ability to purchase and sell both real and financial assets in the Korean economy.[12] There can be no doubt that the balance of power has shifted sharply in favour of capital as a result, with labour unions fighting a losing battle against the government's relentless efforts to undercut the so-called 'privileges' of permanently employed workers by promoting the casualization of labour and the employers' 'right to hire and fire'.

Nor can one doubt that the significance of these changes was clearly recognized at the time. Indeed, in January 1998 a prominent US economist suggested on CNBC that 'Korea is now owned and operated by our Treasury' (Bertrand, 1998: 307) while Larry Summers declared that 'the United States achieved more changes in the Korean economy as a result of the IMF packages than we did in twenty years of bilateral negotiations' (Wu, 2001: 181).

China, despite its communist government and its occasionally nationalist rhetoric, has until recently persuaded neoliberal power brokers that it had rejected the East Asian model and thus posed no threat to their global project. Indeed, having surveyed the available evidence, one prominent commentator concluded in 2004 that there was no need for concern on this front since China was 'developing precisely the type of economic relationships that US strategy has long sought to create ... [having] opened its economy to FDI, welcomed large scale imports and joined the WTO' and that it had evidently joined the global economy on terms that reinforce its dependence on foreign technology and investment and restrict its ability to become an industrial and technological threat to advanced industrialized democracies (Gilboy, 2004).

However, that confidence has recently been somewhat undermined as global financial instability has made China's leaders more cautious about financial liberalization, including liberalization of its exchange rate, and more receptive to the idea that China may need to build strong, national industrial and technological capabilities to provide the material foundation for the 'harmonious society' to which it now officially aspires. Although many undoubtedly continue to believe that this goal can be achieved within a neoliberal policy framework, the current global crisis appears to have persuaded an increasing number in China, as elsewhere, of the need for more balanced national development strategies and more embedded markets. Indeed, internationally the idea has gained ground that instead of focusing on the creation of a level playing field for international capital, the international policy framework should focus on the creation of constructive, mutually beneficial economic links between internally coherent states with enough national policy autonomy to manage their respective embedded markets. Even before the crisis of 2008 had emphasized the risks and weaknesses of the current neoliberal framework, UNCTAD's 2006 *Trade and Development Report* had echoed many others when it concluded its discussion of the challenges facing the developing world at that time by suggesting that

> much depends on the ability of developing countries to adopt more proactive policies in support of capital formation, structural change and technological upgrading, and on the latitude available to them in light of international rules and disciplines. (UNCTAD, 2006, Overview: 1)

Of course, then as now, the main architects of the neoliberal project treat such ideas as indefensible heresies, which is why this UNCTAD report triggered an immediate strong rebuke from the First Secretary of the US Mission to the United Nations in which he deplored the fact that 'several of the recommendations in the Trade and Development Report run counter to the foundations of sound economic and trade policy' (Low, 2006), suggested that the 'concept of policy space ... implies that all developing countries want to opt out of their international commitments', and denounced the report's 'mischaracterization' of 'the Intellectual Property Rights provisions of US bilateral and multilateral trade agreements as being harmful for development'. Ultimately it is the painfully undiplomatic, categorical tone of this response that clearly identifies it as an ideological response to a development that is being rejected out of hand, with no attempt to deal with the wealth of evidence that had led this report, and many others, to its conclusions.

Similarly, when Li Rongrong, the Chairman of SASAC (State Assets Supervision and Administration Commission) announced that China proposes to retain control of a range of strategic industries, a US trade official revealed his government's fundamentally neoliberal policy objectives by denouncing his remarks as 'yet another example of China trying to find new ways to only partially liberalize their economy', and then reminding everyone, including the Chinese government, that the only acceptable outcome is the elimination of all impediments to the ability of 'non-Chinese companies to invest in these [Chinese] companies and compete in these industries in China'.[13] Confidence in that outcome has recently been weakened as China has focused more seriously on the need to establish strong national technological foundations, especially in an increasingly turbulent world, once again raising the fear that 'over time China's economy could come to resemble other

East Asian economies that have favored nurturing "national champions" over free trade'.[14]

Of course, those warning China not to go down the neo-mercantilist road claim that it would not be in China's own interests to do so. When they are reminded, however, that those 'neo-mercantilist' East Asian economies were among the most successful economies in recent history, they will readily change the rationale of their advice from 'it's not desirable', to 'it's not possible', either because China is too large, too decentralized, too rigid and/or too chaotic to manage such neo-mercantilist strategies (Jefferson, 2004), or because such strategies would elicit massive – and 'legitimate' – economic retaliation under the terms of the international obligations that China has now assumed.[15]

The bottom line is that China's efforts to develop a strong national industrial base on which to build a harmonious, high-wage society are being watched closely and with growing alarm by the powers driving neoliberal globalization who remain determined that China must ultimately allow its assets, its resources, its firms, its opportunities and its public sector funding processes to be fully integrated into the global system of finance and trade. And these powers are not passive observers. They will continue to encourage and reward China's deep integration into the global economy so long as they believe that China is committed to such a future, but they will also continue to oppose and punish any indication that China is seriously interested in creating an embedded social market that would allow resources to be invested strategically in support of a harmonious, sustainable society in which the rate of interest – and profit – and hence the distribution of income, could be nationally determined in accordance with the country's own values, priorities and changing circumstances.

4. Thoughts on the political forces shaping China's future

Of course the dream of creating a harmonious society by building a strong, technologically sophisticated embedded market in China, in the face of relentless opposition from abroad – and from powerful internal constituencies – is no more than wishful thinking unless one can identify political forces that might be capable of meeting that challenge. At this moment it is probably easier to argue against the plausibility of this proposition, given that foreign capital now has such a powerful presence in China, that income inequality has risen to chronic levels, that past economic success has by now given rise to powerful concentrations of Chinese capital with close links to government, the military and the international community, that regional imbalances remain a major problem within the country's relatively decentralized administrative system, that Chinese stock markets have become powerful sources of volatility, that social security has been so widely eroded and finally that labour – and especially migrant labour – has become more vulnerable and insecure despite steadily increasing average real wages, as other chapters in this book have shown. Moreover, ideologically many people, and most economists, continue to give market forces the benefit of the doubt in an uncertain world. Many commentators continue to agree with Gilboy's earlier conclusion that China is irrevocably committed to a neoliberal future and can therefore be regarded as a solid ally in the US's efforts 'to promote [economic] liberalism in Asia' (Gilboy, 2004: 38) especially in view of the fact that in late 2008 at least one senior Chinese official argued that the global financial crisis should not slow down China's efforts to liberalize its financial system (Waldmeir, 2008).

On the other hand, it is also true that in recent years – and especially since publication of its eleventh Five Year Plan – the Chinese leadership has come to recognize the urgent need to restore a better balance between capital, labour, society and the environment if it is to deal with the deepening contradictions of its current development model. Moreover, in response to the global crisis, the government has been persuaded to take an important step in this direction by putting far more emphasis on the growth of its domestic economy, although it remains to be seen whether it fully understands the critical need for this domestic growth to be based primarily on earned incomes reflecting rising real wages and earned incomes, and not on debt-creating private or public expenditures, though this is politically more difficult to achieve.[16] One can only hope that the urgency of the current global situation will provide the leadership with the necessary political leverage to meet this challenge, especially since it is almost certain that the much hyped global recovery of late 2009 is unsustainable since it is almost exclusively based on a basically unchanged financial system inflating new speculative bubbles in a real world in which debts have continued to escalate while real incomes are being systematically strangled by unemployment, by pension fund shortfalls and by escalating public sector woes.

Ironically, under these circumstances China's political system, which has been so widely – and often rightly – criticized could potentially turn out to be a source of strength since it might allow China to respond more strategically and coherently to these mounting challenges. Simply put, if the Chinese leadership were genuinely to be persuaded that the country's, and the Party's, future is inextricably linked to the emergence of an embedded market in China, then that leadership would have a direct interest in confronting the admittedly powerful 'special interests' – both national and international – that stand in the way of such a future. There is evidence that this may be happening, including: a renewed interest in industrial policies focusing on the development of technological capabilities that are owned and controlled by Chinese firms working within a national development strategy (Naughton, 2007; Wilsdon and Keeley, 2007); continued resistance to demands for international financial liberalization and a more market-determined exchange rate; continued resistance to political reforms that would effectively strengthen the ability of domestic and international capital to translate economic into political power; reforms intended to strengthen the position of labour and of rural producers in the national economy; and continuing efforts to broaden the base of the international economy by supporting the emergence of a more balanced and internationally managed reserve currency system.

This is not to imply that authoritarian government is preferable to democratic government. Indeed this chapter focuses so centrally on embedded markets precisely because they are deemed a critically important precondition for meaningful democracy in China, as elsewhere. In that context, what is being suggested here is that under current circumstances China's existing leadership could be in a relatively favourable position to lay the foundations for a viable and sustainable future democracy at a time when many democracies are being hollowed out and threatened by growing economic dislocation, hardship, conflict, instability and cynicism. The three factors that will ultimately determine the Chinese government's strategic response to its own growing internal contradictions and the challenges of an increasingly unstable international economy are: (i) the internal structure and dynamics of the Communist Party of China (CPC); (ii) the changing configuration of class forces, as shaped by domestic developments and the international responses to them; and (iii) the capacity of the country's political and administrative institutions to implement policies in support of such a strategy, as a way of managing potentially destabilizing distributional conflicts.[17]

The outcomes that will result from the interaction of these three complex dimensions of China's political economy are inevitably uncertain. All that is possible in concluding this brief discussion is to consider a best and a worst case scenario in order to define the range of possibilities and to emphasize the complex interdependence between these three interdependent sets of conditions.

In the best case scenario, the Party leadership, led by growing concerns about economic and political instability, and responding to increasing popular demand, would resist pressures for further economic liberalization and focus on setting in motion a strategically directed process of accumulation and investment based primarily on high domestic savings and aimed simultaneously at three central objectives: steadily growing, widely dispersed real incomes in a national economy in which economic interdependence provides both rural and urban populations with material reasons for supporting a long-term national development strategy; the development of applied national technological capabilities generating technology rents in support of a fully employed, high-wage economy; and a systematic export drive to prevent the strategy from being strangled by a foreign exchange constraint as growth increases the demand for imports. Pursued pragmatically and sequentially such a strategy needs to focus on changed incentives as the drivers of improved performance within a competitive domestic economy operating within a framework providing strategic direction, safeguards against serious excess capacity problems and financial instability, together with effective labour, social and environmental regulation. If successful, such a strategy could create a political climate in which an active civil society could help to lay the foundations for a meaningful and sustainable democracy so long as corporations could be prevented from usurping the political process by converting their economic power into political power.

In the worst case scenario, the Party would come to be dominated by China's new business elite and, working closely with its international allies, it would continue to liberalize finance, trade and industry. However, an unstable global environment combining erratic and sluggish growth with chronic levels of excess capacity and endemic financial instability would unleash increasingly destructive competitive pressures that would in turn undermine wage and employment conditions within China and curb its ability to promote domestic expansion or to manage growing social and political tensions. Democratization under these circumstances would lead to a divisive and highly unequal struggle for short-term advantage in which national and international corporate interests would further undermine the central government's ability to manage economic and social tensions.

Of course, some would reverse these scenarios, arguing that the more nationally focused policies would be more likely to lead to poor economic outcomes, deeper political cleavages and eventually a more repressive authoritarian government that might be tempted to become an international aggressor in order to divert attention from its internal

244 Globalization and Labour in China and India

contradictions. This could happen, especially if the leading industrial powers meet China's efforts to build an embedded economy with extreme hostility in defence of their neoliberal global corporate agenda, instead of realizing that they also need to rebuild their social markets in order to reinvigorate their democracies and resolve their growing internal contradictions. In this sense, China's future will be jointly determined, shaping, and shaped by, the future trajectory of the neoliberal globalization project.

Notes

1. Strictly speaking that chapter identifies three perspectives but, as explained below, in this chapter the last two are treated as variants of one of two fundamental approaches.
2. Neoliberals define 'special interests' as any interests other than those of international capital – i.e. labour, particular pressure groups, bureaucrats, citizens of a particular nation and even national fractions of capital that seek protection from international capital. The underlying premise is that the empowerment of markets, and hence of international capital, will promote the greater good through the magic of the market. It need hardly be said that this claim cannot be legitimately derived from neoclassical theory, especially when it is applied to an inherently and pervasively imperfect 'real world'.
3. The graphs in Figure 12.1 were produced by United for a Fair Economy, a national, independent, non-partisan, non-profit organization to be found at http://www.faireconomy.org/. The first two graphs on Family Income 1947–1979 are based on an analysis of US Census Bureau data in Economic Policy Institute, *The State of Working America 1994–95* (New York: M. E. Sharpe: 1994), p. 37 and 1979–2001: US Census Bureau, Historical Income Tables, Table F-3. The third graph showing 1979–2000 after-tax family income is from: Center on Budget and Policy Priorities, *The New, Definitive CBO Data on Income and Tax Trends*, 23 September 2003, citing Congressional Budget Office data.
4. For detailed discussions of the dissolution of that system see Bienefeld (1982); Helleiner (1994); James (1996); Best (2005).
5. For a detailed discussion of the debate about the East Asian success stories see Bienefeld (1988); Wade (1990); Perkins (2007).
6. The Mission eventually produced the 1989 World Bank report entitled *Sub-Saharan Africa: From Crisis to Sustainable Development*.
7. The two quotes are from a 1994 paper (pp. 11, 24) written by Ramgopal Agarwala (together with P. N. Schwartz) for a World Bank project assessing its 'Learning Process with Participatory Development'. In the paper Agarwala describes how the 'genuine participation' of non-Bank officials and experts led the Bank team to conclude that the Bank's neoliberal reforms were not working – and would not work – in sub-Saharan Africa because they were inappropriate to that continent's circumstances. It was in thinking about alternative options that the team ended up focusing on the social market as the more appropriate model for that continent.
8. For China this is well known. And, while India's controls are less extensive than China's, they are nevertheless significant (see Schindler et al., 2009).

9. In the 1970s a series of studies led by Dieter Senghaas concluded that the most important determinant of successful development in Europe was the existence of a 'mechanism' that allowed labour to share widely in the incomes generated by early export industries (see Senghaas, 1985). In a paper published in 2000 Joseph Stiglitz mirrored his conclusions in suggesting that one of the most important determinants of successful development was for labour to have a strong voice in the policy process (Stiglitz, 2000).
10. Low interest rates are now decried by some economists as having 'cheated' the savers. But they were the foundation of a successful economy that ultimately rewarded South Korea's 'savers' very handsomely.
11. This is why the demand for national treatment is so central to the neoliberal agenda. Translated into English it means that governments are not allowed to discriminate in favour of national firms and, as global labour markets are integrated, the principle is beginning to be applied in ways that challenge government's ability to discriminate in favour of its own workers, or citizens. The current debate about Sovereign Wealth Funds reflects the same concern, namely that those who manage those funds might have special regard for the interests of 'their citizens' in making their investment decisions.
12. During an extensive visit to Korea in 2001 I asked a series of high-level officials to explain South Korea's decision to liberalize its financial system in the context of that crisis, given that the crisis had clearly been triggered – or, at least, exacerbated – by instabilities deriving from the government's earlier decision to liberalize access to foreign loans by Korean corporations. To my surprise, with the sole exception of a paper given at the Korean Development Institute (KDI), all respondents claimed that Korea had been forced to make those changes, rather than arguing that these changes were desirable in and of themselves, though interestingly enough, the Central Bank asked me to remember that there was a strong pressure group within the government that wanted to move in this direction.
13. Inside US–China Trade (2007).
14. The words are ascribed to Christopher Padilla, a senior US official (see Buckley, 2007).
15. The World Bank's controversial 'Miracle Report' (World Bank, 1993) makes this argument in its concluding chapter as a way of denying that the interventionist policies that had been used so successfully by some of the East Asian economies held any policy lessons for other developing countries (as discussed in Bienefeld, 2000).
16. The critical importance of this issue is discussed in Palley (2009).
17. This echoes Dani Rodrik's conclusion that development success has been closely related to a society's capacity to manage such conflicts (Rodrik, 1998).

References

Agarwala, R. and Schwartz, P. N. (1994) 'Sub-Saharan Africa: a Long-Term Perspective Study', World Bank, Learning Process on Participatory Development (May): 1–32.
Bertrand, Jacques (1998) 'FMI et Baque mondiale', *Relations* (December: 307), see http://www.cjf.qc.ca/relations/archives/themes/textes/mondialisation/mond_bert_9812.htm.

Best, J. (2005) *The Limits of Transparency*, Ithaca, NY: Cornell University Press.

Bienefeld, M. (1982) 'The International Context for National Development Strategies: Constraints and Opportunities in a Changing World', in M. Bienefeld and M. Godfrey (eds), *The Struggle for Development*, Chichester: Wiley, pp. 25–64.

Bienefeld, M. (1988) 'The Significance of the Newly Industrialising Countries for the Development Debate', *Studies in Political Economy*, 25 (Spring): 7–40.

Bienefeld, M. (2000) 'Structural Adjustment: Debt Collection Device or Development Policy?', *Review*, 23, 4: 533–87, Fernand Braudel Center (New York University), Binghamton, New York.

Buckley, C. (2007) 'US Chides China for Worrisome Industrial Policy', Reuters, Wednesday, 10 October, 14:02:49 UTC.

Caprio, G., Jr. and Klingebiel, D. (1996) 'Bank Insolvencies: Cross-country Experience', World Bank Research Working Paper 1620, Washington, DC: World Bank.

Crotty, J. (1983) 'On Keynes and Capital Flight', *Journal of Economic Literature*, 21 (March): 59–65.

Gilboy, M. (2004) 'The Myth Behind China's Miracle', *Foreign Affairs*, 83, 4 (July/August): 33–48.

Helleiner, E. (1994) *States and the Re-emergence of Global Finance*, Ithaca, NY: Cornell University Press.

Inside China–US Trade (2007) 'USTR Examining China's Plan to Maintain State Owned Companies', *Inside US–China Trade*, 7, 3 (17 January).

James, H. (1996) *International Monetary Cooperation since Bretton Woods*, New York: Oxford University Press.

Jefferson, G. H. (2004) 'R&D and Innovation in China: Has China Begun its S&T Takeoff?' *Harvard China Review* (11 August).

Keynes, J. M. (1933) 'National Self-Sufficiency', *New Statesman* (8 and 15 July).

Krugman, P. (1999) 'Depression Economics Returns', *Foreign Affairs*, 78, 1: 56–74.

Low, A. (2006) 'Remarks by First Secretary of US Mission to UN on the UNCTAD: Trade and Development Report 2006', 28 September (4 pp.), available at http://www.usmission.ch/Press2006/0928TDR2006.html.

Naughton, B. (2007) 'China's State Sector, Industrial Policies and the 11th Five Year Plan', Evidence to US-China Economic and Security Review Commission Hearing on 'Extent of the Government's Control of China's Economy, and Implications for the United States', Washington, DC, 24 May.

Palley, T. (2009) 'The Limits of Minsky's Financial Instability Hypothesis as an Explanation of the Crisis', New America Foundation, Washington, DC, 18 November.

Perkins, D. (2007) 'Asian Development Strategies, 1950–2006', paper presented to International Economic Association/Tsinghua University Roundtable Conference on 'The Political Economy of Sustainable Growth', Beijing, 10–11 July.

Rodrik, D. (1998) *The New Global Economy and Developing Countries: Making Openness Work*, Policy Essay No. 24, Washington, DC: ODC.

Schindler, M., Binici, M. and Hutchison, M. (2009) 'Controlling Capital? Legal Restrictions and the Asset Composition of International Financial Flows', IMF Working Paper 09/208, Washington, DC: International Monetary Fund, pp. 1–32.

Senghaas, D. (1985) *The European Experience*, Dover, NH: Berg.

Stiglitz, J. (2000) 'Democratic Development as the Fruits of Labor', Working Paper, Progressive Economics Papers, January, available at http://www.newecon.org/Styiglitz-Jan00.html.

Stiglitz, J. (2001) 'More Instruments and Broader Goals: Moving towards a Post-Washington Consensus', Annual WIDER Lecture, World Institute for Development Economics Research, Helsinki.

UNCTAD (2006) 'Overview', *UNCTAD Trade and Development Report 2006*, Geneva: UNCTAD, pp. i–xxi.

Wade, R. (1990) *Governing the Market: Economic Theory and the Role of Government in East Asian Industrialization*, Princeton: Princeton University Press.

Waldmeir, P. (2008) 'Crisis "May Speed Up" Chinese Market Reform', *Financial Times*, 25 September, p. 17.

Wilsdon, J. and Keeley, J. (2007) *China: the Next Science Superpower?*, London: Demos.

World Bank (1989) *Sub-Saharan Africa: From Crisis to Sustainable Development*, Washington, DC: World Bank.

World Bank (1993) *The East Asian Miracle: Economic Growth and Public Policy*, Washington, DC: World Bank.

Wu, X. (2001) 'Response to Thomas G. Moore: Perils of a Pax Americana', *Asian Affairs*, 28, 3: 180–2.

Part V
Conclusion

13
Concluding Reflections on Globalization(s) and Labour in China and India: a Polanyian Perspective

John Harriss[1]

I take it here that underlying the various conceptions of globalization there is a more or less common view that the term connotes the increased integration of markets – with the principal exception of labour markets – across the world. I also hold that contemporary globalization is intrinsically bound up with, and very largely follows from, the shift that took place towards economic liberalism, through the pursuit of neoliberal policies, starting towards the end of the 1970s (as David Harvey has argued, 2005). Thus it is not at all surprising to me that there should now be concerns about the possible 'end of globalization' in the context of the general retreat from neoliberalism that has gathered pace since the onset of the financial crisis. The chapters of this book are necessarily as much concerned with the consequences for labour of the partial moves towards economic liberalism in both China and India, described in both cases as 'economic reform', as they are with the consequences of 'globalization' *tout court*. There are distinctive pressures, however, specifically associated with the integration of China and India into global markets, and these were etched out in the initial effects in the two countries of the financial crisis and global recession of 2008–9. It was reported early in 2009 that 15 million migrant workers, and perhaps 20 million in total, had lost their jobs in China, and that thousands of factories had closed as a consequence of the downturn in Western demand and the collapse of foreign investment (*The Economist*, 31 January 2009). The figures put on job losses in India were less dramatic but still considerable – Rohini Hensman, in this book, cites evidence that 500,000 workers had lost their jobs in selected industrial sectors during October–December 2008 alone – and the fact that even the most celebrated IT companies have not gone on recruiting in the way that they have been used to is another significant reflection of global recession. In China, far more so than in India, discontent appears to have increased, and it was argued by *The Economist* that 'Whether or not unemployment brings unrest on the scale seen in 1989, the [Chinese Communist] party will be severely challenged over the next few months' (31 January 2009, p. 35). In this context, in common with several other contributors, I find it helpful to view the events of the past twenty years or so in a Polanyian frame, and specifically to enquire as to the working out of the 'double movement' (Polanyi, 1944) as the attempt has been made, in both China and India, albeit partially, to shift towards the self-regulating market.

With regard to China, Marc Blecher argues in his contribution to the collection that rather than holding that the glass is half-full and celebrating the heroic resistance of labour to enhanced exploitation, or on the other hand lamenting that it is half-empty because resistance has been quite limited, we do better to analyse and understand the different patterns in the responses of labour to the forces of liberalization and globalization. The point is well-taken, and yet Blecher also argues that the response of labour in China has been 'broadly quiescent', with some resistance in certain cases, of somewhat different nature as between the most highly globalized south-east and the decaying rustbelt of the north-east. Rather in contrast with this view, Chris King-Chi Chan, Pun Ngai and Jenny Chan present data on the increased incidence of different forms of protest action by workers and anticipate that worker radicalism will be intensified in future, because – as they say in the conclusion to their chapter – 'In concrete, lived space – the workers' dormitories and social communities – Chinese workers are developing higher levels of class awareness and identification ...'

Xiao-yuan Dong, Paul Bowles and Hongqin Chang, however, more in line with Blecher, and writing specifically about rural workers, argue that 'While there have been many instances of peasant protest and backlash, it would be far too much to suggest that there has been an organized civil society counter-movement' – and they refer rather to a counter-movement from above, as the Hu Jintao/Wen Jiabao regime has sought to head off rural protest through prioritizing rural development in their policy pronouncements and the rhetoric of the 'harmonious society'.

Wang, Appelbaum, Degiuli and Lichtenstein in their chapter analyse one specific policy of the Hu/Wen regime, the introduction in 2008 of the new Labour Contract Law that can also be seen as part of a counter-movement from above. This law, implemented in the face of opposition from foreign business associations, and which, on paper at least, provides workers with increased employment security and protections, points to a move away from the reform thrust of ever greater reliance on the market as the regulator. Wang et al. caution us, however, that practice is often different and that the law, where it has threatened business interests, has been subject to various forms of evasion.

The chapters here on India lead to generally comparable conclusions. Ramachandran and Rawal provide a detailed account of the consequences of the rural development policies that have been implemented in the context of India's economic reforms, and show how they account for the crisis in the agricultural economy of the country that has been widely remarked upon. They refer in passing to the apparently increased incidence of suicide amongst Indian farmers in the context of the crisis – which is shown so clearly in some of their data demonstrating the 'near impossibility' of earning sufficient income from farming for very many cultivators. But why should farmers be responding in this way – by taking their own lives – rather than through political mobilization such as occurred in the 1980s, when the farmers' organizations in different parts of the country staged well-supported campaigns for higher prices and lower inputs costs (see Brass, 1995)?

An answer to the puzzle is suggested in work by Jonathan Pattenden (2005). It seems that the intensification of commercial agriculture in the later 1970s and 1980s created circumstances that provided for cross-class mobilization amongst rural people, and the burying of caste and class differences, for the time being, by conflict between the peasantry generally, and the local state and merchants. At the same time the profitability of agriculture made available resources – notably of time, for richer peasants – for engaging in mobilizational activity. The decline in the profitability of agriculture changed all of this, and while it might have been presumed that declining profitability would have solidified the support base of the movements, and intensified their mobilizations, in practice it has contributed to their decline (Pattenden, 2005: 1981). Non-agricultural activities and incomes have become much more important and those more influential people who had been the local leaders of farmers' organizations have become interested rather in 'gatekeeping activities' – roles in which they mediate between other people and the state, and are able to use these roles to secure resources for themselves (for example, from the allocation of ration cards). In sum: 'The sense of togetherness that had accompanied the rise [of the farmers' movements] had been replaced by a growing social fragmentation with people "looking after themselves"' (Pattenden, 2005: 1982) – or, apparently, taking their own lives.

As in China, in India too 'there have been many instances of peasant protest and backlash' – perhaps especially actions such as those that attracted international attention at Nandigram and Singur in West Bengal, where there were major protests against attempts by the state government to take over agricultural land for industrial projects – but 'it would be too much to suggest that there has been an organized counter movement'. This may seem a surprising judgement, in view of the extent of the mobilizations across large areas of the country by 'Maoist' groups, referred to at one point by the Prime Minister, Manmohan Singh, as 'the single biggest internal security challenge ever faced by our country'. This is not specifically a counter-movement against neoliberal economic policies, however, while some ethnographic research shows that the insurgency has roots that are more tangled than the claim of 'class war' might lead one to suppose. Writing of the Maoist Communist Centre in the state of Jharkhand, for instance, Alpa Shah argues that 'the MCC's initial grassroots support is a rural elite – including entrepreneurs who tried to maintain their dominance through their connection with the informal economy of the state' (2006: 309).[2]

In the Indian industrial economy, as Rohini Hensman points out, though the Indian trade unions have succeeded in staving off radical changes in labour laws that were sought by the National Democratic Alliance government, they have not been successful in stemming the contraction of formal employment, and it continues to be the case that the numbers of working days lost due to lockouts by management exceed those lost due to strikes. The organized labour movement in India may not be as weak as it has often been portrayed (see Teitelbaum, 2006), but neither has it been successful in preventing job losses in the extensive industrial restructuring that has been carried through in the interests of global competitiveness. And according to Supriya RoyChowdhury's detailed analysis of labour disputes in Bangalore, in her chapter here, working-class action has become increasingly fragmented. As she says, 'What is absent is both a movement character in the activities of trade unions, and a broad class-based character in workers' struggles.'

It is generally well known, however, that an overwhelming share of all labour in India is accounted for by informal employment of one kind or another (a mapping is offered by Sanyal and Bhattacharya in their chapter here), and there is no doubt that globalization has led, in India as elsewhere, to increasing informalization of labour. But as both Hensman and Barbara Harriss-White point out, the informalization of labour in India long predates the era of globalization – 'the assault on labour rights began long before 1991' (Hensman) – and has many causes, amongst them the deliberate aim of limiting the possible threats from labour organization. Some informal sector workers, however, have themselves latterly become more organized. Rohini Hensman mentions legislation in several states that has 'enabled workers to organize successfully in extremely casualized and apparently unpromising occupations' (see also Agarwala, 2006) – though demands for the extension of these provisions nationally have so far gone nowhere.

Rather than resistance from below, what is more striking, in India as well as in China, has been what Xiao-yuan Dong and her co-authors describe as a 'counter-movement from above'. This has both a strong legal dimension – the chapter by Wang et al. provides a discussion of the extent to which the government in China has recently legislated on labour issues even though it has done little over the whole period of economic reforms in this respect – and one of social security. China under Hu Jintao aims to establish a 'harmonious society'; in India it has been claimed, in the words of one Finance Minister (Yashwant Sinha, in 2000), that economic reforms are being carried through 'guided by compassion and justice'. It seems important neither to take claims of this kind at face value nor to deride them as being all smoke and mirrors – and the chapters in this collection go some way in helping to form a considered assessment of them.

There are 'formidable obstacles' to labour protest, as Blecher says, in China, and they are considerable, too, in India, in spite of the fact that Indian workers do have greater freedom to organize themselves in the space of civil society. Blecher's argument is that the Chinese state has actually taken a measured approach to protests, 'with a carefully modulated combination of harshness towards protest leaders and tolerance and even reward towards the majority of protesters'. The leadership appears to have calculated that it is better off allowing protest that it can manage rather than trying to stop it altogether. These conclusions are borne out in accounts given by Chan et al., of industrial protest in the Chinese south-east (and see Pun and Lu, forthcoming). On occasions the Indian state may respond to protest in much less measured ways, as was the case in the police repression of labour rights that took place in July 2005 against workers at the Honda plant in Gurgaon. Blecher, Chan et al. and Wang et al. all refer to the effort that is being made in China to embed labour relations in a framework of legislation, starting with the comprehensive labour law brought into effect in 1995, and to the attempts that are being made to control the labour situation through reinvigoration of state-run labour unions ('the government has woken up its trade union federation' – the All-China Federation of Trade Unions).

The rise of legalism in labour relations in China, Blecher thinks, represents a genuine attempt to tackle the most oppressive practices in industrial organization, but also the aim of channelling protest towards arbitration and mediation – even though this approach also has its dangers for the state. Workers may be emboldened by knowledge of their legal rights and the fact that the laws are often not enforced may enhance the sense of grievance amongst them. Chan et al. argue, more forcefully, that 'The huge discrepancy between legal entitlement and actual delivery of protection ... was so telling that the legitimacy of the Chinese state is undermined', and they point out that workers' rights of strike, association and collective bargaining are all still absent, in spite of more recent additions to labour legislation. Wang et al. agree that the official trade union remains largely ineffective in improving working conditions despite the additional resources that the new Labour Law may provide it. They do argue, however, that 'it would be a mistake to discount entirely the capacity of the ACFTU to reconfigure itself, especially given the dynamic sense of rights consciousness that China's new Labour Contract Law has engendered among so many of its constituents'.

The authors of these two chapters are perhaps less convinced than is Blecher about the effectiveness in the longer run of law as a mechanism of control of the working class and a means of strengthening the position of the state in regard to labour. These methods may now to be put to the test, when even the manufacturing hub of the south-east 'can't immunise itself against the wave of protest sweeping across China as the global financial crisis batters the country's economy' (Kurlantzick, 2009: 9). So far, the same author argues, 'Beijing has stuck to its battle-tested strategy for controlling unrest, a mixture of co-option and crackdowns', but he also raises doubts about the effectiveness of the economic policies that are being implemented in China, and questions whether police measures will be 'as effective at controlling protest as they once were' in a context in which text-messaging and the internet have provided demonstrators with much more sophisticated tools, and means of avoiding surveillance (ibid.: 13).

India, of course, still has extensive protective labour laws that provide for workers' rights, including those of strike, association and collective bargaining. Much to the chagrin of the most ardent economic reformers, these have still not been pushed back very much at all – though it is a moot point as to whether 'inflexible' labour laws are really as much of a constraint as the reformers maintain. Certainly the World Bank's *Investment Climate Survey* for India (2004) does not entirely bear out the supposition that labour market inflexibility is a major problem – for only 17 per cent of the firms interviewed reported that labour regulation is a bottleneck to business growth, compared with around 20 per cent in China and 57 per cent in Brazil. In any event the existence of the legislation has never prevented egregious violations of labour rights, as at Gurgaon in July 2005, or the kinds of everyday violations that are associated with the informalization of labour in India, described in these pages by Hensman and Harriss-White. There have also been several negative verdicts of the Supreme Court on labour rights (Venkatesan, 2003).

It has been in regard to informal or 'unorganized' labour that the Indian state has been remarkably active, in terms of legislation and new programmes, in the period since the launch of economic reforms in 1991. Mahendra Dev notes four apparently ambitious social security programmes for unorganized workers that have been legislated for by central government in this time: the National Social Assistance Programme (1995); the Janashree Bima Yojana (2000), a social insurance scheme; the National Social Security Scheme for Unorganized Sector Workers (2004); and the Universal Health Insurance Scheme (2004), though he also comments on the lack of awareness about these schemes and the severe limitations to their coverage (in spite of claims to 'universality': see Dev, 2008: 328–33). Most significant has been the passage into law of the National Rural Employment Guarantee Act in 2006, referred to both by Ramachandran and Rawal and by Hensman, which provides rural households with a legal right to 100 days of employment in public works in one year, and holds out the promise of providing some guarantees of basic social security for rural workers (and is realizing them to some extent, in some states at least, according to independent evaluative studies: see *Frontline*, 2009).

An especially interesting development in India has been the establishment in September 2004 of the National Commission for Enterprises in the Unorganized Sector (NCEUS), which includes amongst its members several well-known and left-leaning academic economists. The focus on 'enterprises' in the title of the Commission was a reflection of the government's view, in line with recent development policy arguments, that the key to poverty elimination lies in the entrepreneurial enterprise of the poor. But in practice the members of the Commission have engaged much more substantially, and critically, with the problems of unorganized workers than the title might lead one to suppose. The Commission prepared two draft bills: (a) the Unorganized Sector Workers Social Security Bill, 2006; and (b) the Unorganized Sector Workers (Conditions of Work and Livelihood Promotion) Bill, 2006. These drafts included proposals for legal protection of the labour rights of unorganized workers, as well as for protection of their livelihoods. They were, however, set aside by the UPA government in May 2007, and substituted by a single bill (passed into law in December 2008), much watered down by comparison with the NCEUS proposals, as Barbara Harriss-White notes. Welfare schemes for unorganized sector workers have now been introduced, though without making any financial commitment or setting out any time frame. Rohini Hensman points out that the Unorganized Sector Workers Bill made it clear that it would not be compulsory for employers to register, and that this will 'make regulation of employment impossible'. These criticisms are shared by the members of the NCEUS, who also point to the systematic under-funding of all the programmes introduced by the UPA government in fulfilment of its obligations agreed with other parties in the Common Minimum Programme of 2004. Still, the sheer fact of so much official policy interest in the unorganized sector is remarkable, and seems to show how far the Indian state has been pushed away from the neoliberal model.

India, therefore, presents a rather complex, nuanced picture, with successive governments having apparently felt compelled – sometimes under the pressure of verdicts of the Supreme Court, passed as a result of public interest litigation – to intervene to provide for some legal protection for the mass of unorganized sector workers, and to provide some minimum social security for them, even though they have trimmed and cut away at more radical proposals. An important example of this trimming and cutting has been the way in which the Public Distribution System has been undermined by the introduction of targeting, as Ramachandran and Rawal have explained (though the promises made by the Congress Party in its manifesto for the 2009 General Election suggest the possibility that the PDS will be universalized once more). In so far as India's economic reforms have been 'guided by compassion and justice' this has been granted only grudgingly and as a result of pressure from within civil society and from the organized left (a point that Ramachandran and Rawal emphasize). The programmes that have been introduced can well be seen as representing the management of poverty – limited and non-emancipatory accommodation – and certainly not as making for a social democratic transformation of society. The political task for labour and the left is to increase the pressure for structural reforms.

China now presents a somewhat similar recent history. On the one hand, as Xiao-yuan Dong and her co-authors mention, the Maoist era social welfare system – the 'iron rice bowl' – was destroyed under Deng and 'Ordinary Chinese were left to fend for themselves in a society in which hospitals turn away patients who do not show up with cash, and parents with no money can't enrol their children in a school' (Kurlantzick, 2009: 12). On the other hand, apparently in response to increasingly violent rural protest – partly documented in the *Survey of Chinese Peasants*, by Chen Guidi and Wu Chuntao, suppressed by the Chinese authorities (reviewed in *New Left Review*, 32, March/April 2005) – the current regime has felt compelled to emphasize the needs of rural development and to offer the vision of the 'harmonious society', as Xiao-yuan Dong et al. have explained. More recently the government has announced ambitious plans for the reform of health care. It is proposed to spend $123 billion to establish universal health care, and to provide some form of health insurance for 90 per cent of the population by 2011 (*New York Times*, 21 January 2009). It was widely remarked, however, that this scheme is also a way to stimulate domestic demand. Relieved of their anxiety about insuring themselves against ill-health, Chinese consumers will be ready to save less and to spend more. A similar argument might be made about the linkage effects of state expenditure on the National Rural Employment Guarantee Act in India, the demand-side effects of which may prove significant.

A recent article by Partha Chatterjee, inspired by the work of Kalyan Sanyal whose arguments are presented in this book in the chapter written jointly with Bhattacharya, goes some way towards explaining these somewhat contradictory trends, as both the Chinese and the Indian regimes seem to have twisted and turned, but to have been unable to avoid some movement away from the neoliberal model. Chatterjee, following Sanyal, argues that much of the existing theory of social change and the development of capitalism rests on a narrative of transition, associated with primitive accumulation (the dissociation of the labourer from the means of labour). The theory of the differentiation of the peasantry exemplifies such a narrative. But, Chatterjee argues, and as Sanyal and Bhattacharyya show in their chapter here, 'under present conditions of postcolonial development within a globalized economy, the narrative of transition is no longer valid'. Not least 'the technological conditions of early industrialization which created the demand for a substantial mass of industrial labour have long passed'. Large numbers of people are never going to find employment in the growth sectors of the economy. So although capitalist growth is inevitably still accompanied by the primitive accumulation of capital, 'the social changes that are brought about cannot be understood as transition'. Rather there is an ongoing process of exclusion of labour. The relation of capital and labour to which Sanyal and Bhattacharya draw attention is one which 'defines the new location of labour as one in which the labourer is no longer a source of surplus, but rather the unwanted possessor or occupier of economic resources from which he or she must be divorced in order to free those resources for use in the circuit of capital'. It is this process of dispossession without proletarianization or exploitation that they refer to as 'exclusion'.

But there have also come about by now, Chatterjee (2008: 55) suggests, changes in understanding:

> about the minimum functions as well as the available technologies of government. There is a growing sense that certain basic conditions of life must be provided to people everywhere ... while there is a dominant discourse about the importance of growth ... it is, at the same time, considered unacceptable that those who are dispossessed of their means of labour ... should have no means of subsistence. This produces ... a curious process in which, on one side, primary producers such as peasants, craftspeople and petty manufacturers lose their land and other means of production, but, on the other, are also provided by governmental agencies with the conditions for meeting their basic needs of livelihood.

The sorts of interventions that have been undertaken by the Indian state – interventions such as the National Rural Employment Guarantee Scheme – may be regarded, Chatterjee argues, as 'direct interventions to reverse the effects of primitive accumulation'. The politics of the blocked transition that he observes in India (and describes in some depth in the article) strikingly lacks the perspective of transition, or of social transformation, that was associated with earlier movements of democratic mobilization (in which organized labour played a prominent role), being essentially concerned with negotiations over demands for transfers of resources in support of the livelihood needs of the poor. Another aspect of the politics of the blocked transition, about which Sanyal and Bhattacharya present a rather positive view, is the possibility of mobilizations against dispossession and loss of livelihood – as at Singur and Nandigram – 'rather than against exploitation by capital'. 'Squatting', they explain, has become a new and significant form of resistance.

This wider argument about the contemporary 'double movement' is of course India-centric, but it seems not at all far-fetched to consider that the Chinese state – in spite of the fact that Chinese industrial development, unlike India's growth process, has generated a huge demand for peasant labour – is responding to the same sorts of compulsions as the Indian one.

In short, there is evidence in the chapters in this collection of the existence of the Polanyian 'double movement' in contemporary China and India, reinforcing Bienefeld's contentions about the possibility, at least, that China will resist the pursuit of more thoroughgoing neoliberalism in favour of a strategy for the creation of a high-wage social market economy (that is, in Polanyian terms, a socially 'embedded' economy). The form and dynamics of the double movement are perhaps different from those described by Polanyi with regard to the nineteenth and earlier twentieth centuries – being more a counter-movement from above – but they are not at all inconsistent with the arguments he advances on 'Class Interest and Social Change' (1944/1957/2001: Ch. 13). Here he puts forward the view that though 'The essential role played by class interests in social change is in the nature of things', still, 'class interests offer only a limited explanation of long-run movements in society' (2001: 159). Put rather simply, politics isn't only about economic interests, and 'Precisely because not the economic but the social interests of different cross sections of the population were threatened by the market, persons belonging to various economic strata unconsciously joined forces to meet the danger' (2001: 162). It is an argument that seems apposite in regard to China and India now. The current crisis may well be enhancing the political dynamics to which Polanyi referred, when as we seem to see most clearly in regard to health care reform in China, there are economic as well as social and political interests involved.

Important and fascinating to watch and analyse as this will be, it does also raise the question of what those outside China and India can do both in their own countries and with respect to the internal dynamics of China and India. As Bowles argues in the introductory chapter in this book, how best to respond to globalization and how best to forge solidaristic labour responses globally, depends very much on how 'globalization' is analysed. As he shows, debates over international labour standards, often touted as one of the most useful responses by labour globally, are controversial precisely because they can be interpreted differently depending on how globalization is interrogated analytically.

In this regard, the chapter by Flynn and O'Brien offers a new window on possible global solidaristic responses. They move beyond the international labour standards debate by suggesting ways in which legal mechanisms can be used internationally to affect corporate behaviour.

Just as changes in the law are being experimented with in China and India, Flynn and O'Brien argue that there is an opportunity for labour activists and organizations in the industrial countries to challenge the practices of 'their' corporations through invoking extraterritorial legal provisions. As they put it 'one fruitful way forward for Western labour movements is to put increased energy into changing domestic legal environments so that Western-based transnational corporations (TNCs) can be held accountable in their home countries for labour violations of their foreign subsidiaries and sub-contractors. This is a difficult and complicated task, but putting more emphasis on such a strategy is likely to further labour internationalism by integrating nationalist and internationalist strategies.' This chapter therefore adds an additional twist to the Polanyian theme which runs through this book – how can social agents best protect 'society' from the deleterious effects of the 'self-regulated market' and can legal regulation be one useful component of the 'counter-movement'?

Notes

1. I am grateful to Paul Bowles for very helpful comments on several versions of this chapter.
2. Alpa Shah, who has undertaken remarkable ethnographic research amongst Maoists in Jharkhand, has pointed out to me in correspondence that my statement here seriously underestimates the project of what is now – following the coming together of different organizations in 2004 – the Communist Party of India (Maoist). She argues that it is very much an 'organized counter-movement' and now very actively engaged in struggle against neoliberalism in India. See also the special issue of *Dialectical Anthropology*, 33 (2009).

References

Agarwala, R. (2006) 'From Work to Welfare: a New Class Movement in India', *Critical Asian Studies*, 38, 4: 419–44.

Brass, T. (ed.) (1995) *New Farmers' Movements in India*, London: Frank Cass.

Chatterjee, P. (2008) 'Democracy and Economic Transformation in India', *Economic and Political Weekly*, 19 April, pp. 53–62.

Dev, M. (2008) *Inclusive Growth in India: Agriculture, Poverty and Human Development*, Delhi: Oxford University Press.

Frontline (2009) 'Battle for Work', articles on the implementation of the NREGA, 26, 1 (3–16 January): 4–26.

Harvey, D. (2005) *A Brief History of Neoliberalism*, Oxford: Oxford University Press.

Kurlantzick, J. (2009) 'Taking the Bosses Hostage', *London Review of Books*, 31, 6 (26 March): 9–13.

Pattenden, J. (2005) 'Trickle-Down Solidarity, Globalisation and Dynamics of Social Transformation in a South Indian Village', *Economic and Political Weekly*, 40, 19: 1975–85.

Polanyi, Karl (1944/1957/2001) *The Great Transformation: the Political and Economic Origins of Our Time*, Boston: Beacon Press (second edition, Beacon Press, 2001).

Pun, N. and Lu H. L. (forthcoming) 'Incomplete Proletarianization: Self, Anger and Class Action of the Second Generation of Peasant-workers in Reform China', *Modern China*.

Shah, A. (2006) 'Markets of Protection: the "Terrorist" Maoist Movement and the State in Jharkhand, India', *Critique of Anthropology*, 26, 3: 297–314.

Teitelbaum, E. (2006) 'Was the Indian Labour Movement Ever Co-opted? Evaluating Standard Accounts', *Critical Asian Studies*, 38, 4: 389–417.

Venkatesan, V. (2003) 'The Judicial Response', *Frontline*, 20, 18: 20–2.

World Bank (2004) *India: Investment Climate and Manufacturing Industry*, Washington, DC: Finance and Private Sector Development Unit, South Asia Region, World Bank.

Index